Winds of Evil

Other Titles by Arthur W. Upfield:

ARTHUR W. UPFIELD

Winds of Evil

ETT IMPRINT
Exile Bay

This edition published in 2018 by ETT IMPRINT, Exile Bay

ETT IMPRINT & *www.arthurupfield.com*

PO Box R1906,
Royal Exchange
NSW 1225 Australia

First published 1937
This ett edition published 2018

Copyright William Upfield 1937, 2018

ISBN 978-1-925416-97-8 (pb)

Chapter One

On The Road To Carie

It was a wind-created hell in which the man who called himself Joe Fisher walked northward towards the small township of Carie, in the far west of New South Wales.

Somewhere west of Central Australia was born the gale of wind this day lifting high the sand from Sturt's country—that desert of sand ranges lying along the north-eastern frontier of South Australia—to carry it eastward into New South Wales, across the Gutter of Australia, even to the Blue Mountains, and then into the distant Pacific.

Now and then the dark red-brown fog thinned sufficiently to reveal the sun as a huge orb of blood. That was when a trough passed between the waves of sand particles for ever rushing eastward. The wind was steady in its velocity. It was hot, too, but its heat constantly alternated, so that it was like standing before a continuously opened and closed oven door.

It was not always possible for Fisher to keep his eyes open. Although he could not see it, he knew he was crossing a wide, treeless plain supporting only low annual salt-bush. The track he was following could be seen, on the average, for about six yards. On his left ran a boundary-fence, wire-netted and barbed-topped—a fence which had caught a rampart of wind-quickened dead buckbush, up and over which came charging like hunters the filigree balls of dead and brittle straw.

Quite abruptly, and without warning, a large touring car appeared in the red murk. It stopped at the precise moment that Fisher saw it, and from it the driver clambered, bringing with him a four-gallon petrol-tin.

"Let us hope we will have a good day tomorrow," Fisher shouted back when he joined the driver. "How far are we from Carie?"

"'Bout eight miles. What a day to be on the tramp! I'd sooner be me than you. You aim to get to Carie today?"

"No. I intend going only as far as a place called Catfish Hole, on Nogga Creek."

The driver's sand-charged brows rose a fraction. He was hefty and tough.

He exclaimed with singular inflection of voice, "Well, I wouldn't camp there if I were you—not for all the tea in China. Blast!"

"What is the matter?"

They were standing before the radiator, the tin of water at the driver's feet.

"Take off the cap, will you?" requested the driver.

Suspecting that the radiator was very hot, Fisher gingerly extended a hand, and when his fingers were about an inch from the bright metal mascot, from it to each finger leapt a long blue spark. Beneath the force of the electric shock, Fisher gave a sharp cry.

"There's enough static electricity in that flamin' bus to run a dozen house lights for a week," shouted the grinning driver. "Strike a light! I've only had that happen to me twice before."

"But what is the cause?" inquired the astonished swagman. "I have felt the effect, and seen it, too, so now tell me the cause."

"I dunno exactly. Some say it's the bombardment of the sand against the car's metal-work what creates the electricity that can't get away 'cos the rubber tyres are non-conductors. These wind-storms are fuller of electricity than a thunder-storm."

Not too happy about it, he again attempted to unscrew the cap, and to his fingers leapt the blue sparks.

"What's up out there?" shouted one of the three passengers.

"Come out and try your strength on this radiator cap," he was invited.

The near-side rear door was opened, and a fat man came stiffly out, helping himself to the ground by holding to the metal hood support. Immediately his feet touched earth he uttered a yell of anguish and almost sat down on the track.

"What did you want to let go for?" asked the amused driver. "Why didn't you stay making contact so's the electricity could run out of her?"

"It's a remarkable phenomenon," observed Fisher.

"Phenomenon! Two to one on that word. Reckon you're right, dig. Phew! What a corker of a day. You'll be meetin' another swagman presently. We offered him a lift, but he was too independent to get up. He's about a mile back."

"Well, do we stay here all day?" demanded the fat man. To which the driver replied with a show of impatience:

"I'm not lookin' for a seized engine, Jack. We'll drain off the juice this way."

He tilted the tin of water against the bumper-bar, being careful to release it the moment before it touched the metal. At contact there was a brilliant blue flash. Nothing further happened, and when the driver extended his hand to remove the radiator cap he received no shock.

"Mighty strange to me," grumbled the fat man. "Wonder the car didn't blow up or something. It's good for the rheumatics, anyway. My right leg was aching like hell before I got that shock, and now she's all right."

"The petrol-tank might have exploded," calmly stated the driver, who was now filling the radiator from the tin. "I'm dragging a wheel-chain from now on, like the petrol-wagons drag a chain down in the cities."

"Might be as well," agreed the fat man. "I'd sooner have the screws than be blown up. Cripes! No wonder me wife's mother has to lie down when the wind blows like this. She says the electricity in these storms takes all the strength out of her."

The grin on the driver's face became a wide smile.

"Better get her to wear thick rubbed-soled shoes. Then the next sand-storm will charge her with static till she blows to pieces," he suggested.

"Not a bad idea," conceded the fat man without smiling, but his dust-rimmed eyes were twinkling when he turned back to enter the car. Fisher was chuckling delightedly as he called "Good day" and left the driver fixing one of his wheel-chains to the rear bumper-bar.

The wind sang its menacing song as he plodded northward, a small swarm of flies hovering in the back draught produced by his body and the swag on his back, the left side of his face and his left hand continuously stung by the sand particles. Before and behind him the buckbush charged the fence rampart, sometimes singly and at times like a squadron of horses, many to leap right across the track. Now and then a filigree ball would strike the swagman's head, either to bounce from it or to collapse against it and wrap straw about his face and neck.

The horrible discomforts of this evil day were for a while lessened by thinking of the phenomenon of the electrically charged body of the car. Fisher was not sure that the driver's explanation of the cause was correct, although it was certainly feasible. Petrol-wagons had been known to explode, or ignite, by the static charge generated, so some said, by the constant movement of petrol within the tank. It was certainly interesting. This may be the real cause of aeroplanes exploding in mid-air during great storms. It was, indeed, a problem of interest to a thinking man.

Fisher came upon the swagman mentioned by the car driver. He was trying to boil water in a small billy at a fire partially sheltered by a track-side bluebush. That he was an old man of fixed ideas was already proved by his refusal of a lift this terrible day. At Fisher's sudden appearance he leapt to his feet, with surprising agility, obviously much frightened.

"Good day!" shouted Fisher. "D'you mind me boiling my billy at your fire?"

The old man stretched his bent body, venting a sigh of relief.

"I suppose you can," he consented grudgingly. "You pass a car?"

"Yes. The driver had stopped to fill his radiator, and the machine was so charged with static electricity that he couldn't remove the cap. He said there is more electricity in these wind-storms than there is in a thunder-storm."

"'Course there is," agreed the old man readily. "You don't 'ear no thunder, but the electricity's in the air all right. You get a cat a day like this and rub 'er fur and see the sparks fly! I know a bloke wot gets a terrible 'eadache when she blows, so's he's got to lie down. Where you headed for today?"

"This side of Carie, I think," Fisher replied. "On Nogga Creek. There is water in Catfish Hole, isn't there?"

They were by this time seated on their swags in what shelter the bluebush provided. At the mention of Nogga Creek and Catfish Hole the old man froze, and he leant nearer his chance companion to stare with a fixity which defied the dust.

"Ya-as, there's water in Catfish Hole, I'm told," he said, much more slowly. "You a stranger in these 'ere parts?"

"I have not been this way before," Fisher admitted.

"Ho! But you've heard what's been going on around Carie?"

The old man's billy coming to the boil, he flung into the water half a handful of tea, removed the utensil and waited for Fisher's answer.

"Er—no."

"You haven't, eh? Well, I'll tell you. What's been going on around Carie is what wouldn't let me camp at Catfish Hole for all the tea in China."

"The car driver said the same thing. What is the matter with the place?"

"Murders—two of 'em to date, that what's the matter. Me, I'm George Smith, and I wouldn't camp there for ten million quid. You take my advice and don't *you* camp there tonight—or ever until the Strangler is caught."

"The Strangler?"

"That's what they calls 'im. The year afore last, at this time, he done in a half-caste girl where Thunder and Nogga cricks become Wirragatta River. And then last March he strangled a young feller named Marsh just this side of the township. He's due now to strangle someone else, and it ain't gonna be me. Don't you let it be you."

"What does he do it for?"

"He don't do it for nothink bar the pleasure he gets outer corpsing people. That's the wust of it. There ain't no proper reason. 'Course the police can't do nothink. They can 'ound us about, mate, but they ain't no good at catchin' murderers. Then this strangler, he does his killing at the end of a day like this and when it's certain sure it'll blow like hell again the next day so's his tracks will be wiped out."

"Where, then, did you camp last night?" Fisher asked.

"Me! I camped in the Carie lock-up. They wouldn't let me camp in the stables behind the pub, so I arst the constable to let me camp in the jail. That's about the safest place I know."

Fisher added tea to the water boiling in his billy. To the old man he appeared to be unreasonably calm.

"I'm telling you not to camp at Catfish Hole, or anywheres outside Carie."

"Ah, yes! Thank you for the warning. I will certainly remember it. It all sounds a little unhealthy."

"Unhealthy! Too right it's unhealthy. It ain't healthy to be strangled, is it?"

Although the subject was of absorbing interest to the old man, it was not unduly protracted. It was difficult, for one thing, to talk when sand-laden air and flies competed in entry to one's mouth. The two men parted after the most casual of nods and immediately each was swallowed by the sweeping sand waves.

Joe Fisher was of medium height, slight of frame and yet strong, steady on his feet despite the buffeting of the wind. Like a man long used to the track he carried his swag of blankets and spare clothing within a sheet of stout unbleached calico. The small canvas water-bag gripped by his right hand was stained red by the oozing moisture, and, as the billy was strapped to the swag, his left hand was free to battle constantly with the flies. His face and bare arms were caked by the sand grains. His face and hair below the rim of the old felt hat were dyed a light red. Only the blue of his eyes defied the red fog.

There was a hint of grim tenacity in the dim picture of the shadowy man's determined tramp northward in such bad weather. He could have found shelter, but no comfort, in the lee of the fence, but methodically and at even pace he passed along the track which now did not reveal wheel-tracks; not even those of the car he had recently met.

At last the sun was no longer to be seen in the troughs of the sand waves, for it was too westerly. The wind was losing its strength a fraction, but the sand dust remained as dense. Knowledge of his own part of the country suggested that at sundown the wind would either veer to the south and blow cool and cleanly on the morrow, or lull during the night and at sunrise begin again to blow stronger yet.

Time passed and still he continued the steady tramping to the north, above him the lowering red blanket of sand particles, about him the red-brown fog which now and then was tenuous, and sometimes seemingly solid. Then presently the box-trees bordering Thunder Creek came marching to meet him from out the murk, holding invitation to the traveller with their gnarled and twisted branches.

On gaining their comparative shelter, Fisher found the wind to be much less forceful, but more angry in its song of power. Over the plain it had softly whined; here it bellowed and roared. With quickened pace he crossed the flat, shallow and dry bed of the creek to gain its far bank, when he saw the pine-walled, iron-roofed house standing some two hundred yards back and east of the track. Here the air was clearer, the wind almost conquered by the trees. They circled beyond the house as though purposely planted to keep at bay the vast stretch of open country across which Fisher had been tramping all day.

Despite his statement that never before had he been this way, the man who called himself Joe Fisher knew that when he crossed Thunder Creek he would see the homestead of Fred Storrie's Selection. Dimly in the distance he saw the box-trees bordering Nogga Creek. These two creeks came from the east to join in Wirragatta River less than a mile westward of the fence. And half a mile down the river below the junction of the creeks stood the homestead of the great Wirragatta Station.

In the swagman's tortured blue eyes leapt strange exultation as he strode along the branch track to the selector's house flanked by windmill and reservoir tanks on one side and by sheepyards on the other.

There was that about the front of the house plainly indicating that the door on this side was never used, and, as any swagman would, Fisher passed round the side of the house to its back door. Just beyond this door was a round iron water-tank before which stood a girl gazing vacantly at the terrible sky while water from the tap filled a bucket.

"Good afternoon!" the swagman said, pitching his voice to master the howl of the wind about the roof.

The meeting produced a remarkable result. The girl cried out, sprang about, and then pressing back against the tank stared with undoubted fear shining from her dark-brown eyes. The water continued to gush into the bucket and began to overflow and run to waste along the short brick drain.

"The tap," said the swagman, regarding the running water with a slight frown of disapproval.

Without removing her gaze from his face, the girl permitted herself to sink on bending knees until her groping hand found the tap and so shut off the water.

"You seem to be fearful of something," Fisher said. "I hope you are not afraid of me."

The friendliness in his eyes and the flash of his well-kept teeth had its effect. The ice of her fear began quickly to melt, and it was with evident relief that she asked him what he wanted.

"If you could spare me a little meat," he replied. "I am on my way north and I intend to camp beside the waterhole on Nogga Creek. Catfish Hole, isn't it?"

The girl nodded, normal composure not yet regained.

Fisher gave her time, and presently she said:

"Yes, I can give you a little meat. But … but … Nogga Creek … in this weather!" Again her eyes grew big. "You wouldn't camp there, would you? Not on a night that this is going to be?"

"The wind will not bring rain," he pointed out.

"I know. But … but are you a stranger in these parts?"

"Yes."

"Then you don't know about the Strangler?"

"Well, I have heard of him."

It was, perhaps, his easy smile that brought her from the tank to stand closer to him. Fear still lurked deep in her eyes. Despite the day, she appeared fresh and cool in a house-frock of brown linen. There was character in the moulding of her mouth and chin and grace in the outlines of her body.

"Wait here and I will fetch you some meat," she requested abruptly.

From inside the house a woman called: "Mabel, who's that?"

"Only a swagman, mother. He wants meat," replied the girl, and now more composed she flashed Joe Fisher a half-smile and then hurried across to the canegrass meat-house.

The man's critical eyes took in the out-houses, noting their condition and neat preservation. It was obvious that Storrie's Selection prospered. The girl returned carrying meat wrapped in newspaper, and when she gave it him she again attempted to advise him not to camp beside Catfish Hole.

"Oh, I'll be all right," she was assured. "I've camped often enough in wild country, and to be forewarned is to be forearmed. Besides, the last attack made by this mysterious strangler was last March, wasn't it?"

"Yes. And this time last year, too. You want to be very careful. No one walks about, or camps in the open anywhere along these creeks. I'm going to the dance at Carie tonight, but my brother is taking me on the truck."

"Late in the year for a dance, isn't it?" he questioned.

"Yes, it is so, but then, you see, we haven't any other amusement in Carie."

Again Joe Fisher smiled.

"Well, thank you for the meat. I hope you will enjoy the dance. Do you think I would have a chance of work on Wirragatta Station?"

"It might be worth trying. The Borradales are good people to work for."

"Then I'll try them tomorrow. Good-bye and thank you."

Having raised his hat, Fisher adjusted his swag, picked up the water-bag and continued his tramp to Nogga Creek, now to be seen dusty-green below the red canopy of whirling sand. All the way across the half-mile flat between the two creeks the wind roaring through the trees provided the overture for the coming night of dark terror.

The day was nearly done when Fisher reached Nogga Creek, crossed it, and then strode up along its far bank, hoping to see Carie and not greatly disappointed when all he did see was the netted fence and its barrier of buckbush disappearing into the menacing murk.

Thereafter, he followed the creek eastward for a quarter of a mile, when he arrived at the lower end of Catfish Hole, a long and narrow lagoon of sparkling water lying in the creek-bed. The tip of this waterhole touched a sand-bar, fine and white and dry, and here Fisher decided to make camp for the night.

Now, when the sun must be setting, and the high-flying sand, indeed the very air, was not transmuted for a few moments into the rich colour of blood, Fisher knew that the wind and the dust would be even worse on the morrow. When the rack overhead was tinged with dark grey, when it seemed that the very tree-tops supported this evil sky, he sat on his swag before the fire he had made and ate grilled mutton chops and stale damper, and now and then sipped hot black tea heavily laced with sugar.

With the coming of night the wind dropped to a moaning breeze. The leaden sky came still lower like a material weight threatening to crush the suffocating world. The fire-light painted the near trees against an even black when, an hour later, he unrolled his swag, bunched the blankets into the form of a sleeping man, and then stole away beyond the fire-light to seat himself against a tree-trunk and watch.

He heard the whirr of wings preceding the splash of hydroplaning ducks. After a long time a curlew vented a long screaming cry as it passed above him. There was something almost human in that.

As he carried no watch he had no means of telling the time. He guessed that it was eight o'clock when he heard a car or truck cross the creek on its way to Carie, and he guessed again that it was taking the Storrie girl and her brother to the dance.

After that Fisher dozed fitfully. Some time during the night he heard the curlew scream again, now towards the track by the fence. Quite an hour afterwards the car or truck returned from the township.

It was altogether a most uncomfortable night spent by this swagman, with his back pressing against a tree-trunk. Hence he slept long after the new day dawned. He was eating breakfast when another car reached Nogga Creek from the south. The rising wind prevented Fisher from hearing it. He did not know that it stopped for several minutes when it gained the northern bank of the creek.

Chapter Two

The Ruler Of Carie

Nelson's Hotel stood at the southern extremity of the township of Carie. It was the only two-storied building in the town, and from its upper veranda it was possible to enjoy a wide if, perhaps, not always interesting, view.

Southward from the hotel the track to Broken Hill wound like a snake towards the bluebush covering the town Common, then disappeared among it towards Nogga Creek. A bare quarter-mile distant it passed through the left of two gates set in the Common fence, thence skirted the east boundary-fence of Wirragatta Station for fourteen miles. It was the fence now familiar to Joe Fisher. Just before the Common fence was reached a branch track took the right-hand gate and led one to the homestead of Wirragatta.

Beyond, far beyond the Common fence, the arc of the level horizon of the bluebush plain extended from the eastern tip of Nogga Creek's box-trees round to the north, where lay the distant township of Allambee, and thence farther round to the line of mulga forest, and so to the south and the tall red gums of the river. Here and there over this great plain were low, sprawling sand-dunes which had not been there when Mrs. Nelson was in her teens.

Opposite the hotel was the bakery, and along that side of the straight, wide and solitary street the eye passed the store, the police station, the hall—used as the court house—and then an irregularly spaced row of iron-built houses. Returning along the hotel side of the street, one's eye passed over several more small houses, the doctor's house, the post office. Every building in Carie was skirted by vacant allotments. There was no great house shortage, and the town had ample room for expansion should the shortage ever exist.

The people of Carie were free of class distinctions, and the general happiness stood at a high level. One only among them was the leader, and, in consequence, there was a delightful absence of snobbery.

In any community outside the bush proper, Dr. Mulray would have stood at the apex of the human pyramid. Next to him would have come the bank manager, had there been one, then the postmaster, followed by the senior police officer. But Dr. Mulray cared nothing for society. His interests lay entirely among his patients and in his chess-board. The postmaster had been relegated to a back seat by his considerable family, whilst Mounted-Constable Lee desired only peace and leisure to read novels. As for the storekeeper and the baker and the butcher—well, they knew that to rebel against the leader would preface their examination in bankruptcy.

To dispute with the leader of Carie was to ask for trouble, for the leader held a mortgage over the store, the bakery and the hall. The leader owned Dr. Mulray's house and furniture, the butcher's shop and the majority of the none-too-numerous dwellings. In fact, save for the government buildings, the leader owned almost the whole of Carie, and partly owned several out-lying pastoral properties.

The leader was Mrs. Nelson, the owner and licensee of the only hotel.

On the morning following the last of the winter dances—to be exact, on 30th October—Mrs. Nelson, as usual, arrayed herself in a black silk dress, a white linen cap, black woollen stockings and elastic-sided boots. She was short and stout and something over seventy years old, remarkable for the beauty of her snow-white hair and the brilliance of her dark eyes. Her appearance denoted the essence of respectability, her movements bespoke eternal youth, her personality proclaimed the ever-alert business woman, never to be defeated by circumstances or daunted by advancing age.

With the vigour of a woman twenty years her junior, she stepped through the open french windows to the wide balcony which was so well protected by canvas blinds during the summer months. Half of this front balcony constituted her home. She was seldom found downstairs, and even more rarely went out. It was as though her portion of the upper veranda was her throne from which she ruled Carie.

The sun, she saw, was well above the Common, its colour a sinister deep red. The limits of the plain were drawn close by the thickening red-brown fog, and the dark line of trees to the south marking Nogga Creek was blurred and featureless.

The one street was deserted save for a flock of goats and Mr. Smith, the baker, who was carrying out sacks of bread to load into a shabby gig to which was harnessed a piebald mare. Mrs. Nelson's dark eyes registered no expression when they became focused on the waistcoated figure of the elderly Mr. Smith, whose philosophy of life doomed him to die a poor man.

It was a philosophy frowned upon by Mrs. Nelson.

She was standing with one beringed hand resting on the balcony rail when there came to her a girl dressed in the severe uniform of a maid. The girl's complexion had been wholly ruined by the sun when she had daily ridden after her father's cows and goats, and now it was doubtful if any expertly applied make-up could repair the unfortunate damage. She asked the question she had asked every morning over the past two years.

"Where will you be havin' your breakfast this morning, ma'am?"

Mrs. Nelson turned to regard the girl with eyes that bored through flesh and bone into the soul of her, standing docilely placid.

"The wind is rising, Tilly, and it is going to be another nasty day, but I will take breakfast here."

The girl withdrew, and when again she appeared she was carrying a breakfast-tray. This she placed on a small weather-beaten table before dusting and placing a chair beside it. Mrs. Nelson was dissatisfied with the position of table and chair, and Tilly was directed that they be placed nearer the end of the balcony, where the view of the Broken Hill track would be unobstructed. Tilly lifted the cover from a dish of bacon and eggs; her mistress poured milk and tea into a delicate china cup.

"What time did you get home last night?" asked Mrs. Nelson.

"It was after one o'clock, ma'am."

"Hum! And I suppose you're fit for nothing today?"

"I'm all right, ma'am."

Mrs. Nelson noted the faint colour in Tilly's face.

"If you are, you are stronger than I was at your age. Who did you dance with?"

The faint colour swiftly became a vivid blush.

"My boy, mostly, ma'am," replied poor Tilly.

Mrs. Nelson's attitude imperceptibly stiffened.

"Does your father know that you have a young man?"

"Oh, yes, ma'am. It ... it's Harry West."

"Oh!"

For ten seconds Mrs. Nelson gave her attention to her breakfast. Tilly waited, her nervousness increasing, as Mrs. Nelson intended it should. Tilly both feared and loved her mistress, and in this she was not alone, but she loved and feared her father more. There was nothing of the rebel in Tilly's mental composition. Now, in softer tones, Mrs. Nelson spoke again.

"So it is Harry West, eh? Well, he's steady enough. You could do much worse. You must bring him to see me one evening. You are a good girl, Tilly, and there are things I will have to say to him. Were Mr. and Miss Borradale at the dance?"

"Yes, ma'am. And the doctor, and Barry Elson, and oh! almost everyone, ma'am."

"How was Barry Elson?"

"He was all right, ma'am. He could dance."

"He couldn't dance yesterday afternoon, anyway. Who did he dance with ... mostly?"

"Mabel Storrie. He took her home. They walked home. Tom Storrie drove her in, but when the dance broke up he and the truck couldn't be found."

"So Barry and Mabel have made up their quarrel?"

"Yes, ma'am, I think so."

"You only think so!" sharply exclaimed the old woman.

"Well, ma'am, Barry Elson was very attentive to Mabel all last evening, but she seemed to be keeping back. I don't blame her. Barry had no right to go and get drunk yesterday afternoon. I ... I don't think I'd forgive Harry in a hurry if he went and got drunk just because I gave him a bit of my mind."

"A wise woman never gives bits of her mind to a man before she's married to him," Mrs. Nelson remarked severely. "And what happened to young Tom Storrie and the truck?"

"I think he took Annie Myers home and didn't trouble about his sister, ma'am. Brothers aren't very considerate."

Mrs. Nelson was again devoting attention to her breakfast, and the girl continued to stand patiently to await dismissal.

"What dress did you wear?" was the next question.

"I wore my black crêpe de Chine, ma'am."

"Hum! You were wise there, my girl. Colours don't suit you. How was Mabel dressed?"

"Oh, she wore blue ninon, and her shoes were of blue satin. She looked just lovely, ma'am. I wish—I wish——"

"Well, what do you wish? Out with it."

Tilly faltered and again blushed. Then:

"Nothing, ma'am. Only I wish I was like Mabel Storrie. She looked lovely last night—just lovely."

For the second time since she had sat down, Mrs. Nelson stared hard at the girl.

"Don't indulge in vain regrets, child," she said softly. "You have got one beautiful feature—your eyes. Be careful of them; use them well but sparingly. Now be off. Be sure all the windows are shut and fastened, and that the blinds are lowered three-quarters. Slip down and ask James to come up. Stay in the bar until he gets back."

"All right ma'am, and thank you," Tilly said.

That brought Mrs. Nelson's eyebrows almost together. "Whatever for, child?" she asked.

"For … telling me about my eyes, ma'am."

"Rubbish!" snorted Mrs. Nelson. "Be sure you lie down in your room for two hours this afternoon, or you'll go to sleep waiting at dinner."

Tilly vanished. She was a month or so over twenty-two, compact and sturdy. She possessed the lithe grace given to almost every bushwoman who since girlhood has habitually ridden half-tamed horses. Her constant use of the word "ma'am" was due less—much less—to any sense of servility than to an affectionate respect for the leader of Carie. Like all great men and women, Mrs. Nelson commanded affection mixed with respect.

She now went on with her breakfast, to which, however, she gave less attention than she did to the point where the track to Broken Hill crossed Nogga Creek.

Like a drop of ink, a horse and rider slid over the brown stained carpet of bluebush from the south-east to reach the right of the two Common gates. Behind the horse rose a long finger of dust—dust which became quickly merged in the as yet low-flying tenuous dust-clouds raised by the freshening wind.

The rider opened, passed through and closed the gate without dismounting, then urged his horse into a gallop once again. On arriving at the township he turned down beside the hotel to the stables and yards at the rear. Mrs. Nelson knew him to be Fred Storrie.

It was now ten minutes to nine, and on to the veranda through the sitting-room stepped a white-faced man whose eyes were startlingly blue and whose jet-black hair was lowered over his high forehead in what is known in England as a quiff.

He was rotund, youthful, well under forty years of age. His trousers and open waistcoat were of dark tweed, his dress-shirt was without collar and tie, and on his feet were tan leather slippers. When he spoke London sprang out of his mouth.

"Mornin", ma'am!"

"Good morning, James."

Mrs. Nelson turned slightly in her chair, the better to examine her barman, and James hastily buttoned his waist-coat, then gently flapping in the wind, and endeavoured to hide his slippered feet under the table. James Spinks had been Mrs. Nelson's barman for eight years, and he was, therefore, conversant with Mrs. Nelson's passion for—among other things—sartorial neatness.

"Is the mail on time this morning, James?" he was sternly asked.

"Yes, ma'am. Five passengers. All men. All passengers going through to Allambee."

"Of course everything is ready for them?"

"Too right, ma'am."

"Any trouble last night from Constable Lee?"

"No. No trouble at all, ma'am. Live and let live is Constable Lee. He ain't severe-like on dance nights and Christmas Eve."

"Mr. Borradale—did he call in?"

"Yes, ma'am. He and the doctor slipped in just afore the dance started and then again about midnight."

"Very well, James. After the coach has gone on, ask Fred Storrie to come up for a minute. That will be all."

James accepted his dismissal with a vigorous nod, which made it apparent that the quiff was too heavily greased to come unstuck from his forehead, and he having vanished, as people always seemed to do when Mrs. Nelson had finished with them, that lady proceeded with her breakfast and her watching study of Nogga Creek.

For so many years had she seen, first Cobb and Co.'s coaches, and then the motor mail-cars appear and disappear at Nogga Creek that she knew exactly where the track disappeared among the bordering trees before crossing it. Visibility this morning was exceptionally bad and momentarily becoming worse, and her eyesight now was less good than formerly. Nevertheless, her interest was abruptly aroused by tiny flashes of reflected light at the place where the mail-car was due to appear.

With the agility of a much younger woman, Mrs. Nelson rose and passed into her sitting-room. On coming out again she was carrying a pair of expensive binoculars, and when she levelled them at the reflected lights the blue-veined, china-like hands were trembling.

The glasses permitted her to see the modern motor mail-car halted at the top of the nearer creek-bank. She could not perceive anyone in the car, nor could she see anyone standing beside it who could account for its unusual halt at that place.

It was a circumstance at once arousing the curiosity of a woman habitually in possession of all knowledge connected with Carie and with the mail-cars that passed through Carie. Curiosity so controlled Mrs. Nelson that she experienced no little difficulty in keeping the glasses directed at the motionless car.

At least one minute passed before she saw figures emerge from the box-trees beside the track. They moved together in a bunch to the side of the car, and Mrs. Nelson fancied she saw once a flash of light blue. Then, whilst she continued to watch, the men climbed into the car and it began to move towards the town.

That the halt had not been occasioned by a mechanical breakdown Mrs. Nelson was convinced. Something of an unusual nature had caused the driver to walk right off the track and in among the trees bordering the creek. When she lowered the glasses to the veranda rail her hands were still violently trembling. Her face was almost as white as her hair.

Again seated, she watched the oncoming mail-car seeming to swerve alternately eastward and then westward as it followed the winding track, its wheels and mudguards hidden from her by the low bluebush. A huge volume of dust rose behind the vehicle, to be rushed eastward in a long slant by the wind. Oddly enough, that dust reminded Mrs. Nelson this morning of the old oleograph in the bar parlour showing H.M.S. *Majestic* ploughing an angry Atlantic as great billows of black smoke poured from her two funnels set abreast.

An old man came forth from one of the houses to stand and peer along the track. The uniformed policeman emerged from the police station calmly to survey the township. The usual stray cow and two goats wandered into the single street. And then, beating the sound of the wind, came the rising hum of the mail-car.

As had the drivers of Cobb and Co.'s coaches, so did the youths driving these mail-cars always when arriving from Broken Hill pass the hotel to make first stop at the post office. Having dropped the mail, they then drove back to the hotel, where passengers and driver ate breakfast, and where, in the old days, the horses had been changed.

To the grave perturbation of Mrs. Nelson and to the astonishment of Mr. Smith, Constable Lee and "Grandfer" Littlejohn, this morning's mail-car passed the post office to stop outside Dr. Mulray's house.

Old Grandfer very nearly fell down as he hobbled across the street to reach the mail-car. The baker, the storekeeper, the policeman and half a dozen women, who had seemingly evolved from space, rushed to the house side of the mail-car; while, once more on her feet, glasses glued to her eyes, Mrs. Nelson danced like a willy wagtail. The passengers she saw emerge from the car, and the little crowd appeared to be strangely stilled. Then the robust figure of Dr. Mulray appeared, when there was suddenly much loud talking. The wind permitted Mrs. Nelson to hear not a word.

One of the passengers then pressed to the side of the car and there slid into his arms a crumpled figure in a blue dress. He was a big man, and he carried with ease the limp body into the doctor's house, immediately followed by Dr. Mulray himself.

Mrs. Nelson lowered the glasses. She was repeating over and over: "Oh, dear! Oh, dear! Oh, dear!"

She saw Fred Storrie come racing to the hotel corner in answer to James's shout. He ran on to the doctor's house, and the male portion of the crowd stared after him when he rushed inside.

And then the first of a long succession of sand waves rolled over the township, blotting out Nogga Creek and the Common, smearing into semi-obscurity the bakery on the far side of the street. Mrs. Nelson almost collapsed into her chair. She went on repeating softly as though stunned:

"Oh, dear! Oh, dear! Oh, dear!"

Chapter Three

The Wind

"Martin, aren't you well this morning?"

The strong but well-modulated voice penetrated the consciousness of the young man lying on the bed. About him, washing against him, and against the bed, were the strange and yet familiar vibrations set up by the gale of wind sweeping over and about the stout Wirragatta homestead.

Martin Borradale stirred, opened his grey eyes, moved wide his arms. The light from the tall closed french windows was of tinted yellow. It cast the girl's face in shadow, which was yet no shadow, and it laid a shade of drabness over the interior of the room which normally was very pleasant. Round of head, her dressing-gown-encased body long and beautifully curved and set firmly on small feet, Stella Borradale regarded her brother from the foot of the bed.

"Hullo, old thing! Phew! I feel deadly," replied Martin. "I've got a headache and lots of other aches as well. I might have been playing football half the night instead of dancing."

Stella's next question was without trace of irritation. "How much did you drink in Carie?"

The young man winced.

"Not much, old girl," he confessed. "Four cocktails all told. They bucked me up, anyway. I was not feeling up to scratch all yesterday. I hate these dust-storms. Is it bad again today?"

"It's vile. It is going to be worse than yesterday, I think. I've brought the morning-tea."

"What's the time?"

"A few minutes after ten. There's nothing to get up for if you're not fit."

"Then I'll snooze off again after I've drunk the tea. By the look of it and the sound of it no one of us will be able to work. Has there been a telephone message, or a telegram from Carie?"

"No. You've often asked that question lately. Are you expecting a wire?"

Borradale hesitated for a fraction of a second before saying: "Well yes, perhaps. I've been hoping to receive a visit from a man from Brisbane. Personal matter, you know. I have been expecting him for a month. Oh, well, he'll turn up some day."

"Indeed!"

Stella waited for enlightenment, but did not press for it. When she turned to the windows from which she had a few minutes before drawn aside the curtains, the sinister day-light revealed clear, hazel eyes well spaced in a vital face. Her brother watched her as she crossed to the door, and it did not occur to him that she might be piqued by reason of his secrecy regarding the expected visit. Her dressing-gown was of white and gold, and her light-brown hair hung in two plaits down her back. He did realize how amazingly-feminine she was, and how wisely obstinate in her refusal to have her hair cut.

During her absence from the room he wearily sipped his tea, and when she returned carrying a small bottle he inquired what it contained.

"Aspirin, dear. Two tablets will put you right."

"Hum! Thanks. How did you sleep?"

"I slept all right while I was at it, but I feel I have slept only for five minutes. Coming along for breakfast later?"

"Er—no. I am going to snooze till lunch and try not to dream about this beastly dust-storm."

"Till lunch, then?"

"Until lunch." Martin essayed a laugh. "Sounds like a toast, doesn't it? Confound Mulray! I hate spirits, but he would have me slip across to the hotel with him. He's the kind of man who won't be denied, and one can't drink beer at a dance."

His sister drew the curtains before the windows after standing for a moment to observe the swirling veil of dust without. Softly she left the room and passed to her own room where her maid waited with her morning-tea.

Between these Borradales there existed a real and even affection. They had never been heard in the recrimination not unusual in this relationship. Martin was well set up, slimly athletic, twenty-seven; his sister was remarkably attractive, but yet not beautiful. She was several years her brother's junior. Both were keen on horses and tennis. Both preferred to drive a fast trotting-horse to a car. Both were cultured, having attended Adelaide's best schools, but a university had been denied Martin because of their

24

father's untimely death when the young man was barely twenty. It had necessitated his instant return to Wirragatta.

Having graduated, Stella gladly joined her brother to work in harness with him. Their mother having predeceased their father, the estate had been willed equally to them, but there had never been any suggestion that it should be realized and portioned.

So Martin had settled down to master the details of what is an exceedingly intricate business, and, like his father, he was succeeding remarkably well. He was fortunate in that for the first five years he had had an able mentor in his father's overseer. Only after that canny Scot had died did the young man realize what he owed him and feel the weight of responsibility of which his shoulders, till then, had been relieved.

Stella came home, and quite naturally managed the staff of domestics and efficiently ran the homestead. The world beyond far-away Broken Hill continued on its exciting social and political orbit, but at Wirragatta, as at Carie, it rolled placidly onward from year to year and left no regrets.

Neither of them vegetated, notwithstanding. Wirragatta was not a farm but a principality; the men were not yokels but clever sheepmen and fine horsemen. Many of them were well-read and well-informed. The neighbouring squatters were not country men but people modern in ideas, in dress, in manners. The internal combustion engine had wiped Cobb and Co.'s horse-drawn coaches off the tracks, and now was beginning to span and respan the skies. The great depression was passing and hope burned in the hearts of men.

As these Borradales had agreed, human activities outside the house were stopped by this second day of wind and blinding sand. The stockmen in their huts were unable even to read. The cooks swore and gave up their efforts to protect food. Even within the well-built homestead, even within Stella's bedroom, where she sat reading a novel, the air was tinged with red dust. It was necessary, in order to read, to have the standard oil-lamp burning, there being no electric light at Wirragatta.

The wind boomed and whined about the house, and the colour of the oblong presented by the windows deepened to a sinister dark red as the day aged. Stella's chair vibrated like a harp-string. The lamp smoked if the wick was turned to its normal height. Already her eyelids and the corners of her mouth were sticky with dust. And so, first reading and then dozing, Stella got through the morning.

At noon the maid appeared to ascertain her wishes about lunch. The girl's hair was damp and wispy, and her face was stained by dust and coloured by heat. Knowing full well the terrible conditions faced by the cook, Stella suggested tea and toast. She invariably suggested; never ordered.

"Did anyone ring up this morning—or call?" she asked, reaching for the cigarettes.

"No, Miss Borradale. Oh—but then, of course, he wouldn't count. A swagman came about eleven asking to see Mr. Borradale. Cook told him to go and camp till the wind dropped, as she wasn't going to have Mr. Borradale disturbed a day like this."

"Poor man," Stella said feelingly. "Did cook give him anything to eat?"

The maid shook her head.

"Oh, well, Mary, bring tea and toast. I will slip along to Mr. Borradale and see what he would like."

Stella found her brother standing before the windows gazing out upon the red fog which now completely masked the orange-trees but a few yards distant. Her quick glance found his dressing-gowned figure instantly, noted the unusual orderliness of this most masculine room, its quiet furnishing, the occupant's day clothes neatly folded and hung over a chair-back. Like all other rooms in the house today, the air in this was stale and clammy. At her entry Martin turned.

"Hullo, old girl! Just plain hell outside, isn't it?"

"Just that, dear," she agreed. "I am going to have tea and toast for lunch in consideration for cook and her difficulties—especially her temper."

"That will suit me. Might I have it here? I don't feel like dressing yet. Anyone telephone?"

"No. A swagman called at eleven, and cook told him to wait till the storm had died down. He wanted to see you."

"Oh! Wants a job, I suppose." Martin sighed. "Well, thank the Lord I'm not a swagman."

Assured that her brother had recovered from the exertions of the previous evening, Stella returned to her room and suggested to the maid that a tray be taken to Mr. Borradale.

The afternoon was worse than had been the morning. When many women would have reviled the country and the temporarily uncomfortable conditions, Stella Borradale felt concern and sympathy for the stockmen in their rough huts, the team of dam-sinkers in their unprotected tents, and the two boundary-fence riders who patrolled the netted frontiers of this nine-hundred-thousand-acres kingdom called Wirragatta. She thought particularly of one of these fence-riders, Donald Dreyton, a man who mystified her, and she pictured him crouched in the only shelter provided by stacked camel-saddles.

Yet there was one man who compelled his horse to face the blast of hot, sand-laden wind and ride to Wirragatta shortly after four o'clock. When the maid entered Stella's room with afternoon-tea she informed her mistress that Mounted-Constable Lee desired to see Mr. Borradale.

"This afternoon!" exclaimed Stella, glancing at the windows. "On an afternoon like this! Tell cook I would like her to offer Mr. Lee tea and cakes in the morning-room. Cook will be unable to expose the butter."

Remembering not to frown because of two vertical lines which would appear between her brows, understanding that the cause of the policeman's visit must be serious—otherwise he would have telephoned on a day like this—Stella again entered Martin's room, to find him stretched on his bed reading. What he instantly saw in her eyes caused a tightness at the corners of his mouth, and as she spoke she watched this tightness grow tauter still.

"Lee called?" he cried sharply. "Where is he?"

"Making the best of what cook is able to provide. Will you have some tea before you see him?"

"Yes. I'll dress at once."

He was trying to keep the horror out of his eyes, but she saw it and whispered:

"Do you think—again? Those other two were killed in weather like last night."

For ten seconds both stared at the other. Then Martin's body relaxed, and he said with forced calm:

"Let's hope not. By God, let's hope not."

When, half an hour later, the dust-grimed policeman was taken to the study he found Martin newly shaved and dressed in flannels.

"Ha, Lee! What on earth has brought you here on a filthy day like this?" inquired the squatter, indicating a chair flanking the writing-table. A silver box of cigarettes was set between them, and Lee accepted one. "Nothing serious, I hope?"

Mounted-Constable Lee was phlegmatic. He grinned at Martin, but without humour. Only after his cigarette had been lit did he answer.

Lee was a large, lean man. His hair was sandy in colour and thin, and his clipped moustache was like his hair. Pale blue eyes seemed always to regard the world with wonder, as though his slow but tenacious brain failed to understand why men troubled themselves to break laws.

"Sir," he began, and paused. "Carie has been stirred up again, and remembering how you, as a sitting justice, kindly assisted me with sound advice when Alice Tindall was murdered two years ago, and when young Marsh was murdered last March, I thought you wouldn't decline to advise me about one or two points regarding this last crime."

"Certainly, Lee. What has happened? Not another murder?"

"Early this morning the girl, Mabel Storrie, was nearly strangled to death. This time the Strangler didn't complete his foul work. Before I relate the facts I'd like you to answer a question or two."

"Very well. Carry on. What is it?" demanded the squatter, his eyes narrowed.

"What time did you and Miss Borradale get home last night?"

"I don't really know. Some time after midnight, I think."

"Perhaps Miss Borradale would know," suggested Lee, exhibiting that mental tenacity which his wife termed pig-headedness. "I'd like to know for certain."

"I will ask her. I'll not be a moment."

During Martin's absence Constable Lee produced a long notebook and went over the notes he had made since the arrival of the mail-car from Broken Hill that morning. He was thus engaged when the squatter returned.

"My sister says that we got back at twenty-five minutes after twelve," Martin announced, dropping into his chair and selecting a cigarette.

"Humph! You came to town in the car last night. Which way did you return home?"

"By the direct track."

"That's to say, you took the Broken Hill road to the Common fence, then came through your own gate on to your own country and so direct here?"

"Yes. Why are you so interested in our movements?"

"I wanted to know the way you came home last night because if you had followed the Broken Hill road, to Nogga Creek, turned in there through your boundary gate, and so come home along the creek, you might have seen someone or something of a suspicious nature."

"We saw no one. The last person we saw was yourself standing under the door light of the hotel."

Lee sighed and put away the notebook. Martin could see that he was laboriously marshalling his facts, and that to hurry him would be worse than useless. Even then the constable had to jerk his heavy body upward and the hem of his tunic downward before he spoke.

"Just after eight o'clock last night," he began, "Mabel Storrie and young Tom drove to Carie on their father's truck. When the dance broke up at one-thirty this morning Tom Storrie and the truck were missing. This being so, Barry Elson undertook to escort Mabel home on foot. They were seen to leave the hall, and I saw them pass the hotel shortly after one-thirty.

"When they got a bit beyond the Common gate they fell into argument. Mabel objected to her boy kissing her because he had been drinking. She told him she didn't want his escort, and, in a huff, he left her to go on alone when they were half-way to Nogga Creek.

"Fred Storrie and his missus weren't alarmed this morning when they found that Mabel hadn't got home. They did find young Tom snoring in his bed, and he said he missed Mabel and thought she would be sleeping at her aunt's in town.

"It was one of the passengers on the coach who saw the girl lying about twenty-odd yards off the track. The coach brought the girl into the town, as she was alive, and Dr. Mulray took her into his house, where she is now being nursed by her mother and the doctor's housekeeper."

"Horrible, Lee. Damnable. How was the unfortunate girl when you left this afternoon?"

"Bad. Not only has she been almost strangled to death, she has received a severe blow to her forehead. She hasn't yet regained consciousness. According to her mother, a swagman called at the house yesterday afternoon, got some meat, and said he intended camping at Catfish Hole. He hasn't reached town yet, and when I visited Catfish Hole to interview him he wasn't there."

"Probably the man who called here this morning," Martin cut in. "Wants to see me about a job, I think. He was told to wait until the wind subsided."

The young man abruptly leaned towards the policeman, his face expressing angry determination. "This strangling swine has got to be caught, Lee."

Lee sighed.

"I wired Broken Hill about it this morning," he said, in his voice a hint of despair.

"We can only hope they will send a keener man than last time. Shall I call for this swagman?"

"I wish you would, sir. He may be able to tell us something."

In answer to Martin's ring a maid appeared, and she was asked to cross to the office building and request the book-keeper to find and bring the swagman to the study. When the door had closed behind her, Martin said slowly:

"Two months ago I recalled the fact that the present Commissioner of the Queensland Police Force was an old friend of my father's. I wrote him a long description of the two murders committed here, and asked him if he could have a really first-class man sent from Sydney. In his letter to me he said he would send a man, by arrangement with the New South Wales Commissioner, when that man could be released from a case. Now matters have come to such a pass that no man or woman is safe after dark."

Chapter Four

Joe Fisher

The door of the study was opened to admit two men, the first of whom was the Wirragatta book-keeper. Martin and the constable both ignored the dapper man and concentrated their attention on the swagman. When the door closed behind the retreating book-keeper, the swagman surveyed those at the table. He was of medium height, very dark of skin, very bright-blue of eyes. When he smiled his white teeth emphasized the colour of his skin, and when he spoke Martin's brows lifted a fraction.

"Gentlemen, you wished to see me?" said the swagman.

"Yes, we do," Lee growled. "Sit down on that chair. I've a few questions to ask."

The swagman brought the chair indicated and became seated so that he faced both Martin and the policeman.

"I am an adept at answering questions," he stated lightly, and then, as though prompted by an afterthought, he added, "And at asking them, too. May I smoke?"

At this effrontery Lee frowned heavily and glanced at the squatter. Martin placed the silver cigarette-box nearer the swagman, who took one and lit it, saying:

"Now and then I like a Turkish cigarette, but I have never been able to conquer the habit of rolling my own. My tastes, I fear, are plebeian."

"Never mind your tastes," shorted Lee. "Where did you camp last night?"

"At the lower extremity of a sheet of water called, I think, Catfish Hole."

"What time did you get there?"

"Having no watch, and being unable to see the stars, I cannot reply with accuracy, but it would be about six o'clock. Not later than seven o'clock."

"What did you do when you got there?"

"I made camp and grilled chops I cadged from a young lady at a selector's house. After darkness had fallen I rolled my swag in such a manner as to mislead any evil person into thinking I was sleeping there. Then I stole away and sat with my back against a tree all night. It was most uncomfortable physically, but mentally it was comforting."

"Why did you do that? There are no wild blacks in this State."

"Yesterday I ate lunch with a fellow swagman who had camped the night before in your jail. In consequence of information received concerning an unknown killer, I decided that a nice big tree-trunk at my back would be a blessing."

"Oh! What's your name?"

"Joseph Fisher."

"I don't want your nom-de-track. I want your *real* name."

"Alas, it is one which humbles me. I am unworthy to bear it, but the responsibility is not mine." The twinkle in the blue eyes puzzled Martin and angered Lee. "I am Detective-Inspector Napoleon Bonaparte."

Lee's annoyance was swept away by an expression of astonishment.

"Inspector Napoleon Bonaparte!" he almost gasped.

"If you kindly address me as Bony it will be sufficient. I am not a real policeman, at least not at heart. You are, I take it, Mounted-Constable Lee, and you, sir, are Mr. Martin Borradale. I have a letter for you from Colonel Spendor of Brisbane and an official one for you, Lee."

The contents of the blue envelope apparently were short, for Lee laid it down and stared at Bony until Martin had read the Colonel's much longer one.

"It has become obvious, Lee, that you are officially interested in me as a swagman. Why? Proceed with the questions you intended to ask." Lee remembered himself and stood up. "No, no. Please be seated. As Colonel Spendor delights to impress on me, I am not a real policeman. I will take charge after you have completed your questions."

"Very well, sir. Did— —"

"I insist upon being called Bony," murmured the swagman.

Lee's jaw firmed. Then he said:

"Bony it is, sir. Did you hear anything out of the ordinary during the night?"

"Er—no. Nothing not quite ordinary. At what I think was about eight o'clock, a car or truck passed along the road over the creek going towards Carie. I reasoned that it was the young lady from the selection and her brother, as she told me she was going to the dance at Carie when she gave

32

me the meat. A car or truck returned from Carie about two o'clock this morning. I assume it was the same people returning from the dance."

"You heard nothing more; saw nothing?"

"No."

"You didn't hear a woman scream or cry out?"

"No—o. But wait. Before the day was utterly gone a curlew screamed as it passed over my camp. Then, about an hour before the car or truck passed on its way south, I heard the curlew again. It seemed then to be near or on the road. That second cry might have been a woman's scream. The two are not very dissimilar. Why do you ask that?"

"Because the girl, Mabel Storrie, was strangled almost to death near the road where it crosses the creek, less than a quarter of a mile from where you were camped."

Bony's long brown fingers ceased all movement when rolling a cigarette.

"Indeed! So the third crime of a similar nature has been committed. But please wait. I would like to have the particulars of them in chronological order. Begin with the details of the first."

"You have, then, not seen the letter I wrote to Colonel Spendor two months ago?" Martin asked.

"Oh, yes, Mr. Borradale. I would, however, like to hear all the details from Constable Lee. Now I am all attention, Lee."

"Well, sir—er—Bony, it was during the night of November the tenth two years ago, that Alice Tindall was strangled to death on the bank of Junction Waterhole, which is half a mile up-river from here and just below where Thunder and Nogga creeks join to become Wirragatta River. Alice Tindall was a half-caste, young and pretty, aged nineteen. She lived with her mother and her mother's tribe, who up to then had their home camp beside Junction Waterhole. She had spent the evening of November the tenth with the servants in this house, and the next morning one of the blacks discovered her body on the bank of the waterhole opposite the camp. The night of the crime was just such a night as last night. The post-mortem was carried out by Dr. Mulray, and the coroner's verdict was murder."

"Any proved or probable motive?"

"No. The girl had neither money nor jewellery on her person. Although she was pretty and popular, she had no known enemy. Her character was very good."

33

"Who conducted the investigation? You?"

"I did what I could. Sergeant Simone, from Broken Hill, took over the case. He failed."

The grim lines about Lee's mouth prompted Bony to ask: "Is this Simone a live man?"

"Well, he's a good policeman, I think."

"Ah, but a bad detective, eh? You said that the girl's maternal tribe was camped beside the waterhole. I assume that their gift of tracking was put to full use."

"Yes, but the blacks hadn't a chance to work. As I said, the night of November the tenth was like last night, and November the eleventh was even worse than it has been today. The wind blew away the face of the earth. And then Simone didn't use them right. He wasn't tactful with 'em. They sneaked away a day or two later and they never came back. They got to fear Simone worse than the blue devil, or the banshee, or whatever they call the evil spirit of the bush."

"So neither you nor Simone found one clue?"

"No ... not a blessed lead."

"Well, then the second crime, please."

"The second murder was committed during the night of March the seventeenth this year. There was a young fellow named Frank Marsh, who had returned to Carie the year before, after having served his time to a tinsmith. He turned out to be a good tradesman, and he found plenty of work in this district. At the time of his death he was making water-tanks for Fred Storrie, the selector, and then was camping with the Storries. On the evening of March the seventeenth he visited Carie, and on his way back to the selection he was attacked and strangled to death. Thinking he had stayed in Carie for the night, Storrie didn't worry about his not turning up for breakfast. A swagman found the body about half past nine the next morning. It was lying between the two back gates on the Common fence."

"This time, of course, there were no blacks to call on to track?"

"No. As I mentioned, they had all cleared out. And if there had been any handy to work for us they would have been no good."

"Oh! Why?"

"The weather conditions were exactly the same as when Alice Tindall was killed."

"Is that so! Who investigated?" Bony asked sharply.

"The same officer—Sergeant Simone."

"Results?"

"None! The young fellow had been killed just as the girl had been killed and just as senselessly."

"And last night, or early this morning, in precisely the same weather conditions, this Storrie girl was almost murdered in exactly the same manner?"

Constable Lee nodded gloomily.

"That's it," he assented. "She went with her brother to a dance in Carie last night. The brother and the truck were missing when the dance broke up, so she walked home with her sweetheart. On the way they had a tiff, and they parted when half-way to the creek. This morning one of the coach passengers saw her lying several yards off the track. She had been almost strangled to death and she had suffered a severe blow on the forehead, which has rendered her unconscious ever since. If she lives, she'll be lucky."

"You have communicated with Broken Hill?"

"Yes," answered Lee. "If they send Simone again, they should get their heads read."

Bony chuckled. "If they send anyone—which probably they won't, knowing I am here—we will hope it is Sergeant Simone. Why don't you like him?"

It might have been the fact that Bony was not a member of his own State Police Force that made Lee unusually candid when he replied:

"Sergeant Simone may be a good detective in a city or large town, but he's not the shadow of one when dealing with a bush case. He is too overbearing with bush people. You can't get anything out of bush people by bullying them."

Bony nodded approvingly.

"My opinion of you, my dear Lee, is becoming quite favourable," he said smilingly. "You know, I think I shall thoroughly enjoy myself whilst on this investigation. My thanks are due to you, Mr. Borradale, for drawing my attention to these murders through my revered chief, Colonel Spendor. The Colonel said, 'Bony, the son of an old friend of mine is being annoyed by a blackguard whose vice is strangling people. Go and get him.' I said, 'Do you refer to the blackguard or the friend's son, sir?' and he said, 'Damn you, sir.

Don't you try to be humorous with me'."

Lee's mild eyes now were opened to their fullest extent. He was staring as though his ears were faulty, and Bony chuckled.

"This strangling person uses his brain," Bony went on. "Only the rare murderer does that. In general, murderers are the most stupid of criminals, prone to commit a hundred mistakes. They are more stupid than embezzlers. I believe that it is the fear of the rope which upsets the average murderer and makes him make mistakes. Even the really clever murderer, the odd one in the hundred, will make at least one vital mistake. Not always, however, does the investigator see, or recognize, the mistakes, so that it is always the investigator who fails to sheet home a crime and not the cleverness of the criminal to get away with it. Now permit me."

Bony pushed back his chair and rose. On moving the cigarette-box, he commanded half the table surface.

"We have here excellent sketching materials," he murmured as with a finger point he drew on the dusty surface of the polished table a rough map of the locality. He was as facile as a lightning-sketch artist, and both Martin and the policeman were astonished by his accuracy.

"When were you last in the district?" asked Lee.

"I have not been here before, but when in Broken Hill I studied several large-scale maps. Now please point out to me on this sketch where the three victims were discovered."

With a grimy finger Lee did so.

"Ah!" Bony murmured, and then stood back as though to admire a hung masterpiece. "Yes … very interesting … very. I am glad I came. Thank you, Mr. Borradale. You have put me in your debt. I admire clever murderers immensely—almost as much as I admire myself. Officially I am always delighted to order their arrest. Privately I would like to let them go so that they could commit another murder without making the same mistakes."

Constable Lee's face was a study of outraged law. He glared glassily at the now laughing detective. The twinkling blue eyes beamed on Martin, and the squatter could not forbear to chuckle. He had heard of Bony through intimate friends, and he knew the half-caste's reputation.

"I'm glad that Colonel Spendor consented to get you to lift this horrible shadow from us," Martin said soberly. "Anything we can do to assist you in your investigation will be readily done. The entire community will be grateful to you if you can apprehend this strangling brute."

"Without public collaboration a detective's work is made trebly difficult, Mr. Borradale, and I thank you for your offer of assistance. First, I want my name and rank suppressed. I will work for you, Mr. Borradale, as a casual hand under the name of Joseph Fisher. You can take me on your wages-sheet from now. Set me to work clearing that boundary-fence of dead buckbush. From you, Lee, I require the name of every man and woman in the district. Not now, but later, I would like to study the weather records over the last five years. But to no single person mention who or what I am."

Chapter Five

The Fence-Rider

It was by chance that Mounted-Constable Lee met Donald Dreyton several miles to the west of Carie on the boundary of Wirragatta Station. For five minutes they conversed across the netted barrier, and Dreyton learned of the brutal attack on Mabel Storrie. When Lee went on his business, Dreyton regarded the stiff military figure astride the grey gelding with the manner of one whose eyes are blinded by mental pictures.

Behind the fence-rider stood one riding- and two pack-camels, animals possessing personality and able to think and reason.

Dressed, this first day in November, in khaki slacks, a white cotton shirt, a wide-brimmed felt hat and elastic-sided riding-boots, with face and forearms tanned by the sun, Dreyton had the appearance of being over forty when actually he was but a little more than thirty years of age. Constant exposure, day and night, to the sun and the air had so darkened his skin that the peculiar blue-grey of his eyes was startlingly emphasized. The thin nose and mobile lips, added to the breadth of forehead, indicated intelligence above the average, whilst the two sharp lines between the brows bespoke constant mental activity. He was not a bushman born and bred, but in this was no oddity.

It was seldom that Dreyton troubled to ride. For one thing his riding-camel vigorously objected to being kneeled to be mounted, nor would it consent to be climbed up and down whilst standing. At nearly every wire strain something was required to be done to the fence, and consequently Dreyton walked the ten to fourteen miles every day along his section of one hundred and eighty-three miles. It was doubtless this incessant walking that gave to his body its lithe grace of movement.

Having filled a straight-stemmed pipe with rubbed chips of Yankee Doodle tobacco, having lit the pipe with a match ignited on the seat of his trousers, he resumed his patrol to Carie and the homestead of Wirragatta.

It was almost four o'clock when he arrived at the corner post between the two black gates in the Common fence, there ruefully to observe the long rampart of dead buck-bush built by the wind against the fence running south from that point to Nogga Creek, where his section terminated, and for many miles beyond. So clear was the air he could see the individual trees bordering the creek, while Nelson's Hotel and Smith's bakery appeared to be within easy stone-throw.

When again on the move, headed southward, Dreyton smiled a little grimly. He knew it to be certain that a pair of brilliant dark eyes would be observing him from the south end of the hotel's upper veranda. Between Mrs. Nelson and him existed a kind of armed neutrality, created by her desire to know everything about Donald Dreyton and his determination that she should know as little as possible.

Now he saw the man forking the imprisoned buckbush over the fence and experienced relief that this job he would not have to do before setting off again on another trip. For two hundred yards back from the creek the fence had been cleared of buckbush, and the worker leant on his long-handled fork whilst watching the approach of man and camels.

Blue eyes set widely in a dark-brown face noted every detail of the fence-rider's appearance, and then the thin-lipped mouth beneath the straight nose and the dark brows of this Australian half-caste resolved into a kindly smile.

"Good day!" greeted Dreyton.

"Good day!" responded Joe Fisher, *alias* Bony, *alias* Detective-Inspector Napoleon Bonaparte. "It is a day to be appreciated after yesterday. A glorious wind, that. It has provided me with a job of work."

"So I see," Dreyton said dryly.

"And all day I have been observed, I hope with admiration, by someone on the hotel veranda. He, or she, owns a pair of glasses."

The fence-rider laughed with quick amusement and named the culprit. After that he stared at Bony, and, less openly, Bony stared at him. The result was that neither could "place" the other, and mutual interest quickened.

"Mrs. Nelson is a woman possessed of a remarkably sharp sense of curiosity," Dreyton explained. "She owns almost the whole of the township, and wishes to own everyone in it as well—You're a stranger here, I take it."

"Yes. I came along on the look out for work," Bony admitted. "I—er—put the hard word on Mr. Borradale for a job, and so, fortunately, clicked. Have you heard about the girl, Mabel Storrie?"

"A rumour, yes."

"Ah! You are English, are you not?"

"Of course. My accent, I suppose?"

"Less your accent than your national reserve. I saw Constable Lee riding away along the fence to the west, and it is more than probable that you met. He was bound to talk of Mabel Storrie, and yet you say you have heard nothing more than a rumour about her and of her terrifying experiences near here the night before last."

"You are, then, a sort of bush Sherlock Holmes?"

"I am," admitted Bony gravely.

Dreyton smiled.

"In that case, you have examined the scene of the latest crime?" he said, not without sarcasm.

"Certainly. I, too, have a sharp sense of curiosity."

"And discovered the murderer?"

"Not yet," confessed Bony, still grave. Dreyton laughed good-naturedly.

"You are a strange fellow."

Bony unconsciously bowed. He was thinking that this fence-rider also was a strange fellow. He had seldom met men like this Donald Dreyton—so seldom, in fact, that he was as puzzled by him as he was puzzling to Dreyton.

Then he thought he saw light, and asked, "How long have you been working on Wirragatta?"

"Just two years now. I started here three days before the half-caste girl was murdered at Junction Waterhole. Heard about her?"

Bony nodded.

"Was that your first introduction to the bush proper? he asked carelessly.

"It was. It was not a good moment for the introduction. You see, the detective fellow certainly thought I was the murderer."

So this fence-rider had had no experience of Australian blacks, because shortly after his arrival in the bush those then on Wirragatta had cleared away. And, too, shortly after his arrival, Alice Tindall had been strangled.

"Would you care to see the place where Mabel Storrie was attacked?" asked Bony.

"No, thanks. I am not that much interested in the details. On the road, wasn't it?"

"Yes, on the road," Bony agreed. "She was left for dead on the road."

Again Dreyton laughed good-humouredly.

"I am afraid, Mr. Sherlock Holmes, you are a little out in your statement of the crime," he said. "Mabel Storrie was found some twenty yards *off* the road by the mail-car people."

"Admitted, my dear Watson. Even so, she was left for dead *on* the road. When she recovered consciousness, she walked blindly off the road for twenty-odd yards. Then she tripped over a tree-root, and in falling received a severe blow on her forehead. There she lay till she was found." Dreyton's blue-grey eyes narrowed. "How do you know all that?" he demanded. "Lee doesn't know it."

"Lee? Oh, the policeman! Perhaps not. Perhaps he does and didn't think to tell you. Come with me and I will prove my statement. We must run the grave risk of killing the cat on the hotel veranda. Even then I saw the sunlight reflected by her glasses."

Having vaulted the fence, Bony led the way up along the creek-bank till he halted at the edge of a fairly large sand patch. Across the patch was the upper surface of a tree-root, and on it were the imprints of many feet. On this patch the girl was found. Bony explained:

"Those footprints were made by people who came here early this morning. The imprints left by the coach party and Constable Lee were, of course, wiped out by the wind. Now, the girl was walking home when the night was as black as a stove. Quite naturally, she clung to the road, and on the road she was attacked. Remember, no efforts were made by the murderer to conceal the bodies of Alice Tindall and Frank Marsh: so we may assume—if we take it for granted that Mabel was attacked by their murderer—that he, thinking he had killed Mabel, merely let her slip out of his hands and then fled. There was no purpose in carrying her to the place where she was found, because, although her assailant might have known her brother was due to pass on the truck, he knew that before the dawn the wind would have wiped away his tracks."

"That seems a reasonable argument," conceded Dreyton.

"It is. The Strangler's tracks were quickly expunged from the ground. So were his victim's—save in one place—Come here!"

Motioning the other to follow, Bony led the way towards the road where there was a small wind-swept area of claypan—sun-dried mud of a once-filled surface puddle. Pointing downward, he said:

"On that claypan are the impressions of cuban heels, the heels of Mabel Storrie's shoes. Her walking shoes, for she changed her dance shoes for them before she left the hall."

"My eyes are good, but I can see no tracks," objected Dreyton.

"No? Then step back here a little. Bend low, like this, and look *across* the claypan, not down at it."

The fence-man did as instructed, and at the lower angle he thought he could make out faint indentations. Still— —

"I can certainly see *something*," he admitted.

"I can see heel-marks plainly. Look! I will outline one of the marks."

Standing over Bony, Dreyton watched him scratch the hard grey surface with a match-point, and there grew the outline of a woman's shoe-heel at the position where the woman would have taken her second step to cross the claypan. "I say," he said apologetically, "I'm sorry I chaffed you about Sherlock Holmes and all that. Hang it! You must have eyes like telescopes."

"It is a gift bequeathed me by my mother. You will see that if Miss Storrie recovers, and can recall all that happened to her, she will tell how she got up from the road and walked dazedly away, only to trip and fall and remember nothing more. Now I must get back to my job, or I will be getting the sack at the end of my first day."

Continuing his work, Bony watched Dreyton and his camels travelling down the creek road to the homestead until man and beasts disappeared round a bend and so were hidden by the box-trees. Although mystified by the fence-rider, he had come to form a favourable opinion of him. He was a gentleman by his manner and appearance. Regarded on his present situation, he was a gentleman no longer.

"I wonder what he was, for what he is he has been only for two years," Bony said aloud.

For a further half-hour he tossed the light filigree straw balls over the netted fence, so that the next of the prevailing westerly winds would roll them across the track and away to the east.

It was five o'clock when he shouldered the fork, unhooked the water-bag from the fence, and began his return to the homestead. Along the creek road, plainly to be seen, were the fresh imprints of the camels' feet. Here and there was a solitary imprint of a boot; here and there but a portion of a boot mark. The camels following after the man, almost but not quite, had blotted out his tracks.

Eventually Bony rounded the creek-bend, the bordering track now running to the south-west to Junction Waterhole. On the left of the track grew the line of box-trees, and between their trunks the detective could see, across the flat, the timber bordering Thunder Creek drawing nearer as he proceeded. On the right of the track, two hundred yards round the bend, there grew out on the bluebush plain a thriving leopardwood-tree, in the vivid branches of which a party of crows vociferously quarrelled.

On reaching an imaginary line to be drawn from the leopardwood to the nearest creek box-tree, Bony saw that Dreyton's camels had been halted for some time. Now there was no necessity for the fence-rider to halt at this place, for he no longer was patrolling his section. Bony's mind at once sought for an explanation. Without the smallest difficulty he saw Dreyton's boot-tracks walk off the track to the creek box-tree, and, on following them, he saw where they circled the trunk. He was further astonished to discover marks on the tree-trunk, clearly indicating that Dreyton had climbed it.

Why? Bushmen do not climb trees for exercise or the fun of it. Dreyton was on his way to the homestead after a tiring day, and there must, in consequence, have been something up in this tree to successfully entice him to climb it.

Bony climbed the tree, too. He climbed high to the point reached by the fence-rider.

Later, when he continued the walk to the homestead, he wondered much about Dreyton, and if his climb had had anything to do with the crows quarrelling in the leopard-wood-tree.

Chapter Six

Dreyton Refuses Promotion

The first to be seen of the Wirragatta homestead by anyone following the creek track from the Broken Hill road were the stockyards; and then, as he swung round a sharp bend in what had become the Wirragatta River, there came into view the trade shops, the men's quarters, then the office-store building, and finally the large bungalow surrounded by orange-trees, which in turn were confined by a white-painted wicket fence.

To Donald Dreyton it was like coming to a palm-fringed oasis after a wearying journey over the desert. It was not quite five o'clock and work for the day had not stopped. The clanging of the blacksmith's hammer on iron, the methodical clanking of the two windmills raising water to the tanks set on high staging, and the voices of the birds ever to be found in the vicinity of a dwelling, all combined to give him a feeling of prospective peace and content.

Some distance from the men's quarters, which had first to be passed by anyone wishing to visit, Dreyton turned off the track to follow a pad leading down and across the dry bed of the river and skirting the top end of a beautiful lagoon beside which the homestead was built. On the river's far side stood a small hut given entirely to the use of the two fence-riders.

The camels having been put into their especially fenced paddock, his gear carried into the hut, and he himself shaved and bathed and arrayed in white shirt and gabardine slacks with tennis shoes on his feet. Dreyton again crossed the river and sauntered to the office. The westering sun was gilding the tops of the gums and slanting between them to lay bars of gold on the surface of the waterhole about which the galahs and cockatoos created constant din. The homestead, being built on a shelf below the level of the bluebush plain, the township of Carie could not be seen. In its direction the cawing of innumerable crows indicated that the cowboy was at work killing mutton sheep.

Within the office Martin Borradale and Allen, the book-keeper, were at work before their respective tables, and at Dreyton's entry the squatter

44

glanced up sharply. An expression of slight worry gave quick place to a smile of welcome.

"Hullo, Donald! In again?"

"Yes, Mr. Borradale. I see that I have a day's work along the Broken Hill road assisting that new man."

"You need not trouble about that. He can finish it. How are things outback?"

"All right. I did another two strains of footing over the Channels. Might I suggest that when the bullock-wagon goes out again it takes a dozen rolls of netting and drops them at the Fifty-mile gate? I could get them from there to where the netting is wanted."

"Yes, certainly," Borradale instantly agreed. "The bullocky will be taking a load of rations outback next week." He paused and tapped the table with a pencil end. Dreyton waited. Then: "I think I'll send a couple of men and a horse-dray out there to do that footing. It will take you too long to complete it. Any rabbits along that section?"

"None. But I understand they are numerous less than thirty miles to the north-west."

"That's so. Yes, I'll send men and a dray to do the work. Hear about Mabel Storrie?"

"Yes. Pretty filthy, isn't it? How is she now?"

"Very bad, I hear. She was taken home this morning. Not only was she half-strangled, she was knocked about, too. Every one, of course, has the wind up."

"Naturally. That new man—Fisher, he said his name is—seems to think that the girl regained consciousness on the road and then, dazed, walked away and tripped over a surface root at the place where she was found. Her head injuries, according to Fisher, were caused by that tree-root and not by the Strangler."

"Is that so?" Borradale sighed, then fell to staring at the fence-rider.

"A strange fellow, Joe Fisher," Dreyton said with conviction. "Is he a half-caste?"

"Yes. As you say, he is a remarkable fellow. He was camped at Catfish Hole the night Mabel Storrie was attacked, and he happened to be here when Lee called the next afternoon. Lee and I had him in. He argued like a lawyer and proved that he could not possibly have committed the crime."

Dreyton smiled.

"He should have been a detective," he said. "He's wasting his time as a station rouseabout. Seems quite well educated. Are all half-castes like him?"

"Hardly," dryly replied Martin. "The fellow evidently has had a good schooling. What about your coming back into the office?"

The fence-rider's eyelids drooped before he glanced at the book-keeper. Martin went on:

"Allen wants to leave as soon as possible, because his mother is ill in Adelaide. I thought of you at once. You must be getting sick of the fence by now."

"That I am not, Mr. Borradale," Dreyton admitted smilingly. "Still, if Mr. Allen wishes to leave immediately, I will take over."

"You will? Good man!"

Again the fence-rider flashed his quiet smile. "On one condition," he stipulated.

"And that is?"

"That you really will try to get another book-keeper without delay. Honestly, I am far happier on the fence than I was when anchored to this office."

The quick gratification in Martin's face subsided.

"Very well," he agreed. "I'll do my best. You're a strange fellow yourself to prefer that hard life on the fence."

"It is not so hard. You try it."

"Not I." Martin swung round to face the book-keeper. "When do you want to go, Allen? By tomorrow's coach?"

"Yes ... if possible, Mr. Borradale. My mother's condition is worrying me."

"Then that settles it, Donald. Officially you begin here in the morning. Agreed?"

"Yes. And you will not fail to write to the agency for a new man?"

"Very well," assented Martin ruefully.

He might have said more had not light footsteps been betrayed by the veranda beyond the open door. Into the office came Stella Borradale, dressed in tennis-rig and carrying two rackets. A swift smile broke on her face at sight of the fence-rider.

"Hullo, Donald!" she exclaimed coolly. "Are you really still alive? I

46

wonder you did not choke to death in those two days of wind and sand."

Dreyton's face registered an answering smile, but no longer was his body relaxed in the easy stance of the bushman, and no longer were his eyes unguarded. When he addressed her, he spoke as easily as he had done to her brother.

"I wanted to be a rabbit, Miss Borradale, so that I could burrow deep," he told her. "It was no use wishing to be an eagle. Those I managed to see were perched in dead trees and looked extremely miserable."

"They could not have looked or felt more miserable than I," Stella said lightly, taking the others into her confidence. "In addition to the physical discomforts I was obsessed by the dread that something would happen. It spoiled the dance, and I was thankful to get home. Haven't the detectives arrived yet, Martin?"

Her brother shook his head, and both he and Dreyton noted the look of horror deep in her eyes.

"I hope they send someone better than Sergeant Simone," she said quickly. "He is an obnoxious person."

"I think that half-caste fellow, Joe Fisher, would do better," offered Dreyton.

"I have not seen him," the girl said indifferently, staring at the fence-rider.

She possessed the trick of steady scrutiny without being rude, and Dreyton knew that he was being examined and approved much as his mother used once to do when he returned home at the end of a term at school. Her friendliness, he was well aware, was due to the absence of snobbery in her mental make-up. Her present attitude to him she adopted with all the men. It was never taken as ground for familiarity. It has ever been the general rule for those who live in "Government House" to address the men by their Christian names, and the rule has been in force for so many generations that were a man addressed by his surname he would accept it as an insult.

"Donald is going to take Mr. Allen's place *pro tem.*," remarked Martin, breaking a silence. "Mr. Allen is leaving us tomorrow."

"Indeed!" Again Stella examined the smoothly shaven, not unhandsome face, its keen cut features and the grey-blue eyes now regarding her. Then again she took them all into her confidence. "I am sorry you are leaving, Mr.

47

Allen, and I hope you will find your mother much improved in health. We shall miss your tennis and bridge."

"But we shall have Donald back," her brother cut in, and he could not prevent satisfaction expressing itself in his voice.

"But I have not played tennis for more than a year," Dreyton protested.

"That's your fault," Stella pointed out a little severely. "You would go fence-riding."

The men's cook was pounding his triangle.

"Better dine with us," invited Martin.

"It's kind of you to ask me, Mr. Borradale." Dreyton made haste to reply, "but I am not yet your book-keeper. I must go to Carie this evening to refit. It would be possible for a book-keeper to dress like a fence-rider, but quite impossible for a fence-rider to appear as a book-keeper in his fence toggery. With your permission, Miss Borradale! Hang-dog Jack is so easily upset if delayed in serving dinner."

She bent her head and smiled, and he turned and strode from the office, where brother and sister stared at each other for quite ten seconds.

Dreyton found Hang-dog Jack awaiting him in the long building devoted to the men's kitchen dining-room. Five men were seated on the forms flanking the table. Bony being of their number. Standing at a bench on which stood a large iron pot of soup, and dishes of roast meat and vegetables, was the cook. Hang-dog Jack was an extraordinary person, both in his ability to cook and in his appearance.

He was of cubic proportions. His legs were short and his enormous arms abnormally long. His ugly face was square and crowned with a mop of black hair. A flattened nose, a wide and characterless mouth and a shapeless chin, were redeemed by a broad forehead and steady brown eyes. How he came by his "nom-de-track" no one knew. Some said it was due to his hang-dog facial expression; others that once he actually had hanged an unfortunate dog.

"Soup?" he snarled at Dreyton.

The fence-rider feinted and the cook ducked.

"Lookin' fer fight, eh?" snarled Hang-dog Jack. "You come outside and I'll wrastle you. In two ups I'll dump you six times and give you the aeroplane spin."

"I don't believe in 'wrastling' with you," mocked Dreyton. "Give me soup and a pleasant smile."

The cook ladled soup into a tin plate and Dreyton took it, with knife, fork and spoon, to a place at the table where he met a barrage of greetings and questions.

A young fellow, obviously a horseman, who sat on Bony's right and who was Tilly's "boy", Harry West, wanted to know if Dreyton had seen a piebald mare with a colt running at heels. Bill the Cobbler, an old man without a hair to his head, wished to know if Dreyton was feeling fit enough to write a letter for him to a "widder wot's blackmailing me down in Adelaide". Young-and-Jackson, so named because the famous hotel of that name in Melbourne was the only building he remembered seeing during his rare visits to that city, wished to know if Dreyton had seen Dogger Smith and "'Ow's that old pioneer getting along?"

Beneath their questions was restraint. Dreyton could feel it. He nodded recognition to Bony, who was smiling happily. No one mentioned Mabel Storrie. Harry West asked if Dreyton would take a ticket in the station sweepstake on the Melbourne Cup.

"I don't believe in sweepstakes," snarled Hang-dog Jack.

"Then why did you buy two tickets?" demanded the organizer.

"I don't believe in 'em, all the same."

"What *do* you believe in?" asked Bill the Cobbler.

"I don't believe in nothing," argued the cook as though he enjoyed arguing.

"Not even beer?" mildly inquired Young-and-Jackson, blinking his green eyes rapidly.

"Not even in beer—at sixpence a small schooner."

The scowl on the cook's face was terrific. It amazed even Bony. With deliberate unconcern, Hangdog Jack lit an ancient pipe and casually blew smoke into the soup saucepan. Bony was thankful that the first course was past.

Chapter Seven

The Book Of The Bush

Mounted-Constable Lee and Bony sat facing each other across a small table wholly covered with untidy piles of documents which were partially weighted with sand particles. From the ceiling a suspended oil lamp provided a kind of illuminated passage up which spiralled tobacco-smoke. The time was 9.50 p.m., and the room was that designated as the police station office.

"I don't envy you your walk to town tonight," stated the uniformed policeman. When Bony smiled, but did not speak, he added, "And I envy you less your walk back to Wirragatta."

"Being a still night, there was, and is, no need for nervousness," argued Bony, his ready smile revealing his white teeth, his eyes now almost black. "Have you been informed of the departure of any plainclothes men from Broken Hill?"

"No. I don't expect any notification. Simone will probably be assigned to this last case, as he is in possession of the details relating to the other two."

As he slowly expelled tobacco-smoke, the detective intently regarded the big but lean man who now was frowning.

He said, "What has aroused your dislike of this Sergeant Simone?"

Lee hesitated before answering this question, but when he did he spoke deliberately.

"Simone is a bully. He tries to bully me. He knows that my wife is a Carie woman, and that she would hate to leave here were I transferred. He knows that my wife's father is a semi-invalid, and that her mother is bedridden. He tells me in his sly, slinking manner that I am too popular and that popular policemen are no good to the Force. Knowing that he has us under his thumb, he makes full use of our parlour, and even drops cigar-ash all over the carpet. That riles my wife and annoys me. If I squeak he'll pull strings higher up. Then again, as I said the other day, he's not the shadow of a detective outside a city slum area."

"A rather impossible person."

"You've said it, sir—Bony."

"Well, well, if he comes, he will probably amuse us. If he does not amuse, you and I can send him back to Broken Hill, where, doubtless, he is appreciated. Officious policemen always amuse me for a little while. There is something so naive about them. Simone will certainly want a statement from me as a suspicious character camped within a quarter-mile of the scene of the third crime. Pick up pen and write, my dear Lee, to my dictation. Statements are such necessary documents, you know, to officious policemen."

Lee stared fixedly at this most unorthodox detective from Brisbane, suspecting sarcasm. Then he smiled grimly when he found a pen, the end of which revealed much savage biting. In his breast-pocket was the document signed by his own State's Police Commissioner, instructing him to render every assistance to Detective-Inspector Bonaparte. Already he sensed that he and his wife had a powerful ally against the hated Sergeant Simone, and this was balm laid to his outraged soul.

When Bony's statement had been taken down and signed and initialled by him, the detective said, "Now we can await the gentleman from Broken Hill without mental disturbance. You will not inform him who and what I am, and he will not know. Later we may discuss him again. Meanwhile, please give me your attention and keep secret everything I say now and hereafter."

Constable Lee already had forgotten this extraordinary man's colour. Already he was blinded by the forceful personality of this half-caste who had passed through a university, had risen to high state in his profession—from a police tracker to an inspector—and of whom even he had heard whispers of fine successes.

"Have you prepared that list of persons resident in and near Carie for the last three years?" Bony asked.

Lee proffered several sheets of paper, saying with gratification, "I completed the list just before you came in."

"Ah! The name of every one is here? Yours? Your wife's?"

The other's face took to itself a deeper tint.

"Well, I didn't think——" he began.

"I must add you both," Bony murmured. "Now ... here are the names of some seventy people who have been living here over the period in which two persons were murdered and a third nearly so. If you have not omitted anyone from these lists, other than the two I have just added, then the criminal's name is beneath my hands."

Bony rolled yet another cigarette. There were occasions when he was a chain-smoker.

"I feel pretty sure, Lee," he went on when he had struck a match, "that this case will interest me profoundly, and exercise a brain liable to become lethargic with mundane and sordid murder and other crimes. This strangling series is most promising, and I can find even more pleasure in it, as poor Mabel Storrie is now recovering.

"It may be that the person who attacked her is not the murderer of Alice Tindall and Frank Marsh, but someone who copies his methods. We must not lose sight of this possibility. At this early stage, I think that the same person committed all three crimes. Having perused Simone's reports when in Sydney, and allowing for his magnification of his difficulties in order to save face, I do not wonder at all that he failed. Here in the bush he would be quite out of his element. But, Lee, here in the bush I am well within mine.

"Simone, without doubt, has been trained to discovering clues in the form of revolvers and knives, bloodstains and finger-prints. He has experience in keeping his ear to the ground for criminal whispers, and is facile in putting together information received in the hundred and one thieves' kitchens of any city. I have been trained to use my maternal gifts to see what you white men fail to see on the pages of the Book of the Bush. In that book men and animals, birds and insects subscribe their essays. Added to my inherited maternal gifts are those inherited from my white father. I see with the eyes of a black man and reason with the mind of a white man, and in the bush I am supreme.

"In this bush Simone found no clues. That is not surprising to me. There were no common clues for him to find: most of the uncommon clues remain for me to discover. They are written indelibly in the Book of the Bush on certain pages relative to these crimes I have yet to read. Remember, Lee, that although some men sneer at me on account of my mid-race, I am superior to the blacks because I can reason, and superior to many white people because I can both reason well and see better than they. I have in all my career never arrested a man, black or white. Such work is distasteful to me. As my chief, Colonel Spendor, often says, I'm no damned policeman's shadow. No ... but I am an investigator of crime, and I will demonstrate how I investigate these crimes. You shall learn. You shall gain credit and put the detestable Simone well in the background.

"Now … There is, I believe, coming into general use in America, a method which will bring out finger-prints on clothes. I did think of having Mabel Storrie's clothes sent to America for examination, but time is against me. We shall certainly have one, if not more, sand-storms within the next month or two, and during a sand-storm the strangling brute is active. Let us hope, and hope sincerely, for more sand-storms to come in the near future. Did Simone confide much in you?"

Lee grinned when he awoke from the trance into which Bony's little speech had thrown him.

"Let's say he boasted to me," he corrected.

"Well, then. Did he ever say he thought that the murderer was a tree-climber?"

"A tree-climber! No, he didn't."

"What is your opinion of Donald Dreyton?" was Bony's next question; and now, before Lee answered, his puzzled frown vanished.

"Dreyton is quite a decent man. Never given me the ghost of any trouble. He doesn't drink to excess, and is liked by everyone."

"He appeared to me in that light. And yet. … Tell me all you know about him."

"I have him pat all right. He arrived here from Broken Hill three days before Alice Tindall was murdered. He put up at the hotel, and his luggage consisted of one large port-manteau. The day after his arrival he got work on Wirragatta as a homestead rouseabout. Then, on the very day Alice Tindall was killed, or rather the day preceding that night, he relieved the book-keeper, who left. Dreyton was book-keeping for eight months before he left the office to take on the rabbit boundary-fence. He's been on that ever since."

"Concise! Excellent!" murmured Bony. "What was he before he came here?"

Lee laughed shortly.

"You've got me there. I don't know. And no one else does, either. He has never told us, and, as you know, we bush folk don't ask unwanted questions about a man's past history."

"Hum! When a man does not discuss his past, the past will not always bear discussion. Why did he leave the office for the fence?"

"Got tired of the office, I suppose."

"When he came here, had he had any bush experience?"

"I think not," replied Lee. "No, he was a raw new chum."

Bony fell silent, idly watching a moth circling under the lamp. Lee watched him. Then:

"To use an Americanism, I don't *get* Donald Dreyton. I know, of course, that he is an Englishman, originally a member of what is termed the 'upper class'. But as there are so many degrees within each class of English society—and I mean that word in its widest sense—I, an ignorant Australian, am at a loss definitely to place him. Is he a soldier, a sailor, a lawyer, a churchman, a diplomat? Or rather was he any one of these? I find it extremely difficult to believe that he left the office, and the comforts of life at the Wirragatta homestead, for the opposite conditions of life on a boundary-fence just because he became tired of office work. There is, I think, something more behind that change from one pole to the other than a mere desire for change. I think so still more now that Dreyton has been offered the office work after a long period on the fence, and has declined to take it on permanently."

"May be something in what you say, sir ... Bony. Still, it doesn't seem to have any bearing on these strangling cases."

Swiftly came the question:

"How do you know?" When Lee made no answer, Bony went on, "On the list you have drawn up for me is the name of the man who killed two people and the name of him who nearly killed Mabel Storrie. The actions and the reactions of all those people on our list which are not plain to us must be investigated. Without patience a detective is a block of wood.

"As I pointed out just now, like Simone, I have to begin an investigation without one leading clue. The murderer didn't leave behind him his hat, or his false teeth, or his pipe, or a weapon. He left no finger-prints other than those, possibly, on the victim's clothes. He left no tracks, for the wind wiped them away. He did wear rubber-soled shoes and, for a reason I have not yet established he climbed trees along Nogga Creek the night Mabel Storrie was attacked."

"How do you know—about the——?"

"Please do not interrupt. Listen, note, and don't question me. We will work together, and you will receive a lot of the credit, and score off the redoubtable Simone. Now, from nothing, or next to nothing, let us at least begin to build up the personality of this criminal. That he knows the locality, especially of Nogga Creek and Wirragatta River, is proved. He operates on dark, starless nights. When the girl Storrie is sufficiently recovered to talk to us of her horrific experience, she will tell us that she did not see her attacker because he attacked her from behind as, in the opinion of Dr. Mulray, he attacked both Marsh and Tindall. For the committal of all these crimes he chose a night following a day of wind and high-blown sand, and a sunset indicating that the next day would be as bad, if not worse. He reveals cunning there—marked cunning—and there is, by the way, no fundamental difference of meaning between 'cunning' and 'clever'.

"Now!—Where the road begins to dip down the man-made incline to the creek-bed, the bordering trees meet over it. There is evidence that recently someone climbed up the tree on the Catfish Hole side of the road, and then worked his way along boughs until he gained position over the centre of the road. He dropped from the bough as Mabel Storrie passed under him. He dropped from a bough as Alice Tindall passed under him at Junction Waterhole. To do that he must be agile and strong and sure, and because he was so sure of foot and of hand, I believe it was by no means the first time he reached that position over the Broken Hill road."

"Hang-dog Jack would fit," interjected the sorely-tempted Lee.

"Physically, yes; mentally, perhaps not. Do not forget that the man Marsh was not murdered under a tree, but in the open near the two Common gates. That is a piece of the puzzle which is difficult to place, but I will surely place it. Let us now consider the incidence of time. Each of these three crimes was committed within a period of three hours—from eleven to two o'clock. There may be—I feel sure there *is*—significance in this.

"In this part of Australia we have each year many wind-storms of one day's duration, a lesser number of two days' duration, and a lesser number still of three days' duration.

Here is a point of importance to us. The close of a day of wind and dust will in ninety-nine times in every hundred indicate whether the following day will be fine and clear or windy and dusty. The close of a fine day will not always foretell a following day of wind and dust.

"Let me be clear. Any person having a reasonable knowledge of this part of Australia knows at the close of a day of wind and dust what will be the conditions of the next day. Our murderer has this knowledge. He strangles after a day of wind and dust and when the weather signs at sunset foretell another day of wind and dust to follow. You say that Dreyton was a new chum to the bush, and most certainly a stranger to this part of it, when Alice Tindall was murdered. Therefore, his ignorance of the bush and its weather portents go far towards wiping his name off our list. Hang-dog Jack—how long has he been working in this district?"

"At least five years. He was a sailor at one time, but he is certainly a bushman now."

"A sailor, eh! Hum! Promising. All right, let us try a little harder to visualize this murderer. His climbing exploits indicate great strength, agility and familiarity with certain trees. His mental ability is proved by the fact that he wears rubber-soled shoes, by the fact that he likes to take his victims unawares by dropping out of a tree as they pass under him, and by the fact that he chooses a night for his crime when it is certain it will blow with force the next day. Lastly, and most importantly, by the fact that he does not leave at the scene of his crimes his wooden leg or his braces, his glass eye, if he wears one, or any of the normal clues which occupy such important positions in a normal murder trial. I am not being humorous. There are a hundred clues our strangler could have left behind him, none of which Simone could be expected to discover, all of which I would discover."

"Motive?" breathed Constable Lee.

"I have been expecting you to raise that point," continued Bony. "Motive! By the repetition of his crimes our murderer has made his fatal mistake. Taken separately, each crime could offer several motives, or one of several. Together they point to no one particular motive save gratification of the lust to kill.

"The Strangler's victims have been two women and one man. Two of them were robbed of their lives; the third almost lost hers. Nothing was taken from the bodies, and the three victims were not connected with each other, and could scarcely have been connected with the Strangler through scheme or plot, jealousy or frustration.

"Into this brute's activities chance enters strongly. He may be periodically governed by his lust to kill. It may be—I think it is—that the presentation of the opportunity to kill has to be coincidental with the periodic outbursts of lust. By that I mean that the murderer may have been presented with victims coincidental with a particular weather phase, that he did not choose the dates on which he killed though he must have known that the following day would be stormy. It is possible that every night separating two days of high wind he is out on the hunt for a victim, and that only by chance does he obtain one."

Constable Lee's lips were pressed tightly together and his eyes were gleaming from beneath lowered lids. Bony smiled at him and added:

"So you see, Lee, that no reasonable man could expect Sergeant Simone to succeed. But reasonable men will expect success of me. Who is the oldest resident in this district?"

"Old Grandfer Littlejohn, I think," Lee replied, starting.

"What is the condition of his memory?"

"Poor—when he wants it to be. He's a gossip. Anything you say to him will be retailed to Mrs. Nelson. He is her secret service."

"Oh! Who is the next longest resident here?"

"Dogger Smith, now working on Wirragatta. He has the body of a giant and the vigour of a man of fifty, but the majority of the guessers put his age at ninety. Been here for more years than I've lived. He is never going to die. He'd interest even you with his yarns of the old times. You interested in the old days?"

"The old days of Carie, yes. Very much so. This Dr. Mulray—what type of man is he?"

"He is a pendulum."

"A what?" asked the astonished Bony, and Lee grinned. "He's a pendulum. I was looking into a dictionary some time ago to find out what 'pensile' meant, when I came across the word 'pendulum', which describes Dr. Mulray. He has pendulous eyelids, pendulous cheeks, a pendulous lower lip and a pendulous stomach. Age, about sixty. Height, about five feet nine inches. Circumference at greatest part about four feet. If you can play chess, he'll do anything for you, give you anything. I don't play chess."

Bony broke into low laughter, saying:

"You know, Lee, I think I like you. Do you remember what the word 'pensile' means?"

"Yes. When a man's suspended at the end of a rope he's pensile."

Bony stood up.

"I thought so," he murmured, "but I was not sure. Now I'm off."

Chapter Eight

The Broken Hill Road

To be appreciated, beauty must be felt as well as seen.

To those having the eyes to see and the soul to feel, the great plains of inland Australia present countless facets of beauty: these same plains offer to the man with good eyesight, but a shrivelled soul, nothing other than arid desert.

This early November morning the bush presented to one man at least all its vivid colours, all its allure, to stir his imagination as well as his pulses, to delight his mind as well as to subjugate consciousness of his body. Doing all this, the bush was, indeed, beautiful, for beauty only has the power thus to raise man out of himself.

It was ten minutes to eight when Bony reached the Broken Hill road and the scene of his labours. To the south of him ranged the trees bordering Nogga Creek, the soft breeze tipping each slender leaf with gold, the mass of them supporting the softly azure sky beyond. To the west and east the bluebush merged into a dove-grey carpet, a carpet which stretched away to the foot of the town in the north and rolled by and beyond those significant sand-dunes, which were not there when Mrs. Nelson was a girl.

Bright against the sky lay the red-painted roof of Nelson's Hotel, and, so clear was this crystal air, Bony could actually see the corrugations of that roof. In contrast to its colour the unpainted roof of Smith's Bakery shimmered like faint blue water. Men and cows and goats of Lilliputian size moved about Carie's one street, for the sun was not yet hot enough to create the mirage. There appeared to be a void, not atmosphere, between all those distant objects and the retina of Bony's eyes. It seemed to him, this brilliant morning, as though he had returned from a long sojourn in a dim cavern. This bright world was painted lavishly with blue, green, soft grey, red, yellow and black, colours mixed and laid on in the grand, the majestic manner as only the Master Hand can do it. Eden could not possibly have been more beautiful.

Beyond Nogga Creek came the growing hum of a powerful car. Bony's ears informed him when it was negotiating the far bank of the creek, when it was crossing the wide bed of the creek, when it was mounting the sharp incline before bursting into the sunlight to send to him—and to Mrs. Nelson on her veranda—reflected bars of brightness from its chromium fittings.

It was a big car having especially wide rear seats, driven by a cigarette-smoking youth who wore his cloth cap back to front. Beside him were three passengers. The youth waved a lordly hand, and one of the passengers shouted something as the machine sped by the watching detective like the iron point of a spear fashioned with the red dust raised by it. And in the dust laboured the ghost of a Cobb and Co.'s coach drawn by five straining horses and driven by a wide-brimmed felt-hatted man who wielded a long, snaking whip.

An hour later there emerged from the Nogga Creek trees the figure of a man astride a piebald horse. Tiny spurts of dust rose from the animal's hoofs to blur the legs from the knees down. The rider sat his saddle bolt upright. Methodically his switch rose from and fell upon the horse's right rump, but the horse took no notice of either it or the full voice continually commanding it to:

"Come on, Jenny!"

It was evident to the observant Bony that Jenny long since had decided upon the speed at which she should "come on". Or perhaps it might be that the rider long since had resigned himself to the speed at which Jenny was capable of coming on. Whatever the fact, the horse approached Bony at a steady three miles an hour, and then, without command, when it was opposite the detective, she abruptly stopped and fell asleep.

From beneath pendulous brows a pair of steady grey eyes regarded Bony. Pendulous cheeks were extended as though their owner was winded. The pendulous stomach almost rested on the saddle pommel.

As though the distance separating him from the man at the fence was a full half-mile, the horseman said, "Good day there! Who the devil are you? I've never seen *you* before."

It seemed that for this horseman not to have seen any one before was to be affronted. The switch rose and fell, and the horse again was commanded to "come on". She therefore awoke and staggered off the road to bring her master beside the fence, and then again fall asleep.

"Good morning, doctor!" Bony said politely. "You are out early today."

"Early! Early be cursed! Why, it's after nine." The pendulous cheeks became fully distended as though the accusation had the effect of physical exertion. "Early! Why, I've been abroad these three hours. Who are *you*?"

There spoke the man long used to being obeyed and never become used to the expectation of being obeyed.

"My name is Fisher, doctor. Joe Fisher," replied Bony gravely. "I am a stranger here. That is possibly why you have not seen me before."

"Then how the devil do you know who I am?"

"I have heard your description, doctor."

"Ah ... my description, eh?"

"Yes. You were described to me as a fine figure of a man who rode a piebald mare."

Now were the pendulous cheeks distended twice. The voice became a roar.

"I'll have no word said against my Jenny. She has carried me in foul weather and fine this fourteen years, and she's not going to lie down and die until I do. No, sir! She is the best horse in western New South Wales, and I'll lay this switch across the shoulders of the man who argues the point. So you're Joseph Fisher, eh? You were camped at Catfish Hole the night Mabel Storrie was nigh strangled to death. Did you do it?"

"Doctor ... please!"

"Well, someone did, and it could have been you as well as another. However, you *look* honest enough."

"How is Miss Storrie this morning?"

"She's recovering, poor child. She received a cruel blow to her forehead, and she'll want time, and lots of it, to mend."

"Has she regained consciousness?"

"She has lucid periods. I fear the effects of the blow, as well as the effects of the strangulation, much less than the effects of the shock given her mind."

"The shock to her mind must have been indeed terrible. Has she been able to describe her assailant?"

"No. She didn't see the blackguard. He came up behind her. He joined his fingers across her throat and pressed the balls of his thumbs into the back of her neck. I tell you it's damnable. Here am I paying taxes—here we all are paying taxes on everything we eat and drink and put on our weary backs in order to support a lot of useless world-touring politicians who won't give us real detectives to bring a common garrotter to book. We bush folk are no one's concern, and when we want policemen with brains they send us Sergeant Simone. Oh, a great man is Sergeant Simone. He'll look at you and swear you are the murderer just because he doesn't like the way you part your hair. Tish! He can rant and rave and threaten and look wise, but he's got a brain no bigger than a rabbit's. He tells me he can play chess, and when I invite him to my board he— — The man's an ass."

"So you play chess, doctor?"

"Of course I play it. If I had my way I'd make every policeman play chess for six solid months, with time off only to eat and sleep. Then we would have real detectives sent us when we need 'em. I suppose you don't play?"

"Yes, I play a medium game."

"Ah! So you play, eh?"

Again the cheeks were fully distended. Then the irate manner slowly waned, vanished, was replaced by one of hail-fellow-well-met.

"If that is so, I hope to have the pleasure of your visit to my house. You will find me at home nearly any night. And, sir, at your service. Might I expect you tonight?"

"You are exceedingly kind, doctor. I will be delighted," Bony assented.

"No more delighted than I, but heaven help you if you cannot play better than that wretched Sergeant Simone, for then, should I ever get my hands on you professionally, I'll make you wish you were never born. And don't laugh. Men meet doctors as unexpectedly as they meet death. Good day to you, Joe. Come on, Jenny!"

Jenny opened her eyes and "came on", leaving the smiling Bony gazing after her and her master and in his ears the dwindling command to "Come on, Jenny!"

From the hip-pocket of his drill trousers, Bony extracted the list of names provided by Constable Lee. He felt he was doing a rash thing, but he deliberately crossed off the name of Dr. Mulray.

Towards eleven o'clock he saw, glittering in the sunlight, a smart single-seater car speeding from Wirragatta along the creek to the boundary gate. He was too far distant to reach the gate in time to open it for the woman driver who was obliged to descend, open the gate, run the car through to the Broken Hill road, and then descend again to close it. The car was turned south, and after it had disappeared among the creek trees Bony decided that its driver was Stella Borradale. And then, when a few minutes later the hum of its engine ceased, he guessed that Stella was visiting the Storries.

He had taken his lunch and billy to the trees, there to obtain wood with which to boil the water he used from the canvas bag, when he heard the car returning. Thus it was that, again reaching the gate, Stella found Bony waiting and holding it open for her passage. Having driven the car through the gateway, Stella braked it to a stop and waited for the detective, who presently appeared hatless beside her.

Waiting for her to speak first, he watched her eyes lose their expression of haughty good humour. Absolutely without snobbery as she was, Stella naturally was conscious of inherited superiority over this coloured man, but as her swift gaze moved about his well-chiselled features, finally to become levelled at his blue eyes which were regarding her respectfully she received a queer little shock.

Not till long afterwards did she recognize just what she was now seeing in the depths of his blue eyes. In that first moment of meeting Napoleon Bonaparte, she recognized a mind superior to that of any half-caste she ever had known. She was pleased to think that the new hand did not see the effect, and therefore did not know the cause of the shock. After all, was she not the part-owner of a principality, and was he not a half-caste station-hand?

"Are you Joseph Fisher?"

"Yes, madam, I am he. I regret that I was too distant to open the gate when you came from the homestead."

Without looking away from him, Stella groped about the seat of the car, found her vanity bag and took from it her cigarette-case.

"Where do you come from?" she asked while her fingers blindly removed a cigarette from the case. The question was one she felt she had a right to ask, but immediately she had put it she felt it to be an impertinence, and no longer could she encounter Bony's eyes. She was becoming angry with herself, not at having asked the question of a half-caste, but for asking it of this man whose clear blue eyes regarded her so gravely. With a quick movement, she thrust the cigarette between her lips—and then found a burning match held in service.

"I am a native of Queensland," stated Bony, now smiling. "At the beginning of things for me I was found beside my dead mother in the shade cast by a sandalwood-tree. I was taken to a mission station where I was reared by the matron—the finest woman who ever lived."

Stella now was looking at Bony with a singular expression, an expression which at once troubled him because he could not define its cause.

"You speak well," she told him. "You must have received a fair education."

"Yes. I worked my way up through—Yes, I had quite a good education."

"Indeed! And your name is Joseph Fisher?"

Bony bowed the lie. And then Stella Borradale laughed.

"But why have you come all this way to work? This is a long way from, say Banyo, which I am told is on the railway between Brisbane and Sandgate?"

She saw now the blue eyes blink, and at once was assured of his identity.

"Banyo!" he repeated. "Did you say Banyo, Miss Borradale?"

"I did. You know, Joe, I don't like your alias at all. It is not nearly so nice as your real name, Mr. Napoleon Bonaparte."

Defeated, found out, Bony chuckled.

"The victory is to you, Miss Borradale," he said quickly. "Now please tell me how you guessed."

"By putting two under two and adding them. My brother has long been expecting a mysterious visitor. Then you arrived. Then he and Constable Lee and you held long conference in the study. Those two points make number two. When you said you came from Brisbane and mentioned the sandalwood-tree and the matron of the mission, you gave me the second number two. When I added them up to make four I at once recalled what my dear friend, Mrs Trench, of Windee, told me about Detective-Inspector Bonaparte. (*The story is told in The Sands of Windee) I should have known you were no ordinary bush worker three seconds after I saw you just now. Being so facile at inductive reasoning, I'm sure I must be right in saying that you are here to investigate two horrible murders and a very near-murder."

"Now that you know, may I depend on your co-operation?"

"Most certainly. Anything I can do I will do gladly."

"The only people who know my real name and vocation are your brother and Lee. I chose to adopt an alias and work as a station-hand through no urge to be melodramatic. My task is to find a monster hidden among a community of normal people, and as a station-hand success will be less difficult to attain. It is really essential that no one other than your brother and the constable, and now you, should know me for a detective."

"I will not so much as breathe it," Stella affirmed earnestly.

"To no one?"

"To no one. You may depend on me. Having heard such wonderful stories of you from Mrs. Trench and Dash Trench, the gloom cast by this strangling beast seems already lighter. Do you think you will find him?"

"Naturally. I never fail."

"And may I—in private, of course—call you Bony, as Mrs. Trench does?"

"Assuredly. I shall insist on it."

To them the hum of a car came from Carie way. Turning, Bony saw it at the Common gate.

"This," he said, "may be Sergeant Simone. He arrived last night."

"Oh!" the grey eyes narrowed and the keen blue eyes did not fail to notice it. "Then I will get along, Bony. Sergeant Simone disapproves of women smoking cigarettes, and I am not going to throw away a half-smoked one. I think it such a pity that Sergeant Simone always arrives here after one of these terrible crimes and never before one is committed."

"Might I ask why?" inquired Bony.

"Because then Sergeant Simone might be the victim. *Au revoir*. I'll keep my mouth shut about it, never fear, And please, please tell me from time to time how you are getting on."

For a moment the detective thrilled at her laughing face, and as he looked after the car and its rising dust he remembered the list of names in his possession. Stella Borradale's name was down on that list. It was absurd to have it there, but then the name of Mrs. Nelson was there, too. He crossed to rebuild the fire for the tea making, and he was busy with it when the car from Carie pulled up with screaming brakes.

A harsh voice shouted, "Hey, you! Come here!"

Chapter Nine

Detective-Sergeant Simone

Just beyond the closed gate stood three men. Bony instantly recognized Constable Lee and the slight young man whom he had met the previous evening, but the hugely fat man dressed in light grey flannels was a stranger. It was this fat man who shouted:

"Hey, you! Come here!"

He was like an old-time sergeant shouting at a private when men in the ranks were less important than the regimental mascot, and the singular thing about this man's voice was the clarity of his articulation when his teeth were clenched on a cigar. It says much for Bony's sense of humour that he instantly obeyed the summons with a distinct twinkle in his eyes. He was careful to close the gate after having passed through it. He now saw with interest agate-hard strong white teeth biting viciously on a large cigar and green agate-hard eyes glaring down at him from a superior height.

"What's your name?" rasped Sergeant Simone.

"I am Joseph Fisher—as Constable Lee has doubtless told you," Bony replied lightly. On observing that his tone and careless indifference at once aroused the unreasoning animus of a beast, he added, "And who are you?"

"Never mind who I am, and never mind what Constable Lee might have told me. You answer my question and no slinking round corners. What's your name?"

"Joseph Fisher."

"You were camped at Catfish Hole the night Miss Storrie was attacked and left for dead?" the question shot out.

"That is so," replied Bony, further fanning a smouldering fire.

"What time did you make camp that night?"

"That I couldn't say."

"Well, what time did you leave camp the next morning?"

"That I could not say, either."

"Well, you had better say, and mighty sharp, too, or you'll be for it. I don't stand no nonsense from nigs and half-castes. You're a likely looking bird to have done this last crime. And you are wasting my time."

The slight young man was looking at Bony miserably, but the face of Constable Lee registered a flash of genuine happiness. Bony's calmness gratified him, and now he was mentally licking his chops.

"My dear sergeant——" began Bony, when Simone cut in:

"Don't you 'dear sergeant' me," he roared without removing the cigar from his mouth. "What time did you camp that night at Catfish Hole?"

Bony sighed with emphasized despair.

"I tell you I don't know," he said. "There was no sun visible and I had no watch. Because I had no watch and because later the stars were invisible, too, I could not state the time that the truck crossed Nogga Creek on its way to Carie and the time when it came back."

"Then guess the time—do you hear me?"

"I can guess and be nearly correct. I camped about half-past six o'clock. It was about eight when the truck passed on its way to Carie, and it was about half-past two when it returned. It was about a quarter to two that I heard the curlew scream from about here. It was a wild night, and I was dozing when it screamed, and, as I told Constable Lee, it might just as well have been Miss Storrie screaming as that bird. It is all down in the statement I made to the constable here."

"Humph!" grunted the hugely fat sergeant from somewhere deep in his stomach. He took a fresh bite on his half-masticated cigar. Then:

"I don't like that statement. To me it smells fishy, and I've got a good nose for fishy statements. I didn't rope in Moorhouse Alec and half a dozen other crooks without knowing a thing or two about statements. Yes, my lad, there is a lot queer about your statement."

"I trust that I omitted nothing," murmured Bony.

"What's that? Omitted nothing? You might have done. I reckon you made up that statement, and what's more I reckon you spouted it from memory, having been learnt it by someone else."

"Why do you think that?" Bony inquired mildly.

"I'll tell you, my lad, why I think it," Simone vouchsafed, at the same time bending forward and leering down at the detective. "I gotta sister what reviews novels in a lit'ry paper, and you and that statement is what she'd say wasn't in character."

"Dear me! I hope all the participles were correct."

"What's that?"

"I said I hoped all the participles were correct," Bony replied. "I was always weak on participles."

"I suppose you are trying to be funny. Well, I'll tell you where you and that statement don't square. It is too well put together for a half-caste swagman and fence cleaner."

"You relieve my mind, sergeant. For the moment I actually thought you had discovered an error in the participles," Bony said gravely, and even the slight young man forgot to be miserable. "Really, I did dictate the statement and Constable Lee really did take it down."

"All right. We'll return to the statement later on. Come on with me and no tricks, or I'll come down on you like a ton of bricks. I want you to show me just where you camped at this Catfish Hole, and where you sat all night with your back to a tree—according to your statement."

The four men walked under the bordering box-trees to the lower extremity of the sheet of water called Catfish Hole. There Bony pointed at the charred embers of his fire, now partly submerged by wind-driven sand. Then he indicated the big tree-trunk, around which no man could have reached to strangle him. Simone expectorated with practised neatness before again glaring down at Bony from his superior height.

"Where did you come from?" he roared, to add without a pause, "Come on, now! Out with it!"

"I came up from Broken Hill."

"You don't belong there. I've never seen you before."

"Oh, no. I came across to Broken Hill from Barrakee Station. You see, I was working at Barrakee."

"Barrakee, eh! We'll soon check up on that. Who owns Barrakee?"

"Mr. Thornton."

"Humph!" Again came the devastating grunt. Then Simone turned to the slim young man.

"Now, Elson, what time was it you left Miss Storrie to come on alone?" he barked.

"I don't know the time exactly," replied Barry Elson, who was dark, good looking, dapper, a horseman writ large all over him. "It would be about twenty to two in the morning."

"It was a nice thing to do, any'ow, leaving a poor defenceless young woman to come on home alone a night like that, with this strangling brute in the offing," Simone said insultingly. "To date we've only got your word that you didn't go hurrying after her—if you parted with her at all—and try hard to do her in. Oh, yes, you can fidget, Elson. I've got two eyes and a bit right on you, same as I got 'em on Mister Fisher, here."

"Let us hope you will not contract eye-strain," Bony murmured.

"What's that? You talking to me?"

"I am under that impression, sergeant. You have been staring so hard that you fail to see certain facts. Miss Storrie was attacked by the man who murdered Alice Tindall and young Marsh. When Alice Tindall was murdered, Mr. Elson was on holiday down in Adelaide, and I was not within hundreds of miles when either of the two crimes were committed."

Simone for the first time took from his mouth the now almost completely eaten cigar. His lips creased to express heavy sarcasm.

"Quite the detective, eh? So you and Mister Elson can be acclaimed innocent little lambs? Now let me tell you that the feller who attacked Mabel Storrie wasn't the bird who done in them other two. If he had been that bird, he would have done the job on the Storrie girl good and proper. As it was, she was attacked by an imitator of the murderer, and a darned poor imitator, too. I'll tell you two some more. The real gent is strong. The feller who attacked Miss Storrie wasn't so strong. That's why he failed to kill her. So don't you two think you're gonna get out of it as easily as all that."

"There are, of course, other facts," Bony said carelessly. He was enjoying himself thoroughly, and Lee, guessing it, was enjoying himself too.

"I don't want to hear about *your* facts and *your* ideas," shouted Simone, viciously flinging to the ground the remains of a once beautifully symmetrical cigar. He was now standing rule-straight, his head thrown back, the velour hat appearing to be much too small for his bullet head, three layers of fat welling over his linen collar. "I'm head serang (*The boatswain of a Lascar or East Indian crew.*) of this investigation, and you are gonna know it before I'm through.—Now then, you, Fisher! How did you know Mister Elson was down in Adelaide when Alice Tindall was done in?"

"I'll tell you," Elson began to say when he was cut off like water gushing from a tap.

"You'll tell me nothing till I ask you to tell me things, and then you'll be mighty quick off the mark," Simone snapped. "Now—you——"

"I met Mr. Elson in Carie last night," explained Bony with unruffled calm. "It appears that a good many people regard him with grave suspicion, and so I asked him if he remembered just where he was when both Frank Marsh and Alice Tindall were murdered. As their murderer undoubtedly tried to murder Miss Storrie, when it came out that Mr. Elson was not in the district when either of those other two were murdered, it seems very unlikely that he murdered the girl he is in love with. That's obvious."

"And it's obvious that you and him have been in collusion," sneered the sergeant. "Oh, no, my bucks! That won't go down. The feller who attacked Miss Storrie wasn't as strong as the bird who did the murdering. And I can see two gents right now who ain't so very strong. Now we'll have a squint at the scene of the crime."

Huge though he was, Sergeant Simone walked with strength and easy carriage. A bull-doggish appearance gave to him a personality not possessed by the easy-going Constable Lee, albeit a personality rudely overbearing and ruthless. He would not be lacking courage when dealing with armed desperadoes, but as a detective dealing with a bush case and with bush people he was a freak.

Lee managed to wink appreciatively at Bony before striding off at Simone's side, and at half a dozen paces behind them walked Barry Elson and Bony.

"Thanks, Joe," whispered the young man.

Bony smiled. His first impression of this overseer who was employed on a neighbouring station named Westall's had been very favourable. It was continuing to be favourable, but a wide experience had taught him not to value a first, or even a second, impression. The reason why he had crossed the doctor's name off his list was his conviction that the Strangler possessed agility above that of the average man. Mulray was long past physical agility up to the standard set by the average man. So was Mrs. Nelson and Grandfer Littlejohn and many others, and their names would be erased in due time.

What had impressed Barry Elson's innocence on Bony had been the young man's sincerity when, the previous evening, he had made open confession. Then, his handsome dark eyes and quivering lips bespoke sensitiveness and frankness. He explained how, for several years, he had been the Don Juan of the district, and how, when he finally and honestly fell in love with Mabel Storrie, his reputation rode him like an old man of the sea.

Without foundation, Mabel had accused him of flirting, and she rashly presented him with his ring. To make matters worse, he had then got drunk on the day of the dance, but before the dance actually began he was sobered and had striven to "make it up" with her.

Then had occurred the walk following the non-appearance of Tom Storrie and the truck. At the Common Gate Elson had made another desperate attempt to obtain forgiveness, whereupon the still unappeased object of his adoration complained about his drinking. All the evening Mabel really had been as miserable as her lover, and even at this late hour the ghost of his reputation haunted her. It was that wretched ghost, and not the fact that he had been far from sober during the day, which had withheld her forgiveness. They argued for the next several hundred yards, and then, as Elson confessed, he blackmailed her for a kiss or two, with the threats of a dark night and a prowling strangler.

Mabel Storrie, however, was not the girl to be intimidated by threats of such a nature. She was no shrinking miss. She called Elson's bluff and refused his escort farther; and he, as he said, like a fool, took her at her word and walked back to the township. No one had seen him arrive at the hotel, and no one had seen him enter and go to his room.

So now, as the policemen and the suspects walked back to the place where Mabel had been found by the coach people, Bony inquired of himself if Barry Elson could have been made strong enough by the emotion of anger to strangle into unconsciousness, at least, a healthy and robust young woman. "Anger giveth strength," as someone might or might not have said.

"As far as I remember, Lee," Simone was saying, "this Mabel Storrie is quite a hefty wench."

"She'd weigh about a hundred and fifty pounds," Lee estimated as the party arrived at the sand patch examined by Bony in company with Donald Dreyton.

"Humph!" grunted the sergeant, and then he glared at a kookaburra impertinently watching them from a nearby bough. "It was dark that night?"

"As dark as a rabbit's hole."

"That being so, I can't understand why she walked off the road. You'd think she would have stuck to the centre of the track. Of course, she might have been dragged off the road by her attacker. That seems likely enough when we pass out the murderer of them other two and reckon she was attacked by an imitator. The murderer made no attempt to conceal the bodies of them he done in." Baleful green eyes glared at Bony and Barry Elson alternately. "No, she didn't walk off the road to this place. She was dragged off it by the imitator, who expected her brother to pass on the truck."

The kookaburra at this moment chuckled throatily.

"But she *was* attacked on the road and she *did* walk off the road, to trip over that root and stun herself," Bony said lightly.

"You're mighty fly, ain't you, Mister Fisher? How do you know that? Bit of a tracker, eh?"

"You really would like to have proof?"

"You spout your stuff and give less lip."

"Very well." Bony detailed the movements of the girl after the Strangler had let her slip from his hands, concluding with: "On that small claypan are the imprints of her shoes."

"Show 'em!" snapped Simone, striding to the claypan.

Bony pointed to the outline of one shoe-heel he had made more plain with a match point.

"Someone drew that," Simone said scornfully.

"I did," admitted Bony. "But here is another, and here another, which I have not touched."

The sergeant squinted and could see nothing.

"Like hell, there are. You drew that mark on purpose to mislead the police."

"If you stand here and bend low and so look along the surface of the claypan, you will see four heel-marks beside the one I have outlined," urged Bony politely.

With ludicrous effort, Simone stooped and screwed his eyes to pinpoints. Then he jerked straight and snorted:

"I can't see no heel-prints. They ain't there, and you know it. Oh, no, Mister Fisher! You've had your little joke."

When he moved away, Constable Lee took his place and bent low. After a little period of strain he said with semi-conviction:

"I think I can see them."

"You can't see nothing, Lee," raged the sergeant. "You imagine you see tracks 'cos this nig said they was there. Come on! Enough of this. We'll go and interview the victim. You come, too, Mister Elson, so's you can see the results of a dirty piece of work. That goes for you, too, Mister Fisher. And don't either of you ever forget that I can reach out and take you in just when I want to. This time I'm not going back to the Hill without a prisoner."

And then that kookaburra opened wide its beak and cackled and screamed and chuckled, paused for breath and then gave himself a hearty encore.

Chapter Ten

Winged Allies

As Bony had explained to Constable Lee, the detection of criminals in a city is much easier than the detection of the rarer criminal in the bush. Detectives engaged on city crime receive many important clues from the underworld itself. The allies of a city detective are many, because the criminal operates against a static background, such as a house interior, or even a street. The city detective, trained to follow defined lines of investigation, is out of his element when his background of crime changes from the static to become composed of ceaselessly moving sand and the surface of the virgin earth which is exposed to the constant action of sun and wind.

The keen city detective goes to science for assistance as well as for establishing proof. The camera, the microscope, acids and reagents, all are allies of the city detective. Without these scientific allies, in addition to innumerable human contacts, the city-trained detective is lost when investigating a really well-planned crime in the wild bush. Actually, Sergeant Simone was judged harshly for his failures at Carie, for here in the bush he was without his customary allies.

Bony had allies of an entirely different kind, but many of whom were to him as valuable as scientific apparatus is to his city colleagues. For assistance, he called on the birds and the ants, vegetable growths and natural processes. Phenomenal eyesight and the gift of calm patience contributed largely to his successes. Of all his many assistants, he regarded Time as the most important. It was his firm belief that the passage of Time never buried a crime. It was invariably the criminal who strove to bury his crime, and Time which removed the earth and exposed it.

The day following his meeting with Dr. Mulray, Stella Borradale and Sergeant Simone, Bony began an exhaustive examination of the trees along Nogga Creek, beginning with those meeting over the Broken Hill road and that climbed by Donald Dreyton. The wind, having that pressure designated by seamen as a breeze, constantly agitated the foliage. For this he was thankful, as he did not want sharp eyes glued to the business ends of binoculars to observe his movements through the unnatural movement of tree-branches. Even as it was, he was obliged to work carefully in order to conceal his activities from the curious Mrs. Nelson.

High in the tree climbed by the fence-rider, he found a living branch sucker snapped close to the parent branch and hanging by a strip of its smooth bark. The resilience of the sucker was of such strength as to defeat the strongest wind to break it. A mischievous galah or cockatoo had not done the damage, because the break was too broad, and Bony decided that it had been done by a man climbing into the tree.

Himself wedged between a branch and the tree-trunk, the detective closely examined the broken ends of the sucker and the strip of bark holding them together. The bark still retained its soft green colouring, but it was the degree of remaining sap which led Bony to the conviction that at least ten days had passed since this sucker was damaged. That meant it had been broken by a man's body or boot days before Dreyton had climbed the tree and several days before the attack on Mabel Storrie.

Why the fence-rider had climbed the tree was a question now nagging for an answer. Had Dreyton seen something among its branches, causing him to climb the tree? Had the party of quarrelling crows flown to the leopardwood-tree from this tree at Dreyton's approach, and thus had led him to the object over which they quarrelled? Any strange object in a tree would ultimately be discovered by the crows, who would announce the discovery by their cawings. That the crows had not returned to the box-tree after Dreyton had left it might indicate that the object of their insatiable curiosity had been removed by him.

However, all this was conjecture of less moment than the fact that someone had climbed into the tree before Mabel Storrie was nearly murdered. Allied to this fact was the evidence that someone had climbed into the trees overhanging the Broken Hill road and, almost certainly, had dropped from a branch when she was passing beneath them.

Which of the many people living in and around Carie would climb trees? Boys and many girls, too, are great tree-climbers, and of boys and girls Carie had its normal share. But these trees were a full mile from the township. Nevertheless, a mile, or even more, is nothing for healthy youngsters to walk after birds' eggs and bees' honey. There were no children at Wirragatta or at Storrie's Selection, but there were two youths employed on Wirragatta who were capable of climbing trees after young galahs.

Then Bony's next step was to ascertain if the galahs' nests had been robbed, and to do this he did not propose to make inquiries of the townspeople or those at the station.

From introspection his brain again took charge of his eyes. They probed the green-clothed branches of the tree in which he was perched and those of neighbouring trees that were almost interlocked. His gaze moved with deliberate system, moving along each successive branch from trunk to extremity. Thus it was eventually that his gaze became applied to a particular section of a particular branch of the tree next his. Without difficulty, or danger of falling, he passed from tree to tree, and thus was able to bring his gleaming eyes to a point twelve inches from the section of branch which had caught his attention.

For some time he studied this section of living wood, brows knit, brain working to establish the cause of a certain phenomenon. For a distance of eighteen inches the bark of the section was of a different tint. He gripped the same branch with both hands a little beyond the tinted section and began to rasp it. The action produced exactly the same tint—soft rust on the background of grey-green.

The result of the experiment pleased him.

At no little risk of accident, the detective climbed and swung himself from branch to branch, on which he was able to see the same discoloration, for some sixty yards, when he reached a point in the line of trees where there was a break. Down the last tree he slowly descended, and on the trunk he found unmistakable evidence it had often been climbed.

The evidence provided by the trees went to prove that a party of boys had often played follow-my-leader by swinging themselves along the branches of at least twenty trees. Either the boys, or one man, had made a kind of tree-trail over a long period of time, on each occasion making much the same jumps and using the same hand and footholds.

Along the dry bed of the creek Bony walked to the Broken Hill road, knowing himself safe from observation, his eyes glittering when the sunlight shafts fell on them. For two hours he climbed trees, and at places trod a blazed trail among their branches, a trail blazed for such as he to see and reason upon.

At odd hours throughout the whole of the next week, Bony climbed trees, finding in them many things of profound interest which had no possible bearing on his investigation. He came to know Nogga Creek from Junction Waterhole to Catfish Hole and up along Thunder Creek almost to Storrie's house. His work resulted in astonishing knowledge having a direct bearing on his investigation—knowledge given him chiefly by the galahs and their habits.

These rose-breasted, grey-backed parrots favour box-trees in which to nest, those along the two creeks joining to become Wirragatta River having been especially favoured for countless years. And this was the story told by the galahs. ...

*

During the late summer, autumn and winter these birds congregate in large flocks, when they feed together on the distant flats and roost together in adjacent trees. Towards the end of July the units comprising the flocks become imbued with the nuptial madness. Their harsh cries become more harsh and louder still. Their feats of wing become more daring and brilliant, it appearing to the observer that they determinedly "show off" like the male lyre-bird and the male peacock. Then, within the space of a week, the flocks break up into pairs, and during the courting period the old nesting-holes in the trees are cleaned out and prepared for the eggs and the young birds.

Countless generations of birds use the same nest-holes every spring. The holes, of course, have their genesis in the work of the borer and the bardee (*A beetle larva of Australia, Bardistus cibarius, that bores into plants and is used as food by Aborigines.). The rain continues the rotting of the wood, which is pulled out by the birds back to the living walls of wood. To the bottom of these nest-holes is sometimes the length of a man's arm.

The only enemies of the young birds were formerly the wild cats, and now the domesticated cats run wild, and the defensive measures taken by the parent birds to defeat the cats will be attributed to instinct or reason according to the views of the reader. Like all close observers, Bony voted for reason.

When a nest-hole is first prepared, the birds tear away the bark from about the entrance, and, if the hole is at the junction of a branch with the trunk, they clean off the bark about the branch for several feet. With distended combs and much vociferous screeching, they beat and beat their wings against the exposed wood until it is polished to the glass-like surface of a dance floor. No cat, therefore, can possibly find foothold to reach the nest-hole and then claw out the squabs. Every year thereafter the bark-cleared spaces are repolished in this manner.

As previously stated, Bony found many galahs' nests in the trees along Nogga and Thunder Creeks. At this time the nesting-season was well past, and the young birds, having learned to fly, had with their parents joined into flocks.

Along Thunder Creek and along Nogga Creek, eastward of Catfish Hole, the nests provided the detective with indubitable evidence that they had housed young birds this last season, but in those nests in the trees from Junction Waterhole to Catfish Hole there was found no such evidence. Instead, the wisps of grass and feathers deep in these particular holes were old and brittle. Not only the last nesting-season, but at least the season before that, the birds had not used the nest-holes along this section of creek.

It had already become obvious that along this section of trees—from Junction Waterhole up to Catfish Hole—in which the galahs had refused to nest, a party of boys played follow-my-leader and had blazed an easily followed trail among the branches. Either boys, or one man, had made and subsequently used this trail.

The age of the trail was established for Bony by the galahs. About the edges of the wing-polished spaces the bark had grown and overlapped them. With his knife, the detective conducted countless experiments on this overlapping bark until he proved to his entire satisfaction that the birds had not nested along this section of Nogga Creek for four years. The boys, or the single man, by climbing from tree to tree repeatedly, had frightened them from doing so. The trail, therefore, was at least four years old—from two years before Alice Tindall was murdered.

Bony never seriously considered the trail to have been made by a party of boys playing follow-my-leader. He had become convinced that it had been made by a man, and, too, the man who had killed Alice Tindall and attacked Mabel Storrie.

Why did this man climb these trees and swing himself along from branch to branch? Why had he not done his tree-climbing along other sections of the creeks? What, indeed, could be his object? No man would be likely to experience pleasure by doing this. There were no bees' nests to rob of honey, and for years there had been no young galahs to take from the birds' nests. His object could not be to leave on the ground no tracks at those times he killed, for did he not always select a night when the next day was certain to be wildly stormy?

And so the galah's story presented Bony with a singular problem. Why, for at least four years, had a man used the trees along a section of Nogga Creek as another would use a garden path? Try as he might whilst he worked, cleaning the boundary-fence of buckbush, Bony could not solve it. The only man he could imagine doing this "tree walking" was the Wirragatta cook, Hang-dog Jack, and Hang-dog Jack, besides being a human travesty, was also a terrific contradiction.

Bony's mind was still gnawing at this bone late one afternoon as he walked down along the creek road to the homestead after a day's labour, when there overtook him young Harry West astride a fearsome brute of a horse all a-lather with sweat and still sprung with viciousness despite a gruelling gallop.

"Good day-ee, Joe," shouted Harry, even as he slid to earth to jerk the reins over the beast's head and fall into step beside the detective.

Harry West was young and tall and graceful as Adonis, if not so handsome. He was reputed to be the best horseman in the district, and the discerning Bony had quickly noted Harry's natural ability to do well those things he liked doing. With a small-bore rifle Harry could bring down crows on the wing. With a stockwhip he could flick away pins stuck into a table without disturbing the flour scattered about them. But, although he had attended school until the official leaving age, he was unable to compose a simple letter. He was remarkably proficient in counting hundreds of sheep passing through a gateway, but was beaten by a simple problem sum. In his opinion, any work not able to be done from the back of a horse was exceedingly degrading. Bony was considering the removal of *West, Henry,* from his list.

"She's come, Joe," Harry said, the blood mounting into his tanned face even as his hard elbow prodded Bony's ribs. The smart felt hat was pushed back and there was to be seen a greased "quiff", which, however, was a poor sort of thing compared with that so carefully and expertly trained by James

Spinks, Mrs. Nelson's barman.

"Who has arrived, Harry?" Bony asked mildly.

"Who? Why, you know. The ring! She came by this morning's mail."

"Ah!" murmured the enlightened detective.

One of his first tasks at Wirragatta had been to advise Harry West about an engagement ring, and with a jeweller's catalogue to aid him he had chosen a platinum ring set with a square-cut diamond.

"She's a humdinger," Harry announced with tremendous enthusiasm. When recalling the price paid, Bony thought the ring should certainly be that, and more. Harry ran on: "If they had sent a ring with a round diamond, I'd have sent it back with my opinion on 'em. That was a natty idea of yours, thinking of a square diamond. Can't say I ever seen one before."

"It is because they are not common that I urged you to purchase a ring set with one. That you simply had to buy a platinum setting was against my advice. A hundred guineas is a great deal of money to spend on a ring."

"It ain't too much to spend on a ring for my Tilly. A thousand-quid one wouldn't be good enough for her. Any'ow, if we fall hard on bad times, this ring will pawn for a goodish bit."

"I admire your forethought, but not your pessimism, Harry. Having had the pleasure of meeting and speaking to your young lady, I concur that a cheap ring would be an insult."

"Thanks, Joe," Harry said as another man might when accepting a knighthood. Hazel eyes regarded Bony with bashful intensity. "Cripes!" he burst out. "I wished I could talk like you."

"Practise, my dear Harry."

"I ain't got no time."

"Then let us talk about Tilly. Do you intend to marry her one day?"

"Too flamin' right I do," came the prompt reply. "I heard only yesterday that old Alec, the boss stockman, was pulling out, and aimed to retire to the Hill. He's occupying one of the married cottages, you know."

"The married cottages! Oh, you mean one of the cottages occupied by married people on the far side of the river. So you think you may obtain the occupancy of one?"

"I ain't sure, Joe. I sorta hinted to the boss this morning that I'd like to get married and settle down on Wirragatta. I'm a bit young yet, I suppose, but if old Alec leaves, I'm as good as the next for his place. Like to see the ring?"

"Yes, I would."

With approval, Bony noted Harry's firm chin and the straight nose. For two minutes, whilst the horse whistled and stamped and tugged at the reins looped from Harry's arm, they stood to admire the expensive ring. The price paid was enormous for a station-hand.

"Think she's good enough?" asked Harry with swift doubt.

For an instant Bony thought he referred to Tilly, the maid-guardian to Mrs. Nelson. Then:

"Why, yes," he replied. "It is a truly beautiful ring. So you really want to marry her and settle down for life?"

"Too right—with Tilly. She'll do me, Joe."

"Then, married to Tilly, if you always play the game of life as it should be played, you will never regret it."

For a space, they walked in silence. Then Harry said earnestly:

"What d'you think of my girl, Joe?"

"When she smiles, she is lovely," Bony told him, remembering Tilly's plainness of features and beauty of eyes. "It will be your life-long vocation to keep her smiling. How old were you when you first came to Wirragatta?"

"Seventeen. I bin here a bit over five years."

Bony plunged.

"I suppose that you, like most boys and young men, have often climbed these creek trees for galahs' eggs?"

"Can't say as I ever had the time," replied Harry. "I was more keen on horses and things."

For a little while they walked in silence, and then for a little while they again discussed Tilly. Eventually Bony suggested:

"When the blacks, who used to camp hereabouts, suddenly left, you must have noticed the quietness at Wirragatta. I understand that the tribe was quite a large one."

"Too right! There musta been half a hundred all told when mustered: After poor Alice Tindall was murdered they all cleared off. I don't blame 'em. Old Billy Snowdrop, the head man, tipped something like that would happen. He was a funny bloke, all right. He uster reckon his tribe was cursed by a special banshee or ghost wot lived in the trees, and after they all cleared off and went outback I seen him one day, and he asked me if I ever seen or heard the banshee after he got Alice. The banshee, I mean, not Billy

Snowdrop. Get me?"

"Yes, I think I do. That is all very interesting," Bony remarked softly.

Chapter Eleven

A Strange Fellow

Hang-dog Jack was beating his triangle, calling the hands to dinner, when Martin Borradale stepped into the office to find Donald Dreyton at work on his books.

"Hullo! Time to knock off, isn't it?"

Dreyton, looking up, smiled.

"I was beginning to think so," he said, and reached for his pipe and tobacco plug. "Have the Storries got away for Adelaide?"

"Yes. Stella and I have just got back from seeing them away. They made Mabel very comfortable on the truck, and her mother and Dr. Mulray were able to sit with her. Mulray is going down as far as Broken Hill. Mabel seemed bright, but the terrible shock she received is still painfully evident. Mrs. Nelson has been very generous to her."

"You were not particularly mean," Dreyton said dryly. "I remember drawing up your cheque for a hundred."

"They will want it. Mrs. Nelson gave them another hundred and let Storrie off paying the half-yearly interest on her mortgage, which was due this week. What with all that and the sixty-odd pounds raised by public subscription, Mabel should not lack the very best surgical and nursing service. Old Mulray says he thinks one operation at least will be necessary."

"Simone done anything yet, do you know?"

Martin shook his head, saying, "I have heard nothing. It is time something was found out about this strangling swine. Even Stella is getting jumpy, and behind old Alec's leaving, I think, is his wife, who is terrified to leave the doors unlocked after dark. Anyway, I dropped in to speak about a quite different matter."

Borradale paused, and Dreyton noted the flush swiftly mounting into his face. When he again spoke the words came quickly.

"Look here, Donald. My sister and I have been discussing you."

"Indeed!" Dreyton said politely.

"That's right! Counter my—or rather *our*—damned rudeness with suavity," Martin burst out. "You are the most even-tempered fellow I know. Anyway, we discussed you in no critical manner, I assure you. As a matter of fact, we would like to know your real reason for not wanting to remain permanently in the office. It may be none of our business. It probably isn't. On the other hand we might be able to remove a bar to your undertaking the office work for good."

There was but little physical resemblance in Martin to his sister, but a great deal in mannerisms. His eyes were clear and steady—so like his sister's. Dreyton wanted to look away, for he was finding it difficult to meet Martin's gaze. As the temporary book-keeper hesitated to speak the younger man proceeded rapidly and with evident embarrassment.

"I am going to be perfectly frank," he said. "Allen was a good book-keeper, and quite a good fellow, but he was wholly unable to forget he was a book-keeper when out of the office, when over in the house or on the tennis court. We have missed your conversation, your dashed good society, and never before or since you were with us have we been able to accept anyone so entirely without reserve."

Dreyton's brows now were raised a fraction, and still he made no attempt to speak.

"Hang it, man! You're a mystery," Martin exclaimed. "You talk about everything but yourself. You leave a comfortable job and decent living conditions for the life of a fence-rider, which is tougher than that of any stockman. Surely you must be sick of it by now?"

Dreyton's stony expression melted into a slight smile. He stood up and deliberately stretched.

"By no means," he said. "Look at me! I am as tough as leather. I am as healthy, as fit as a Melbourne Cup winner. I see the sun rise every morning, and I can lie abed and look at the stars before going to sleep at night. I can read with profit, for I have the time and the peace to think of what I have read. I miss the tennis, of course, and the good food and the agreeable society, but, Mr. Borradale, I think I have gained more than I have lost."

Dreyton looked all that he said he felt. Compared to him, Martin appeared dapper, and he was endowed generously with physical strength.

"Then, Donald, you won't come back—permanently?"

The other fell to filling his pipe, and having lit it he sat down and said with slow impressiveness, "You know, Mr. Borradale you are being extremely decent to me. I was a-hungered and you gave me food—and all the rest of it. You make me feel an ungrateful dog, and so I would like to put you right on one point where you appear to be wrong. You seem to think that outside the office I forget I am the book-keeper. I don't forget it. I don't forget it for an instant. Neither do you or Miss Borradale, but you are both too splendid ever to let me see or feel it.

"You say I am a mystery. I cannot solve that mystery for you, but I will tell you this much. What *you* have I once had. Seeing what you have poignantly reminds me of the estate from which I have been cast out. To people of that estate book-keepers are considered small if worthy fry. The wounds on my soul given it by my fall are still capable of being scarified by the salt of your affluence—if you will permit the crude simile."

"I have suspected that," Martin said softly. "It's hard luck, but I think you should not let it govern you."

"I most certainly am not worrying about it, or whining about it, Mr. Borradale. I am explaining this now because I cannot be but constantly reminded of your exceptional kindness. It is something like this with me. Alone, with my camels for companions, I can feel a true man. On that fence, when renewing rotten ground-netting, when cutting posts, when tracking my camels, I can forget the past and live the present, be my own master and crave for nothing I haven't got. When in close association with Miss Borradale and yourself I cannot forget or cease to be envious of you. And that doesn't do, as you will agree. I am happy to be able to repay in small measure by undertaking this office work when you are in need of a book-keeper."

The ghost of a scowl which had been growing on Martin's face abruptly vanished.

"I am glad we have been candid," he said, rising. "What must be cannot be helped. Stella and I both like you immensely, and you have only to hint you are tired of the fence life and the book-keeper's billet is yours. Perhaps in time you might be able to change your mind. However, let's pass to something else. Westall's cousin has come up from Melbourne for a holiday, and we have invited him and Westall over for the week-end. We should have some really fast tennis."

"Good! You will have to practise that backhand of yours. As for me— well, I have become a perfect dud."

"Oh, rot, Donald. Hop into your things and come along for a singles. I'll be waiting for you. By the way, I consented to let Joe Fisher borrow the weather records. He has some idea of being able to foretell droughts and good years by a study of them."

Dreyton was locking the books away in the safe when, a few minutes later, Bony entered.

"Good evening, Mr. Dreyton," he said, being careful to address the book-keeper, not the fence-rider.

"Hullo, Joe! What can I do for you?"

Blue-grey eyes encountered deep blue eyes across the book-keeper's writing table.

"I have called for the weather records Mr. Borradale said I could have to study," replied Bony.

"Here they are. I am, however, to point out their value and to ask you to be sure to return them intact."

"Mr. Borradale can depend on me," Bony said with assurance, although he was positive that Borradale had never thought to be so particular.

Dreyton was now openly looking at the clock, but the detective pretended to be dense.

"One is able to foretell with reasonable certainty a dry season or a big rain by observing the ants and the birds, especially the parrot genus," he went on. "I have noted a singular thing about the galahs in this district. Although they have nested with unfailing regularity along Thunder Creek, from Catfish Hole down to the river, along Nogga Creek, they have not nested for at least four years."

Not a muscle of Dreyton's face betrayed his quick interest.

"Indeed!" he said carelessly, and Bony felt the national reserve of the Englishman fall like a cloak about the book-keeper. "What would account for that, do you think?"

"Ah ... it is hard to be positive, Mr. Dreyton. It is so interesting that I would really like to be sure. Galahs, like many other birds, use the same nesting-holes every year, and one cause which may determine their abandonment of their nest-holes would be the systematic robbing of their nests of eggs and young birds. —Do you collect birds' eggs?"

Dreyton laughed, genuinely amused. "Of course not."

"Or obtain young galahs to send to friends in the city?"

"Again, of course not."

"That being so, I was wondering—pardon my unmannerly curiosity—why you climbed one of the Nogga Creek trees that afternoon we met on the boundary-fence."

"How do you know that I climbed that tree?" Dreyton asked, a degree too quickly.

"Your tracks shouted the fact as I was passing on my way back from work. They even told me that you exercised the greatest caution not to permit Mrs. Nelson observing you through her glasses from the hotel balcony."

It was as though Dreyton held his breath whilst Bony spoke. It was the barely audible sigh and not his eyes which betrayed mental strain.

"You're a strange fellow, Joe," he said slowly, but with steel in his voice. "As a matter of fact, I thought I saw something unusual up in that tree. It was nothing, after all. A piece of newspaper."

"Something which had attracted the crows," Bony suggested.

"Er—yes. They were kicking up quite a din as I neared the tree, and they flew away when I came under it. Now be off, there's a good fellow. I'm due at the tennis court, and I am late already."

"A piece of newspaper!" Bony echoed, a note of disappointment in his voice. "I was hoping you would say that you found a piece of grey flannel cloth caught in the ends of a broken sapling."

That brought the temporary book-keeper close to the half-caste, to glare down into the blue eyes from a superior height.

"Just what do you mean?" he asked, and for an instant he looked ugly.

"Mean? Why, what can I mean?"

"What the deuce have my actions to do with you? Are you trying to blackmail me?"

"No, most decidedly not," Bony replied calmly. "I suffer one vice, a curious mind—or should I say a mind enslaved by curiosity? You know, your discovery in that tree is very interesting, Mr. Dreyton. I wonder how that piece of grey flannel—dark-grey, I think it was—came to be impaled by a broken sapling situated at least thirty feet above ground. From the trousers of a bird-nester, I suppose. Probably he accounted for the galahs not nesting about there."

"There's no doubt about that," Dreyton said with forced carelessness.

"Now do go away, Joe. I have to change for tennis."

"Ah … of course. I am sorry I have detained you," murmured Bony. "I suppose … I suppose you would not consent to show me that piece of flannel cloth?"

"You suppose right, Joe. Forget it. It is of no importance to you or to anyone else. If you think I go about collecting pieces of cloth attached to tree suckers, you must have an extraordinary opinion of me."

"Very well, Mr. Dreyton. Thank you for the records. I will take great care of them. Perhaps if you should come across that piece of grey flannel—dark-grey, wasn't it?"

"Yes … yes. Come on, now! Out you go. I want to lock up."

Then the telephone-bell rang shrilly. Dreyton swore, and Bony sauntered out to the veranda. He was smiling. He had certainly discovered a wisp of grey fibre adhering to the broken ends of a tree sucker in that tree climbed by Dreyton, but he had not known until Dreyton informed him without the aid of words that what the crows had quarrelled about was a small portion of dark-grey flannel.

He had but reached the end of the office building when Dreyton called:

"Joe ahoy! Just a moment."

Bony went back.

"Constable Lee is on the phone and wishes to speak to you," Dreyton said with asperity. "Hurry up, please."

At the telephone, Bony announced his presence. Lee said:

"Sergeant Simone went out to Westall's station this afternoon. He has just returned, bringing Barry Elson with him. He has arrested Elson and charged him with the attack on Mabel Storrie."

When Bony did not speak, Lee said anxiously, "Hi! Are you there?"

"Yes, Lee. I am astonished by Simone's action. When does he propose to take his prisoner to Broken Hill, do you know?"

"Tonight. He's at the store filling up with petrol. Elson is in the lock-up. My wife is preparing his tea now."

"Will you take it in to him?"

"Yes."

"Then tell the young man not to worry about the future. I shall probably see you early this evening. *Au revoir*."

Having replaced the instrument on its hook, Bony turned to find Dreyton standing at his table, waiting.

"That was Constable Lee, Mr. Dreyton," Bony explained. "He rang up to say Sergeant Simone has arrested Barry Elson for the attack on Mabel Storrie."

"Then Simone is a confounded fool," Dreyton said, his eyes beginning to blaze.

"Perhaps. Perhaps not. Now, he *would* have been a confounded fool had he arrested *me*."

Chapter Twelve

The Night Rider

A treeless plain has its wardrobe of dresses, a wardrobe much better stocked than that possessed by a forest. Unlike women, nature dons a dress to suit every mood, and not one to create a mood. Some of her moods call for ugliness, colour dissonance, even drabness.

On this particular evening in the second week of November the bluebush plain surrounding Carie wore a dress of orange and purple, for the setting sun had drawn before its face a mantle of smoky crimson bordered along its topmost edge with ribbons of gold and of pale green.

This celestial drapery was beyond Mrs. Nelson's range of vision. She was sitting in an easy chair at the extreme south end of the balcony of her hotel, the knitting with which she had been employed now idle in her lap, her small, white, blue-veined hands resting upon it. Even so, she could command an excellent view of the one and only street.

It was an evening to calm anyone's troubled mind, but the mind of Mrs. Nelson was by no means untroubled. In fact, it was greatly excited by recent events.

To the south, a bar of dark green was Nogga Creek, and after the sun had set it became a bar of darkling colour fading gradually into the dove-grey sky. From the wide eastern horizon, coming inward towards the town, the grey of distance merged into purple—a purple slashed by streaks of orange where the sun's aftermath caught the lines of tobacco bush—a purple which flowed about the greater splashes of light red, beneath which lay the thousands of tons of fine-grained sand deposited by the winds since Mrs. Nelson was a girl.

Smith's Bakery opposite, and all the town to the left of the hotel, was stained with dull reds and browns—stains which obliterated the harshness of iron roofs and weathered walls of wood, of iron, of petrol-tins, of chaff-bags. Along the street had been driven a flock of goats, and, as though their passage had been transmuted into an imperishable mark, minute sand particles raised by their cloven hoofs now hung steadily in mid-air, forming a nigger-brown varnish, which coloured old Grandfer Littlejohn, talking excitedly with Mr. Weaver, the many playing children, and the unusual number of gossiping women standing on the footpaths. Even the figures of Bony and Mounted-Constable Lee, talking outside the police station front gate, were tinted with this umber shade.

What an afternoon it had been! The little woman on the veranda was feeling almost exhausted by the strain of the excitement. She had, of course, watched the departure of Sergeant Simone on the track to Allambee, and for two hours she had found much enjoyment in speculating on his destination and the purport of his business. Then she had seen the sergeant's car returning along the sole street, had watched it turn just before it reached the police station and so disappear in the direction of the lock-up. And in the car with the sergeant had been Barry Elson.

It was as well that, despite her years, her heart was robust, because the subsequent wait and the suspense were hard to bear. That old fool of a Littlejohn had hobbled to the police station corner and stood there to stare at the lock-up instead of coming to tell her if Elson really had been arrested. Mrs. Nelson was about to send for James and order him to go and ascertain what it was all about when Sergeant Simone drove out to the street and pulled up before the petrol pump outside the store.

After that, for an hour, the car was parked outside the police station whilst that annoying brute of a man was inside talking mysteriously to Constable Lee. People began to animate the usually empty street, and they stood like statues staring across at the lock-up when the sergeant drove his car to it, and out of Mrs. Nelson's view. Ah, and then he had suddenly reappeared with Barry Elson at his side, and had driven away, to vanish under the Nogga Creek trees on his way to Broken Hill.

Tilly came on to the veranda and told her in hushed voice all that she had guessed. One could see the look of amazed relief in Tilly's homely face. One could tell by the movements of the people in the street that at long last the shadow of the Strangler had been lifted from Carie.

And then, about half-past seven, that stranger half-caste working on Wirragatta had appeared at the Common gate, to walk into Carie to the police station, where he had been for the last half-hour. Oh, what was he doing in the police station? What was he talking to Lee about? Mrs. Nelson sent for James. And James received certain orders.

Mrs. Nelson's dislike of Sergeant Simone was due less to his profession than to his refusal to inform her of the progress of his investigation. She disliked Donald Dreyton because he avoided acquainting her with his past history. With Joe Fisher, she was positively angry, for not only was she unable to find out whence he had come and who he was, but he had not even called at the hotel for a drink and a yarn with James. Old Grandfer Littlejohn had been ordered to come up for an interview, but to hide his ignorance of what was going on the old fellow had cackled about nothing.

The plain was swiftly changing its gown for one of dark grey and indigo blue. From two dozen tin and debris-littered back yards hens were quarrelling for roosting-places. Mr. Smith sat down on his doorstep, and Grandfer Littlejohn arranged himself on his petrol-case set at the edge of the path outside his son's house. And then Bony left Constable Lee, and, on his way towards the hotel, was stopped by Grandfer. … Five minutes later Bony entered the hotel, and the watching Mrs. Nelson sighed and settled herself to receive a visitor.

No longer could she see the division of land and sky. Far distant a bright light burned steadily as though through the uncurtained window of a stockman's hut. Not being interested in the stars, Mrs. Nelson could not name this one. Nogga Creek was now a dark fold in a deep cloth of velvet.

The minutes passed unnoticed by the watching woman. Sounds of town life slowly became hushed as the plain nestled beneath the blanket of night. One by one the sitters rose and passed beyond doors. Lights within the houses winked out to stare at Mrs. Nelson and from below came the familiar sounds made by the hotel yardman when placing steps in position and mounting them to light the lamp suspended over the main door. By now the Common gates had been eaten up by the night and the plain was sinking swiftly into a pit.

Came presently a swish of starched clothes. Tilly appeared. Behind her came the new Wirragatta hand, Joseph Fisher.

"Here is Mr. Fisher, ma'am," Tilly announced, and Bony said, advancing, "It is indeed kind of you to ask me to come and see you, Mrs. Nelson. I trust I find you well?"

The old woman's eyes gleamed like glinting water. The soft, pleasing voice astonished her. She had known many half-castes and quarter-castes. Most of them had spoken pleasingly, but this man's voice contained something deeper than mere vocal sounds.

"I like to meet all my customers personally," Mrs. Nelson said lightly. "Tilly shall bring a chair for you—if you will consent to stay for a few minutes and talk to a lonely old woman."

"There is nothing that would please me better. Permit me to fetch the chair."

Bony turned back to take the chair Tilly was bringing from the sitting-room. From the moment James had informed him that his employer would like him to visit her, the detective was, to use a word he himself always barred, intrigued.

"May I smoke?" he inquired whilst arranging the chair with its back touching the veranda rail.

"Certainly."

"Thank you. I am mentally sluggish when unable to smoke."

"They tell me, Mr. Fisher, that you were camped at Catfish Hole the night Barry Elson nearly murdered poor Mabel Storrie. Did you know about the terrible crimes that have been committed near here?"

"Yes. But who would want to strangle a poor half-caste station-hand? I suppose that you, like every one else, are glad that Elson was caught at last?"

"Of course! We shall all be able to sleep peacefully tonight," replied Mrs. Nelson. "What part of the State do you come from?"

As Bony expected this leading question, he was decided to save time. He said:

"For many years I was working on Barrakee, on the Darling. Before that I was farther up the river, above Bourke. You see, I was born north of Bourke. I left the river to escape my sponging tribal relations. I have never before been out this way."

"By the sound of you, you have received a good education."

"Oh, yes. A Mr. Whitelow saw to that."

"Your father?"

"That, madam, I am unable to answer," gravely replied Bony. "Mr. William Shakespeare, or some other, wrote something about the wisdom of the man who does know his own father."

Just how Mrs. Nelson would take this Bony was uncertain, but interested. There followed a distinct silence before Mrs. Nelson said:

"You are caustic, Mr. Fisher, and I do not approve of caustic people."

"Your pardon, Mrs. Nelson. Do you really think that young Barry Elson attacked his sweetheart?"

"Who else? I have thought it all along," she conceded, evidently pleased that they had successfully skated across thin ice. "He is a young man I have not liked, but until the attack on poor Mabel Storrie I had certainly not connected him with those two terrible murders. I suppose Sergeant Simone questioned you severely?"

"'Severely' is the correct adverb," Bony admitted with a low laugh, and he wished he could see his questioner's face. The sequins decorating Mrs. Nelson's black silk blouse gleamed now and then as they caught the light of the hotel lamp reflected upward from the wide light-sword flung across the street.

Mrs. Nelson waited for Bony to proceed, and having waited vainly she said, "You would get on better with Constable Lee. What does he think of Sergeant Simone arresting Barry Elson?"

"Lee is too good a policeman to tell *me* what he thinks."

"I don't know about that," swiftly countered the old woman. "Lee is just a grown-up boy. There's nothing bad in him like there is in Sergeant Simone. Lee's policy is to live in peace and let live in peace. Simone told me that Lee is too popular to be on duty in a bush town, and that he considered it advisable to get him transferred."

"Indeed!"

"Yes, indeed. And so I gave Mister Sergeant Simone a piece of my mind. I'll tell you just what I said to Sergeant Simone, because I would like you to tell Lee some time and so ease his poor mind. Both his wife and him are scared to death that he might be transferred, and then what her father and mother would do I don't know. Don't let him know I asked you to tell him. Mention it casually."

"Yes. I understand perfectly," Bony agreed, the sound of the cash register and the murmur of voices in the allegedly closed bar drifting up to them. It appeared that many after-hours customers were celebrating the departure of Sergeant Simone, or the arrest of the supposed Strangler. Lee certainly was leaving people to live in peace.

"Very well, then. I said to Sergeant Simone only last night, and up here on this veranda— 'Simone,' I said, 'like all government servants, you and your Commissioner think you have got the boss hand. I, a little old woman, would break you like a straw. I own the majority of the shares in the *Sydney Post*, and I'd have a reporter sent up and tell him how you have failed in your duty of catching the murderer of Alice Tindall and consequently let Frank Marsh be murdered. I'd make the people of New South Wales laugh at you first and then hunt you out of the State. So, you see, you don't know me, my man. I'm the boss of this district, and don't you ever forget it.' "

Bony laughed softly. Another silence fell upon them. Far away towards Nogga Creek there came to Bony's abruptly straining ears the rhythmic drumming of a horse's hoofs pounding on the earth track. The animal was being furiously ridden.

Bony sensed, rather than saw, Mrs. Nelson's fragile body stiffen in her chair, and he knew that she, too, heard the thudding hoofs. Together they listened, Bony trying to decide if the rider was coming from Wirragatta or from Storrie's selection, and whilst he listened he watched the sequins glinting on Mrs. Nelson's black blouse and noted that their movement was becoming more rapid.

Then he said slowly and softly, "I wonder, now!"

It caused Mrs. Nelson to ask sharply, "At what do you wonder?"

"I wonder if Sergeant Simone had his prisoner handcuffed."

"I don't understand you, Fisher," Mrs. Nelson said, become so agitated that she omitted the courtesy title. "Do you think this horseman is coming with news of another — —?"

"Supposing that Barry Elson was not handcuffed, wouldn't it be possible for him to strangle the sergeant and escape in the car, and for this horseman to have found the body on the track?"

"Don't be a fool, man!" snapped Mrs. Nelson. "Why, Simone could eat his prisoner. Still—still—I fear— — Which direction is the rider coming from?"

"I cannot determine," answered the thrilling Bony. He stood up to peer into the black void hiding the Common. "I think he is now at one of the gates."

For three seconds the silence of the night surrounded them. Then from out the void the hoof-beats again came to them, quickening to a wild thrumming pounding. Which of the two gates had the rider just passed through? Which one?

"I—I—oh, I hope there hasn't been another murder done. I couldn't stand …" Mrs. Nelson cried softly, the fire with which she had described her threats to Simone burned to cold ash.

"What's that?" Bony demanded, his entire attention centred on the possibilities of the horseman's errand. His body, to Mrs. Nelson, was silhouetted against the sword of light cast across the street by the hotel lamp, and she saw it stiffen. From along the Broken Hill road, swiftly rising in tone volume, came the pounding tattoo on sandy ground of the animal's hoofs. Both half-caste and white woman could picture the rider crouched along the horse's neck, a great horror on his ashen face.

It seemed that Mrs. Nelson no longer could bear the suspense engendered by the oncoming horse and rider. She rose from her chair and stepped quickly to the veranda rail at Bony's side, there to clutch the rail with small beringed hands.

Somewhere in the void beyond the end of the street came to them a sharp metallic report which further agitated Mrs. Nelson and sent Bony hurrying below. Mrs. Nelson heard men's voices raised, and out through the main door of the hotel ran James, the barman, and his several customers. Mr. Smith appeared in front of his shop, his rotund figure illuminated in the light-sword cast by the hotel lamp.

The pounding of hoofs rose in crescendo, but no faintest indication of horse and rider was to be seen in the black void of night until man and animal abruptly burst into the light-sword, to be followed by a rolling cloud of dust. A stockwhip cracked like a machine-gun, metallically. The horse was reined back upon its haunches, and then its rider sat and stared at the gathering of men outside the hotel, which now included Bony.

"What's up?" demanded James Spinks.

The little crowd moved towards the rearing horse.

"Look out!" someone shouted. "Harry's ridin' Black Diamond."

"What's up?" shouted the youthful Harry West. "Nothink's up. Can't a bloke ride to town without all the population wantin' to know what's up?"

"What do you mean by riding to town like that?" James wanted further to know, and Bony saw that his face was drawn and ghastly white.

"Well, how was I to come? Think I was gonna lead this devil of a horse?" complained Harry. "Stiffen the crows! It's a bit thick if a bloke can't ride to town to see his girl without being roared at. You draw me a schooner of beer time I get in from parkin' this cross between a lion and a tiger-cat."

"Drat him!" Mrs. Nelson cried softly. "Drat him! He gave me quite a fright."

Chapter Thirteen

A Dangerous Man

The day following that evening when Harry West, mounted on Black Diamond, had so perturbed Mrs. Nelson and Detective-Inspector Bonaparte was Sunday. There was no faintest wind this day, but the sky was tinged with an opalescent white, hinting at wind within a few days.

The quietness which governs a city on Sunday also governs a station homestead, especially during the afternoon. Even the birds seem to respect the Sabbath. The morning had been spent by Bony and the other hands washing clothes and cutting hair, and then, although Hang-dog Jack said he did not believe in cooking on Sundays, he presented the noonday meal with the air of a man quite ready to accept congratulatory remarks as his due.

There was no afternoon smoko tea for the hands on Sundays, and, having made his own tea and shared it with Bill the Cobbler and Young-and-Jackson, Bony quietly gathered together the Wirragatta weather reports, a writing-pad and a pencil, and crossed the river to the camelman's hut on the far side.

This was a small corrugated-iron hut, but fortunately a drop-window in the wall, opposite the door, when opened provided a cooling draught of air. Under the window was a roughly made table, and along each vacant wall was a roughly made bush bunk. For a seat at the table there was an empty petrol-case. Bony found this hut, occupied only by the two fence-riders when at the homestead, to be an excellent retreat.

With the hundred and twenty monthly weather sheets before him, the detective began to continue his study of them. Each sheet duplicated data supplied to the State Meteorological Bureau, and each day of every month the station book-keeper-in-office had entered the number of points of rain fallen, if any, and general remarks on the conditions of the weather. From all these records Bony completed the plotting of a graph showing throughout the ten years covered by the reports the incidence of wind-storms; and, as he expected, the index curve rose to its highest point in late October and early November. After these two months the number of wind-storms was greatest in September; then in March, and least of all in February.

It will be recalled that the three crimes now occupying Bony's attention were committed—the first during the night of 10th-11th November, the second during the night of 17th-18th March, and the third during the night of 30th-31st October—all during a period of twenty-four months.

On each of these dates the wind had blown with hurricane force, and Bony's conclusion from this, as well as from his observations among the Nogga Creek trees, was that the significance of the dates might have been produced not by the activities of the Strangler so much as the opportunities presented him by a chance victim. The fellow could go out in the weather conditions he evidently liked fifty or a hundred times and meet with a victim but once.

On the other hand, and this appeared the more likely, he might well have known the approximate time when a victim would pass a certain way. Quite a number of people would know that Alice Tindall spent her last evening of life in the kitchen of the Wirragatta homestead and that she would be walking back to the camp at Junction Waterhole. Quite a number of people knew that Frank Marsh was in Carie that last night of his life, that he was working for and living with the Storries, and that he would be walking to the selection from the township.

An even larger number of people knew that Mabel Storrie was at the dance in Carie, but all these people knew she had been escorted from her home by her brother on the truck, and all these people thought that she would return home on the truck with her brother. Only when the dance was over were Tom Storrie and the truck missing. Only by chance, or seeming chance, did Mabel part from her lover when half-way home, to go on alone.

Sergeant Simone certainly had some grounds for arresting Barry Elson, but Bony considered them not nearly sufficient. That the lovers did part company, that Mabel did go on alone and Elson return to the hotel, Bony was morally certain.

He proceeded a step farther. A man knew that Alice Tindall would be returning to her camp from the homestead late one night. Weather conditions promised another day of wind and dust to follow. Knowing the character of the girl, this man knew she would refuse an escort. Therefore, pre-knowledge and not chance had given him the opportunity to strangle her. The same reasoning could be applied to the murder of Frank Marsh committed in the identical weather conditions. But in Mabel Storrie's case it must have been chance, not pre-knowledge, which had presented the Strangler with his opportunity to attack her.

Two of these three cases, therefore, were alike with regard to presuming that the murderer had pre-knowledge of his victim's actions. It raised again the possibility that the attack on Mabel Storrie had been done by an imitator of the murderer of the other two, but telling against this possibility was a third fact. Alice Tindall and Mabel Storrie had been attacked from the branch of and under a tree along the same creek, whilst Marsh had been killed three-quarters of a mile from a tree, near the Common gates.

Here, however, there was room for argument. Marsh had been found close to the Common gates, but there was no shred of proof that he had been strangled to death where his body was found.

Bony's mind went back to the first two cases, those of murder. These bore similarity and favoured pre-knowledge.

The prevailing weather was an inducement to people to stay at home. Assuming that the murderer did have pre-knowledge of his victim's movements, he must have been at Wirragatta homestead the evening of that night Alice Tindall was killed, and he must have been either at Storrie's selection or in Carie the evening of the night Marsh was murdered.

Now if it could be established that someone resident in Carie or at Storrie's selection was visiting Wirragatta when Alice Tindall was murdered, or if it could be established that a resident at Wirragatta had visited Carie or the Storries the evening that Marsh was murdered, then the name of a man, or men, who knew the movements of both these unfortunates could be regarded as that of a person having the pre-knowledge the murderer almost surely had.

Bony came to favour this pre-knowledge theory at the expense of that which assumed that the murderer obtained his victim only by blind chance, like a thug waiting at a dark street corner for the casual pedestrian to come within striking distance of him. The chance of meeting a lone walker on such nights was so infinitely small as to be put aside in argument as unworthy of consideration. Only in the case of Mabel Storrie had chance given the killer a prospective victim, and again only through chance had she escaped death.

Bony felt he was on safe ground to reason thus. He must find if there were any visitors to Wirragatta the night Alice Tindall was murdered, and if there were any visitors to Carie or to Storrie's selection from Wirragatta the night that Marsh was murdered. Anyone out visiting on either of these two windy nights could be held gravely suspect.

Outside the hut wherein Bony was pondering these theories a willy-wagtail shrilly chirped its warning call, and, thus warned of someone's approach, he quickly stacked the weather reports and was wrapping them in their brown-paper covering when Stella Borradale appeared in the open doorway. From Bony, now on his feet, her cool gaze fell to the table.

"Do I interrupt you?" she inquired pleasantly.

"An interruption *can* be much appreciated," he replied, advancing to her. "Might I be of service?"

"I saw you come here an hour ago, and I have suspected that you make this hut your writing-room," she said smilingly. "Would it, do you think, be permissible for me to enter? I have a message for you."

"Back in 1900 it might not have been. In this year, certainly, Miss Borradale." Bony turned back and rearranged the petrol-case seat. "If you will be seated—I am sorry I cannot offer you a cigarette. I make my own, and badly, too."

"I have cigarettes, thank you." Stella became seated and Bony held a match for her use. "I have had quite a long letter from Marion Trench, and she and her husband and Mr. Stanton all wish to be remembered to you. I hope you did not mind me mentioning to her that you are here?"

"By no means—if you stressed the fact of my incognito. I recall many pleasant incidents of my stay at Windee. There I achieved my greatest success—and sacrificed it."

"Oh! How, may I ask?"

"I cannot, of course, speak of the case, which was delightfully baffling. Miss Marion Stanton, as she was then, is both physically and mentally a beautifully woman. For the sake of her happiness I confessed to my colleagues my first and only failure to finalize a case."

Stella Borradale was regarding the detective pensively.

"Marion and I have been friends for years," she said. "Some time back she hinted that her present happiness was due entirely to you. They ask me to tell you how much they hope you will call at Windee before returning to Queensland."

"That would be like the people at Windee. Did Mrs. Trench mention

Father Ryan?"

"Yes. She said she thought you would like to know that Father Ryan always talks of you when he and they meet. Are you a Catholic?"

"No. But I admire Father Ryan immensely. He is a wonderful man—a splendid man."

Through the smoke of her cigarette Stella watched the dark face now animated and lit with the lamp of enthusiasm. She tried very hard to keep out of her own eyes her increasing interest in this half-caste who behaved and spoke as well as any man she had ever known. His vanity was obvious, but her interest was not based on his fine face and modulated, cultured voice. Just what it was based upon puzzled her.

She said impulsively, "May I ask why you are continuing your investigation after the arrest of Barry Elson?"

At once Bony's face became a mask.

"You are asking a conjuror to show how he does his tricks," he said chidingly, the smile again lighting his eyes. "But I will answer your question—in strict confidence. I am almost, but not quite, certain that Barry Elson did not attack his sweetheart."

"I am sure he didn't," she said emphatically. "But ... but could you not have prevented his arrest?"

"I could have done, I think."

"Then why didn't you? Think of the state of his mind at this moment if he is innocent, as I am sure he is."

"Barry Elson admitted to me, Miss Borradale, that he did a caddish thing when he left Mabel Storrie to walk on home alone, most especially after those two terrible murders. He must learn his lesson and then, perhaps, he will be given the opportunity to re-establish himself with the Storries and with everyone else who knows him. I regret that I cannot enlighten you further on this matter."

"Well, will you appease my curiosity by telling me if you have made any progress in your investigation? We seem to agree that this strangling beast is still at large. Sometimes, chiefly at night, I become horribly nervous. One never knows when that terrible person will again attack and kill."

"I can assure you that I shall not return to Brisbane and my family until I have located him. I wonder, now—would you assist me by frankly answering a few questions I would like to ask, in strict confidence?"

"Most certainly."

"I do not think it absolutely essential but I believe it will be of assistance to maintain my slight deception on the people here," Bony said in some kind of preface. "Nearly everyone will talk more freely to a private individual than they will to an investigating police officer. Why, I don't know, but it is so. Other than to Mrs. Trench, you have not revealed my identity?"

"I passed you my word about that."

"I stand reproved, Miss Borradale. Now may I begin the inquisition? No one will disturb us, as my sentry is on duty."

"Your sentry!"

"A willy-wagtail. He informed me of your coming. Now for my first question. Please go back in your mind to the night when Alice Tindall was murdered. Were both you and Mr. Borradale at home that night?"

"Yes. I remember it quite well."

"Alice Tindall left the homestead for the blacks' camp shortly after eleven o'clock, did she not?"

"The time she left was settled for ever by Sergeant Simone," replied Stella. "It was twenty-five minutes after eleven. It had been a dreadful day, and about nine o'clock it began to thunder and lighten badly. There was no rain, but we expected it, and Alice stayed with the cook and the maids until the thunder had passed on."

"Were there any visitors at Wirragatta at that time?"

"No, no one."

"I suppose you cannot recall who the men were then working at the homestead?"

"Not all of them. Hang-dog Jack was here, of course, and Harry West and Young-and-Jackson. Mr. Dreyton had just gone into the office as book-keeper."

"Ah, yes! Mr. Dreyton is a man of breeding and education. He reminds me constantly of Mr. Trench at Windee."

"Oh! In what way?"

The expression of pensiveness on the dark face was banished by the slow-growing smile.

"When first I met Mr. Trench," Bony said, "he was a rabbit-trapper and kangaroo-shooter on Windee. As you would know, that is not a trade for a man of refinement to follow. Mr. Trench provided me with quite a little mystery, and I think I run no risk of breaking a confidence when I tell you that the reason he was a fur-and-skin getter was due to the condition imposed on him by Mr. Stanton. Wishing to prove him before accepting him as his son-in-law, Mr. Stanton made it the condition of his consent that Mr. Trench should apply himself to the hardest work on the run for two years.

"There is a certain similarity between Mr. Trench and Mr. Dreyton. Both are gentlemen and both are English. Their manner and speech prove rearing and education above that of the average man. Can you tell me why Mr. Dreyton prefers working on a boundary-fence to working in an office?"

The abrupt question, following the reference to Trench proving himself for love, caught Stella's breath. Try as she might, she could not conquer the betraying blush, and Bony felt he had been indelicate.

"Forgive me!" he exclaimed. "Do not, please, answer that impertinent question."

"But I must," she said quickly, breathlessly. "There is nothing like that of the Trenches between Mr. Dreyton and me. Neither my brother nor I know why Mr Dreyton prefers the fence work. Or rather we do. We wanted him in the office because he is such a good tennis player and bridge player, and then the other day, when my brother made a direct appeal to him, he explained that living with us, even as the book-keeper, reminded him too acutely of the status in life he had enjoyed and lost before coming to Australia."

Bony now was sitting motionless, gazing absently out through the drop-window.

"Don't you believe me?" Stella Borradale asked coldly.

"Er ... of course, Miss Borradale. I fear I am being very rude." Again the quick smile. "I am often rude when I am thinking. Now let us come forward in time to the murder of Frank Marsh. Can you recall that night?"

"Easily. Sergeant Simone questioned us all enough to make us remember it all our lives."

"Then I owe something to the redoubtable sergeant," Bony said laughingly, and his smile was so disarming that it made Stella momentarily forgetful of that dangerous ground to which he had led her. "Tell me, please. Who slept at 'Government House' that night other than the cook and the maids?"

"Only my brother and I. Mr. Allen, who was then book-keeping here, occupied the book-keeper's room in the office building."

"There were no visitors?"

"None."

"At that time Mr. Dreyton was fence-riding. Was he here at the homestead or not?"

"Yes, he was. He was camped in this hut," Stella answered, obviously trying to perceive the objective of Bony's questions.

"You are being very patient with me," she was told. "You had no visitors when Alice Tindall was murdered, and you had none when Frank Marsh was murdered. Did you go out the night that Marsh was killed?"

"No. It was a bad night."

"Did you play bridge?"

"No. My brother was away part of the evening. He went to the Storries to discuss with Fred Storrie a deal in sheep."

"Can you tell me what Mr. Dreyton did that evening?"

"Yes … due again to Sergeant Simone. Mr. Dreyton visited Carie, where, for some time, he played chess with Dr. Mulray. But tell me! Surely you do not think that Mr. Dreyton——"

Bony chuckled.

"You will be accusing me of thinking that either Mr. Borradale or Mr. Dreyton is the Strangler. Men like they do not commit murder without a sound motive. Besides, you can tell me, I am sure, what time they returned to the homestead. In your brother's case at least."

"Yes. He returned shortly before ten o'clock. He had been poorly all day and he went straight off to bed."

Bony rolled and lit another cigarette.

"I have, of course, a reason for asking all these questions, and when you decided to come here this afternoon with Mrs. Trench's message you let yourself in for them. You see, I have to solve a jig-saw puzzle, and my questions can be termed the pieces of the puzzle. Would you be able to forgive me if I were very candid with you?"

She could, subsequently, never understand how this man swamped her natural reserve to the extent of compelling her to tell him that he could be as frank as he wished. He went on:

"I find it difficult to believe Mr. Dreyton when he says that his reason for preferring the fence to the office is the pain he feels when in contact with luxury, comparative to his previous financial and social status. I find it difficult, too, to believe that your brother's desire to have him in the office is due to Dreyton's social accomplishments."

Quite slowly Stella expelled her caught breath. She was become fearful that she would once more betray herself. To prevent this she hurried into an admission.

"I also find it difficult to believe that," she said, and Bony did not fail to note that her coolness of demeanour was temporarily shattered. "I have long suspected a stronger reason than bridge and tennis and good company. I think that sometimes my brother feels the responsibility of running this property too heavy to bear, and I think his load is lightened for him when he can discuss his difficulties with Mr. Dreyton. As you know, Mr Dreyton is only a few years senior to my brother, but he is decades older in worldly experience. Martin takes after our mother in many ways. Our father was much more rugged and hard than is Martin."

"Hem! I can understand that running Wirragatta successfully is not an easy task. And then your brother left school to return home direct to manage this property, and therefore missed that hardening process induced in one's character by what is cynically called sowing one's wild oats."

"If you do not believe Mr. Dreyton's reason for preferring the fence life, what do you think could be his reason?"

The indifference with which this question was put was not genuine, and Bony's sharp ears detected it. Stella now was semi-masking her face by lighting a cigarette from the match he held in service, but having guessed the secret of her heart he knew her reason for asking the question.

"I will not attempt to answer your question, Miss Borradale," he told her as his eyes twinkled. "It may be that Mr. Dreyton is being very foolish. As to that I cannot say."

For the second time this afternoon Stella Borradale felt the warning heat creeping to her face, and she was not alone in blessing Hang-dog for beating on his triangle at this moment. They rose together. Bony gallantly escorted her to the door of the hut, but despite the cook's interruption and the detective's gallantry the blush would betray her.

In a frantic effort to overcome it she said laughingly, "I think you are a very dangerous man, Bony."

It made Bony laugh delightedly, and when they stood one on either side of the doorstep he said, "Dangerous, Miss Borradale? Never, never dangerous, I earnestly assure you."

Chapter Fourteen

Retrospect

It was a thoughtful man who walked across the river's dry bed to the men's quarters. Bony's inquisition of Stella Borradale had brought out several facts, only one of which at the moment appeared to have any significance relative to Bony's investigation. This was the fact that Donald Dreyton must have known that Alice Tindall was walking back to her camp and that Frank Marsh was walking back to the Storries' house.

Martin Borradale knew this, too, and it was likely that yet others would be discovered who knew as much. Yet this series of crimes began shortly after Dreyton arrived at Wirragatta. It was he who climbed trees, to discover a piece of grey flannel in one, and it was he who for some mysterious reason preferred life on a boundary-fence to the comparatively luxurious life at the homestead.

And yet — — It was as difficult to believe Dreyton capable of such terrible deeds as to think it of Martin Borradale, of Harry West, or of Bill the Cobbler. Bony had detected a kindly streak even behind the exterior of Hang-dog Jack. He was searching for a ferocious beast, and no one he had yet met came near his mental picture of this beast. Almost despite himself his mind kept reverting to Dreyton, for there was the keen suspicion that the temporary book-keeper knew certain facts and suspected others which he had never divulged.

When Bony entered the men's dining-room Harry West and the horse, Black Diamond, was the subject under discussion. Harry was reviling Constable Lee for reporting him to the boss of Wirragatta for riding Black Diamond into Carie.

"Fair towelled me up, he did," Harry complained.

"You deserved it," Bony asserted as he seated himself at the table. "Pass the beetroot, please."

"Oh, I ain't whinin' about it, Joe, only it's a bit thick to be chewed for ridin' a moke I can manage with one hand."

"Why did the boss order that no one was to ride Black Diamond?"

inquired Bony of everyone in general.

"'Cos he's a man-killer," replied Hang-dog Jack. "That 'orse has already killed one bloke and injured two others. Give the boss his due, he done quite right to declare Black Diamond an outlaw. 'Arry here is the only bloke wot ever rode him, but to go and ride 'im in the dark—well, he deserves what's coming to 'im."

"There's no law against riding a measly horse to a township, is there?" Harry demanded hotly. "Lee's a liar to say that I rode to the public danger. Why, I only got as far as the pub corner. Didn't I, Joe?"

"It was far enough. You might have ridden down someone on the road."

"Someone on the road!" came the withering echo. "Ain't every man, woman and child in the district afraid to go out after dark?"

"But Simone's nabbed Barry Elson," Bill the Cobbler pointed out.

"You're a bigger fool than I take you for if you think Barry Elson done all them murders," Harry flashed out.

"We don't think it, and neither does anyone else wot's got any gumption," put in Young-and-Jackson. "Didn't Simone tell Hang-dog Jack that he reckoned he was looking at the murderer of Alice Tindall?"

"Perhaps he spoke a true word when he spoke in jest," Harry heatedly got in, and then ducked when the bone of the leg of mutton carved for the meal whizzed past his head.

"You 'int I done them murders again, Harry West, and I'll break you inter little bits," snarled the cook, crouched now at the head of the table, his face hideously convulsed with rage, his long arms curved and his hairy-backed hands opening and snapping shut. Yellow teeth were bared in a ferocious grin.

"If we all took the sergeant seriously," Bony said in effort to pour oil on troubled waters, "then I would not sleep o' nights. Sergeant Simone told me that he thought I was the murderer, and I cannot understand why he did not arrest me instead of Elson. Come, now, don't let us lose our tempers over what the sergeant said. Harry, sit down."

The quiet authoritative tone succeeded. Harry sat down and the rage slowly passed from the cook's face. Hang-dog Jack turned back to his serving-bench, and thereafter the meal was eaten in silence.

"You should not have said that about truth and jest," Bony reproved Harry West as they walked across to the bunk-house. "When controlled by such a gust of anger, Hang-dog Jack might do you a serious injury. Once he got his hands on you, you would be lost."

"I didn't think," confessed the young man. "Besides, I was riled at him for backing up the boss. The boss sorta hinted that I'd lost me chance of one of the married houses for riding that black devil against his orders. Ah, well! Poor old Hang-dog Jack ain't a bad sort. I'll go back and apologize to him. No bloke can be responsible for his dial."

"To apologize requires courage," averred Bony, glancing quickly at Harry's fearless face. To that face came a grin.

"To apologize to Hang-dog Jack certainly does," Harry said. "Say, are you going to town tonight?"

"Yes, I promised to play chess with Dr. Mulray."

"Good-oh! When you startin'?"

"Just after sundown."

"That'll do me. We could arrange to meet and walk back together. I don't like the idea of coming on alone in the dark—on foot."

"Very well," agreed Bony, and Harry returned to the kitchen to prove his courage and raise himself high in Bony's estimation.

The sky was aflame to the zenith, and the vociferous birds were winging about the homestead and river trees when the detective and Harry West left for Carie. The track to Carie ran beside the river for a quarter of a mile before branching off from the creek track just above Junction Waterhole. When they arrived at this splendid sheet of water Bony halted beneath one of the huge red-gums which was the third last to the first of the creek box-trees. A gentle easterly breeze rippled the crimson-dyed surface of the water, and when a fish jumped for a fly its gleaming scales gave back crimson fire.

"It was here where poor Alice Tindall was found, wasn't it?" Bony asked.

Harry West shrugged his shoulders without knowing it. "Yes," he said, to add quickly: "Come away, Joe. I hate this place even in daylight."

"Why, it is entrancingly beautiful," Bony objected. "What a waterhole! It must have been a great camping-place for all the blacks in this district. Water! Cool and precious water now that the summer is come again. Shade! Real shade cast by these trees which suckered before Dampier ever saw Australia. There was loving and fighting, chanting and feasting for years upon years, Harry, all about this waterhole. Then the white man came, and for still a few more years the blacks lived their unfettered lives. But there was no more hunting and, because the white man's tucker was easy to get—by working for it—there was no more real feasting. Finally came the dreaded bunyip to drive them all away, and this beautiful place now is desolate."

"Aw, come on!" urged Harry. "We can talk about 'em on our way. Yes, there was always blacks hereabouts before Alice Tindall was strangled. After that, when Simone had finished roaring at 'em, not a one would come within fifty miles of the place. And I don't blame 'em, bee-lieve me."

"She was a nice-looking girl, wasn't she?" Bony said as they strode away from the river, across the bluebush plain.

"Too right she was. As you know, she was a half-caste, but like you she had sharp features. Old Dogger Smith—you ain't met him yet; he's the biggest character in Noo South—told me she was born white and didn't begin to colour until she was past twelve. That sounds funny, but it's right, maybe. But pretty! Gosh—she was just lovely."

"How old was she when——?"

"Getting on for eighteen. She was a corker. She had blue eyes, lighter in colour and brighter than yours, Joe. She had long straight hair what hung down her back in plaits. She wasn't too dark of skin, either. Well, Miss Borradale always took a great interest in Alice. She wanted Alice to be a maid at 'Government House', but Alice wouldn't take it on. Still, that didn't make no difference with Miss Borradale. She encouraged Alice to visit the maids at 'Government House', and she gave her clothes and showed her how to wear 'em. Alice often went with Miss Borradale out riding and sometimes in the car, and it was because of Miss Borradale that Alice grew up as good as she was pretty. Blokes would no more look cross-eyed at Alice than they would at their sisters.

"'Course all the blokes were after her. When she was a baby, according to old Dogger Smith, there was a lot of talk about her being taken away from the tribe, and people reckoned she would have been took, only her mother uster cook at 'Government House', and she got old Borradale to put a spoke in somebody's wheel. Anyway, as I said, Miss Borradale had a lot of influence over her, and she wouldn't have anything to do with any bloke, black or white. I fancy meself a bit, and I tried pretty hard to hang my hat up on her, but it was no win. Even Hang-dog Jack uster shiver and shake when she spoke to him, and the funny part about it was that she wasn't afraid of him. You'd think she would have been scared stiff by a bloke with a dial like he's got. There was one man, though, who could have got her if he had thought about it."

"Oh! Who?" purred the interested detective.

"The boss. I seen her looking at him more'n once when he wasn't looking at her, and she didn't know I was looking at her. She uster stand still—quite still—and look at him … like … like. …"

"Like what?" Bony softly asked.

"You ever been in love, Joe?" surprisingly asked Harry West, and he appeared to find the distant town interesting as he put this question.

"Of course. I am still in love."

"Well, then you'll understand. Alice uster look at the boss with her blue eyes shining like stars—like—like my Tilly looks at me sometimes. I tries to remember how she looked them times, not as she looked when me and the boss saw her dead."

The young man fell silent, and, having given him a few seconds, Bony urged him to proceed.

"The evening before, Alice had been up at 'Government House' jabbering with the maids. It came on to thunder and lightnin' and the night was as black as the ace of spades. Anyhow, Alice stayed put till the dry storm had passed over, but even then the air was thick with sand. We blokes had gone to bunk. It was no use any of us asking to take her to the camp, because she would have refused and run off, and even I couldn't catch her. I tried one afternoon, kiddin' I'd kiss her if I caught her, but she left me at the post.

"At the time, a recent flood down the creeks had left filled to the brims both Junction and Station waterholes, and there was a wide stream of water connectin' them. Alice had to walk up this side of the river and cross it above Junction Waterhole to reach the camp, which was on the far side. Not one of the blacks heard her scream out—if she ever did—and the camp from the place where she was strangled was only sixty-odd yards away. Anyway, old Billy Snowdrop, wot's supposed to be the king of the tribe, came running to the homestead, where me and the boss and Dogger Smith was talking by the stockyards.

"For quite a bit, Billy Snowdrop kep' up a jabbering we couldn't understand about a banshee or bunyip what lived in the creek trees near the camp. After Dogger Smith grabbed Snowdrop's whiskers and shook him up we gets it that early that morning Sarah was on her way to the homestead to do the washing, not having enough gumption to know there wouldn't be no washing done that day, when she finds Alice dead under a gum-tree. Well, we ran back with Billy Snowdrop to the body. Aw—it was crook all right. It mightn't have been so crook if Alice had been old and ugly. I don't like thinking about how she looked that morning. No, not even now."

"Did no one know who was her father?"

"Not that ever I heard."

"What was done after you were taken to the body?" Bony asked.

"The boss sent me back to the homestead to drive the car into Carie and bring back Lee and Dr. Mulray. He wouldn't let me go near 'Government House', or tell Donald Dreyton to telephone from the office, for fear of upsetting Miss Borradale, who got upset bad enough when she did hear. As I was leaving, the blacks were rushing across the river above the waterhole, and Billy Snowdrop was yelling for all of 'em bar one or two good trackers to keep back."

"Did they find any tracks, Harry?"

"By then the wind was raging like hell let loose. There was no tracks for even them to find, and it started them off talking about the bunyip."

For a spell they walked in silence.

Then Harry said, "'Course, we all reckons a bunyip is a kind of blackfeller's bush ghost. When Simone heard of it he laughed at the blacks, and when they kept it up he roared at 'em and told them to shut up about their fool banshee. Ever since then I have thought there might be something in that bunyip idea. Old Dogger Smith reckons there is, anyway. He fell out of Ma Nelson's pub one night a bit the worse for wear, and he got slewed and ended up at Nogga Creek, where he thinks it's as well to camp. He swears he dreamed hearing a banshee or bunyip laughing at him from up in the tree he was camped under. Queer old bird, Dogger Smith."

"In what way?"

"Well, for a start, he's about a hundred and fifty not out. Then, when you camps with him, he keeps you up all night talking about murders. He's great on murders. There ain't no one in this district he don't know all about. He knew 'em when they was babies, and he knew everything about their pa's and ma's before 'em. He's a corker all right, but he's got sense with it."

The sun's flaming aftermath was drenching the township with colour, and they had vaulted the boundary-fence in preference to opening and shutting one of the gates, when Bony asked:

"What men were at the homestead when Alice was murdered?"

"Men? Oh, me and Dogger Smith, Bill the Cobbler and Hang-dog Jack."

"Only four of you? How many were there when Frank Marsh was killed?"

"Lemme think! Yes, the same four and Young-and-Jackson and Waxy Ted. Cripes! That was a night!"

"Indeed!"

"Too right! The day before Frank Marsh was killed Waxy Ted got a fiver from Tatt's. What does he do but invite all hands to town that evening Frank was murdered. It happened that Lee was upset about something and wasn't in a good mood, and Mum Nelson gave orders to James that the bar wasn't to be opened up to the general public. It was no good Waxy Ted trying to get a drink, 'cos when he's half-stung he will insist on singing 'The Face on the Bar-room Floor'. So me and Bill the Cobbler, we took the fiver to the back door and persuades James to hand out thirty bottles of beer, which we takes to the mob parked at the Common gates.

"Hot? It was a hell of a night, and after we had necked more'n half the beer we wasn't even cheerful about it. So we decides to stagger back to the men's hut and polish off the rest, and just as we were about to start, along comes Frank Marsh. He was a decent bloke. He was working and camping at the Storries', making water-tanks. Anyway, when he arrived on his way to town we had to open up another round of bottles, so that by the time we parted from him it must have been around ten o'clock. Gosh! We didn't think then that poor old Frank would be lying dead at them gates next daybreak. You know, Joe, things are getting worse than crook. Me and Tilly is afraid to walk out after dark."

"You don't think Barry Elson committed these crimes?"

"No, I don't, as I said at dinner. The bloke wot's doing them must be strongish. Alice and Frank and Mabel were reasonably well set up, and it would take a stronger man than Elson to kill them with his bare hands. Tilly backs me up in that."

"Ah, Tilly! Did she like the ring?"

"Too right, she did. She's still talking about it. She reckons it's miles better than the one Ma Nelson gave Mabel Storrie, and that was a bonzer."

Chapter Fifteen

Iron Hands

At dawn the following Tuesday the wind began rapidly to freshen from the north, and when the pale-yellow sun rose sluggishly above the rim of the world it cast not black, but dirty grey shadows. By noon the sand waves were rolling over the bluebush plain, and the dead buckbush again lay piled against the fence that Detective-Inspector Bonaparte had slaved to clean. The sun went down in a brown murk, but among the men opinions of the next day's weather were divided.

Darkness arrived half an hour before due time, and Bony, who had most reluctantly decided to maintain an all-night vigil, slipped away from the homestead at five minutes to eight. He had prepared for a night's absence from the men's quarters with the story that Dr. Mulray and he were still fighting a game of chess and that they had determined to sit up till morning, if necessary, to finish it.

The night was not quite so evil as that he had spent at Catfish Hole. The stars could be seen, if faintly, and the darkness was not absolute. The wind had dropped to a strong breeze, and, the temperature of the sand-particles being lowered by the going down of the sun, the wind had now no power to raise them off the ground.

With the cunning and the silence of his maternal ancestors, Bony moved without sound. Never a dead stick broke beneath his feet. He saw obstacles into which a white man would have blundered, over which a white man would have tripped, into which a white man would have plunged, with risk of broken bones.

On leaving the homestead he walked due north out on to the bluebush plain. Here he could not see the river trees, but he could see the weak spark of light which was the oil lamp suspended outside Nelson's Hotel. The wind moaned and sighed dolefully about the bushes that appear so desirous of preserving their individuality by demanding plenty of space around them. Although Bony was forced to walk erratically to avoid them, he yet succeeded in keeping to a predetermined course.

Without once seeing either the river gums or the creek box-trees, he arrived at that solitary leopardwood-tree in which the crows had been quarrelling that afternoon he had tracked Donald Dreyton up into a box-tree. The Three Sisters and the Southern Cross announced the time to be a few minutes after nine o'clock.

Standing close to that side of the handsome, spotted trunk nearest the township, Bony made a cigarette, and then, with his coat removed and enveloping his head, he struck a match to light it. Thereafter he sat with his back to the tree, facing Carie, and smoked, confident that the west wind would not carry the scent of tobacco to the creek.

It was just such a night for which he had been waiting—a night when the aborigines' bunyip could be expected to walk, or swing along from tree to tree. Notwithstanding, Bony felt nervous and could not banish his nervousness. Here he sat trying to calm his nerves with cigarette-smoke, wearing a dark cloth coat with the collar turned up and pinned at his throat so that no portion of his white working shirt would be visible. In the right-hand pocket of the coat lay an automatic pistol of small calibre, and in the other was a reliable electric torch.

Who was this strangling beast who behaved like a monkey in trees, who killed with no motive save to gratify a lust to kill? Was his name on the list of persons supplied by Constable Lee? Was he a man, or was he, after all, the bush bunyip? Bony's aboriginal blood tingled, and Bony's white man's mind fought to still the tingling. After a moment's struggle the mind conquered the blood.

At this point of the investigation he was presented with several pertinent questions for which he could not supply the answers. He was decided that as the three crimes had been committed south of Carie the criminal must live in the township, or at Wirragatta or Storrie's selection, and of the list of Lee's names he had struck off all but eleven. These eleven men were "possibles", but no one of them was a "probable" save, perhaps, Hang-dog Jack. They were:

HANG-DOG JACK, the cook
DONALD DREYTON, the book-keeper fence-rider
BILL THE COBBLER, station-hand

HARRY WEST, station-hand
FRED STORRIE, the selector
TOM STORRIE, the selector's son
MARTIN BORRADALE, the boss of Wirragatta
CONSTABLE LEE
WEAVER, the storekeeper
JAMES SPINKS, the barman
DOGGER SMITH, the trapper

One of these men was the murderer of Alice Tindall and Frank Marsh, and the attacker of Mabel Storrie. They all had pre-knowledge of the movements of each of the three victims. There were names on the list struck off because, although the owners had pre-knowledge of the movements of one victim, it was proved that they had not this knowledge of the movements of the other. One of the eleven "possibles" was the murderer.

That the man who swung himself from tree to tree along certain sections of Nogga Creek was the person he called the Strangler, Bony was reasonably sure. The obvious reason for this singular method of locomotion appeared to be the desire to leave behind him as few tracks as possible. Yet in this case the obvious might not be the correct basis for argument. The assumption that the crimes were premeditated might be wrong. They might have been begotten by Impulse allied with Chance.

More than a third of the names remaining on his list he could with excuse have rubbed out, but, although the law assumes a man to be innocent until proved guilty, it is the detective's duty to regard all suspects as guilty until investigation proves which of them are innocent.

Bony had not yet met Dogger Smith. Lee was a "possible", because he admitted he knew that Alice Tindall was visiting the Wirragatta homestead the night she was killed. And, of course, he knew when Marsh and Mabel Storrie were in the town.

Of only one thing was Bony absolutely sure. The Strangler was no ordinary criminal. He had made only one mistake, which was the repetition of his crimes. This proved that his motive was the primal one, the lust to kill. He belonged to the terrible class of maniacs who can successfully conceal their mania from those about them—by far the most dangerous units of human society.

Perhaps it is no wonder that this half-caste Australian was fearful.

The cigarette having been consumed, he pushed the glowing stub into the soft, deep sand on which he was sitting, rose and stepped from the friendly tree, mentally girding his loins. Two minutes later he reached the creek track to the Broken Hill road, crossed it whilst his skin prickled and came direct to that tree into which Dreyton had climbed to retrieve the piece of grey flannel. It was the end one of fourteen trees forming one of the sections along which the "bunyip" progressed from branch to branch.

At the foot of this tree Bony determined to spend the night. He sat down with his back against its trunk, facing the north and the township, now masked from him by the intervening bluebush. No one could pass along the creek track without being observed. The circumference of the trunk at his shoulders was about five feet, and the knowledge was comforting that even a gorilla could not attack him from its far side and throttle him. Because of his dark clothes and skin, no one could see him from the branches this black, humid and sinister night. Yet, to him, anyone up among the branches would be silhouetted against the sky.

When he had taken up this position, Bony's nerves became less taut. He felt much less vulnerable to attack than he had done when walking to and from the leopardwood-tree. He was not a powerful man—not even a very robust one—and he knew that he would be no match for a man who could strangle with his hands a young fellow like Frank Marsh.

It says much for Bony that he essayed this vigil. The fears and inhibitions of his mother's people were in his blood, and like all clever men his imaginative power was much too strong for this kind of work. Reasoning is for daylight, when the primal man in each of us can be, and is, forced back into the mists of time. Like many a white man who knows his bush, Bony believed in the bush spirit named by the blacks as "bunyip", the spirit that gloats over the unfortunate who, alone, meets with accident, the spirit which lurks close by to a dry waterhole and watches the arrival of men without water. It is everywhere, the bunyip. It watches from the heart of every bush, from behind every tree-trunk, from the summit of every sandhill and from the foot of every mirage.

There was something about this foul Strangler which was almost supernatural. In the wind and the dust of night he pounced and slew until

117

his lust was appeased. Supposing that his crimes were not premeditated, that he was not one of those now remaining on Constable Lee's list? Supposing that he had the head of a dog and the body of a kangaroo and the arms and hands of the kangaroo?

Reason opposed such a notion, but the idea was nourished by the darkness and the wind hissing among the trees. Much of reason is evolved for the express purpose of comforting men who live life like those who shoot unknown rapids in frail barks. A coward can easily deny his God when he is young and the sun is shining, but it is the believer in God who can command courage as he dies. Then it is faith, not reason, that takes the hands of a man to lead him on.

So, even as Bony thrilled at his triumph over fear, so did he wish himself back in his bed in the men's bunkhouse.

The Three Sisters were above him now. He could see them as the wind-swayed branches moved. The Southern Cross was not visible, it being masked by the creek trees. It was ten minutes after eleven o'clock.

One of eleven possibles! Which one *the* Strangler? Of course it was a man and not a bunyip. Come away! cried Bony's mother. Stick it, old man! urged his father. Dreyton, Donald Dreyton. He knew when Mabel and Frank walked alone. He was camped only four miles away when Mabel walked alone. If he was innocent, why did he conceal, keep the piece of flannel and not at once hand it to the police? Tom Storrie! He was a strong youth, with hands like legs of mutton. Fred Storrie, his father! He was tall, lean and as strong as a bull. He knew when Alice walked alone, or could have known. He knew when Frank walked alone. Did he mistake his daughter for someone else, and then, discovering his mistake just in time, release her from his hands and, thinking her dead, leave her? Physically and mentally, Hang-dog Jack was the most likely of all the possibles. He could——

Abruptly Bony ceased to breathe.

The back of his head rested against the trunk of the tree, and the trunk had received a distinct blow. ...

Continuing to keep his head pressed against the trunk, Bony slowly turned it so that his left ear came to be pressed against the rough bark and he was able to look up into the swaying branches.

Among them he could see no fantastic shape. The skin at the nape of his neck was prickling, while the feeling in his legs drained away like blood. His hair felt dry and brittle. Now he could faintly hear a regular tattooing on the trunk, but he could not locate its origin. When the tattooing ceased he heard a soft rasping noise as though something was sliding down the bark to reach him.

Yet he could see nothing, and the horror gripped his muscles and tortured his nerves. Stilled to stone, Bony waited with his right hand caressing the pistol and his left hand gripping the torch. He looked for, but failed to see, either man or bunyip. The rasping noise ceased, and he dared to free his pent breath. His straining ears hurt and then felt exquisite relief when they caught the sound of a sharp hiss.

There was someone or something on the far side of the trunk against which the detective was pressing his head. The strange tattooing began again, and Bony recognized it for what it was. It was being produced by a nervous man's fingers, and this man, too, was pressing himself against the tree-trunk. The wildly staring half-caste saw the outline of the man's head bulge outward from the trunk line, slowly, deliberately, until he saw half a man's face. Swiftly Bony's eyelids drooped to mask the white of his eyes.

The seconds passed, and neither man moved a fraction of an inch. The unknown continued to stand peering round the trunk; Bony continued to lie perfectly still, watching the half-face exposed to him. Had his own face been white he must have been seen, for now intuition rather than visual proof assured him that he was not discovered.

Even whilst he waited thus, Bony was experiencing admiration. The unknown had not arrived via the tree-branches and then down the trunk to his present position. He had come along the ground. He had come as silently as an aboriginal along the edge of the creek-bank which passed the tree only three or four yards beyond it. Bony knew that his super-sight and hearing had not been at fault. For a white man it had been an achievement, and that he was a white man was proved by the faint gleam of white face protruding from the trunk of the tree.

From the direction of the homestead Bony now heard the unmistakable sound of footfalls. To turn his head or to make the slightest movement would have betrayed him to the man on the other side of the tree, but presently the detective knew that a third man was coming along the creek track. He was now close. Now he was passing. Then the half-face vanished behind the tree, and swiftly Bony changed the angle of his head so that he could see the opposite line of the trunk and watch the track as well.

Walking the track was a man. He was walking towards the Broken Hill road, and for an instant of time he became silhouetted against the sky above the township. His shape, his gait, the manner in which one arm was swinging, all informed the detective that he was Hang-dog Jack.

The next moment the Wirragatta cook had vanished into the dark of the night. Bony waited, listening with all his power, to hear, if not to see, the fellow on the far side of the tree move away from it. Still more seconds passed, and he heard no sound nor saw any movement other than the waving branches above. Hang-dog Jack's footfalls faded into the night as his shape had done. Still Bony waited, certain that the other man had not moved his position.

The moment arrived when he could wait no longer. With the pistol now free of the coat-pocket, he slowly and noiselessly drew up his legs, and then he began the operation of raising his body whilst still pressed against the trunk. Up and up, inch by inch, and so till he gained a standing attitude, still pressed to the tree.

With the pistol ready for instant work from the hip, the detective slowly sidled round the tree, his head a little in front of his body, his right eye seeing past the trunk and his left eye blinded by it.

There was no one behind the tree. As silently as he had come so had the white man departed.

The Wirragatta cook had disappeared in the direction of the Broken Hill road, and Bony dared not use his torch to ascertain if the unknown man had trailed Hang-dog Jack or was still close by. The silence of the unknown's departure was astonishing, because, unlike his arrival behind the tree, his departure had been listened for. From this vigil so far, one fact stood out in great importance. Hang-dog Jack walked the creek track in the middle of the night without the smallest effort at concealment or even silent movement.

Bony felt no uneasiness about the cook—if he were not the Strangler. Hang-dog Jack was exceptionally strong and he was, too, an expert wrestler. No man was better able successfully to resist physical violence. The detective reviewed his own actions in the immediate past. Should he have bailed up the unknown who had watched the cook pass by? Had he done right by making no attempt to apprehend the unknown for identification? Yes. To have done this would not have proved the unknown to be the Strangler, for

Bony had not seen the fellow up among the tree-branches. He could not be charged with vagrancy, or with being on enclosed land or with any one of the hundred charges used for the purpose of holding a suspect.

Who he was Bony naturally would have liked much to know. Yet he would prefer to remain in ignorance of his identity if the knowledge did not prove him to be the Strangler. The pressing matter at the moment was to learn the direction taken by the watcher from the tree. To Bony an examination of his tracks would provide evidence of his identity as sound as that of fingerprints. Once he saw them he never would forget them, and would surely recognize tracks made by the same man at any future date. That he had followed the cook Bony was inclined to believe, but until he had proof he could not know if this were so. He might be within a few paces of him, and to use the torch to examine tracks at this stage would be foolish.

Accustomed to the noises created by the wind, Bony failed to notice its increasing violence until a stronger gust came roaring along the creek. It was ominous. It came, this gust, like an express train, and like a train it roared its passage towards the Broken Hill road.

Continuing to press his body against the trunk of the tree, his head and his eyes incessantly moving, Bony listened and endeavoured to register sounds made by human agency. He could detect nothing moving save the smaller branches of the tree above him.

One thing was obvious. Hang-dog Jack at least would return to the homestead, having come from it, and it was more than probable that he would follow the creek track again rather than return by another way unmarked by track or pad. If the unknown watcher was on his trail Bony determined, at the least, to see his shape.

The only way of seeing an object on a particularly dark night is to get it silhouetted against the sky, and so Bony sank to the ground, and like a stalking fox he crawled from the tree to the edge of the creek-bank, at this place five feet above the creek-bed and sharply steep.

Employing extreme caution not to get too near the edge of the bank, where he might be precipitated with noise to the gravelly bed, he worked his way towards the Broken Hill road, still on hands and knees, for some fifty to sixty yards, when he reached a point midway in the break of the bordering trees. Now he could look towards the plain and see clearly the line it cut against the lighter tinted sky. Between that line and himself passed the creek track, and no living thing could use the track and not be seen silhouetted against the sky.

The detective knew this place well. He was lying along the edge of the creek-bank, and an attack could not be delivered from that side, nor could it come from a tree, because the sky above him was clear of branches. For the first time since leaving the stately leopardwood-tree he felt safe.

A lightning mind was probing for the reason of the cook's midnight walk. Hang-dog Jack's destination was as mysterious as the open manner of his going to it. This latter argued that he was not the Strangler, but opposed to it was the assumption that were he the Strangler he would have nothing to fear. If met and questioned, he could say that being unable to sleep he had chosen to take a walk. There was no law in existence to forbid it. He was even keeping to a semi-public road.

The wind gusts were appreciably stronger when, an hour later, Hang-dog Jack returned. He was actually humming, and the sound reached the tensed Bony before the fall of the cook's boots in the soft sand of the track. As he passed across Bony's skyline there was no possibility of mistaking his squat, powerful figure and the long, swinging arms. He was walking at a comfortable pace, like one to whom time and circumstance are of no moment.

The ugly figure disappeared towards Wirragatta. Still tensed, Bony waited as motionless as a blue-tongued lizard waiting to trap a fly. As distinctly as he had seen Hang-dog Jack he saw the second man run along his skyline, following, not the track, but the tree-line and passing the detective within less than five yards. He ran crouching so that he appeared not unlike a giant crab. Only during a space of four seconds was Bony able to watch him, and, although he was quite unable to determine the fellow's identity, he did know that the cook was being stalked.

Who was this second man and why was he stalking the cook? Always suspicious of the obvious, Bony reasoned that he might be, like himself, merely an observer. That the stalker was not Constable Lee, Bony was sure. That he was not Donald Dreyton, he was much less sure. Had it been anyone else who walked the creek track save Hang-dog Jack, Bony might have hastened after him to render assistance if necessary. He scarcely felt uneasy, on the cook's behalf, as it would have required much more than hand pressure on Hang-dog Jack's throat even to inconvenience him.

What was of greater importance was the fact that the second man had walked across the break in the tree-line and therefore had left his tracks there. Yet Bony continued to lie at the bank edge and wait. To see those tracks he must use his light, for by dawn they would certainly have been wiped out of existence by the wind, but to use the light would betray his presence if not his activity. And for the moment Bony knew this to be unwise. He waited fully thirty minutes, and he would have liked much to wait longer before he decided that if he further delayed in examining the tracks he would never see them at all. Up the creek was coming a heavy gust of wind with the roaring of a great waterfall.

And the wind beat him even as his light showed the line of tracks but a few feet distant.

Like a thousand devils the wind howled among the trees and plucked at their branches to tear many from the parent trunks and lay them violently on the ground. It threatened to throw the detective off his feet, and when it passed it left him gasping.

The line of tracks was still distinguishable, but each of the footprints was become blurred and almost filled in. It was quite impossible accurately to estimate the size of the boot or shoe worn by the unknown, although it was possible to establish that the size was six or seven or eight. The little, but important, tell-tale marks proving how the man walked and what part of his soles was given most work were gone, destroyed by the wind, perhaps before that last gust.

Bony had not time to feel to the full his disappointment when he made a discovery. Although he could quite clearly see his own tracks along the creek-bank, he could not discover the tracks made by the unknown after he left the tree to stalk the cook towards the Broken Hill road. There were his tracks running westward after the cook, but there were no tracks running eastward. An examination of the road revealed Hang-dog Jack's double line of tracks, but no others. How, then, had the unknown man left the tree-trunk round which Bony had observed him watching the cook?

As silently as the stalker of the cook, so did Bony walk back towards the tree against which he had sat for so long. The absence of the stalker's first line of tracks worried him, because there was suggested a further complexity. The double line of the cook's tracks proved that the wind could not have erased from the earth the stalker's first line of tracks. Yet the stalker had left but the one line, that of his passage towards Wirragatta. Was the stalker, therefore, not the unknown man who had watched the cook from behind Bony's tree. Had he been for a long time farther towards the Broken Hill road waiting the coming of the cook? If that were so, then it appeared that the stalker was not the unknown, that the unknown had not gone after the cook towards the Broken Hill road and was still between Bony and the homestead. Were there four men along this creek tonight, not three—Bony, the unknown, the cook, and the stalker?

Then came the attack—swift and silent and sure. ...

His caution overcome by chagrin and the problem set him by the tracks, Bony failed to keep watch on the branches beneath which he was walking. He heard the light impact of feet on the ground immediately behind him. Nervous tension having been relaxed, the communication between eardrums and brain was lethargic. Before he could turn and defend himself, before he could begin the attempt, vice-like hands encircled his throat and neck.

Instantly his breathing was stopped. The primary pressure was terrific. It was a band formed by interlocked fingertips across his windpipe, hand-palms pressed to the sides of his neck, and two thumbs cruelly crushed against either side of a serial segment of the spinal column.

As the overwhelming horror flooded his brain before the air stoppage began to take effect, Bony abruptly went limp. He drew up his legs, but his body was held on its knees by the two hands at his throat. A throbbing hum was in his ears, but beneath this inner sound he heard distinctly one having an exterior origin. It was low, throaty laughter—a dreadful, gleeful chuckling telling unmistakably of the lust to kill. The power of the life-destroying hands was equalled by the power of the arms supporting his weight.

Instantly Bony's hands went upward to tear away the band of bone and flesh about his neck, and it was then that he became conscious of the automatic pistol in his right and the torch in his left hand. Tautened muscles rather than intent pressed forward the light switch, and the strong beam moved to and fro between the branches like a searchlight hunting an aeroplane.

The pistol cracked even above the roar of the wind and the roaring in Bony's ears. He doubled it round and against his side, and at terrible risk to himself endeavoured to shoot his assailant. The night was now becoming unnaturally dark to Bony's starting eyes, and then swiftly the threshing branches against the sky faded into a general void.

Again and again the pistol cracked, but, although his fore-finger could still continue to press and release the trigger, Bony could not move the angle of his body more than was permitted by the muscles of his neck below the Strangler's hands.

He began to slide downward into a pit. Once again the pistol exploded. Then he felt himself flying across immeasurable space. In his brain a light flickered with astonishing rapidity. When it stopped, pain ceased. Consciousness ceased, too.

Chapter Sixteen

The Doctor's Patient

So limited was the scope of Dr. Mulray's practice that to receive a night call was unusual. He was awakened by a persistent knocking when the dawn was breaking on a new day of high wind blowing coldly from the south.

The doctor's bedroom was the front room, left of the tiny hall; his study-cum-consulting room was opposite. He was, therefore, not difficult to awaken by the knocking on his front door in a township where electric lighting and bells were notably absent. The temperature this early morning was lower than it had been for weeks. With the fall, the wind's power over the sand particles had waned to vanishing point. The air was bracing, even in the doctor's bedroom, and as he heaved himself off the bed, Dr. Mulray knew that while he had slept a cool change had arrived.

"All right! All right! I'm coming!" he shouted when the knocking continued. Breathing heavily, the old man struggled into a worn dressing-gown, picked up the oil lamp he had lit, and thudded out to the hall and the front door. The wind caused the lamp to flicker badly, but standing outside he saw the burly Constable Lee and the much smaller Joseph Fisher.

"Admit us, please, doctor. I am in need of your services," urged Bony. The tones of his voice caused the doctor to stoop to glare at him, and then he abruptly straightened and turned to the study door.

"Come in and let me have a look at you. Shut the door, Lee," he commanded. Within the study, having put down the lamp, he watched the detective lurch into the room, and then gently assisted him into one of the two old but comfortable leather armchairs.

"Humph!" he grunted, not unkindly. "What has happened?"

Bony, looking up into the weather-beaten, pendulous face, stretched his neck.

"I have been within an ace of death," he said with difficulty. "The Strangler attacked me while on Nogga Creek. Please examine my throat, doctor. Then, perhaps, a sedative. ..."

"Ah!" The exclamation was expressive. "Don't you talk any more till I say so. Know anything about this, Lee?"

Dr. Mulray had unfastened the pin at Bony's coat-collar and was already examining his neck while he was taking the detective's pulse.

"No, doctor," replied Constable Lee. "This man has just roused me out and asked me to bring him to you."

"Humph! A nobbier of brandy with a plentiful dash of milk, Lee. Brandy in the sideboard cupboard. Milk in the cooler on the back veranda. Get it, please. Now then, Joe! We'll have your coal and shirt off. The strangling brute got you, did he? I knew damned well that that fool of a Simone arrested the wrong man. Humph! Ah! Yes! Humph! Your coat-collar saved your neck from external laceration, Joe. There is only faint ecchymosis. I doubt that you could articulate if the hyoid bone was fractured, as it was in the cases of Tindall and Marsh. Mabel Storrie's windpipe was split in two places, so I have heard from Adelaide. I can't tell the condition of your windpipe without X-rays, but I am hopeful that you have escaped that most serious injury. Mabel had no clothing protecting her throat. Neither had the other two. Ah, good, Lee! Here, Joe, sip this brandy and milk. Take your time. You, Lee, help yourself to a bracer."

"Thank you," Bony murmured weakly. "I'll be better presently. Fright, you know."

"'Shock' is the correct word for your mental condition," argued the doctor. "I know; *you* don't. You will stay here today. I have a spare room. You will go to bed now. Think you can walk with assistance? Help him, Lee. I'll show you the way."

While the policeman was helping Bony to his feet the doctor rushed out of the room, across the hall and to his own bedroom, from which he appeared a moment afterwards with a clean pair of pyjamas. Taking up the lamp from the study table, he directed Lee and the patient along the short passage to a rear bedroom.

"Did the brandy sting more than usually?" asked Mulray. Bony shook his head.

"Good! It augurs well for your windpipe. Those neck muscles will be bruised. I'll foment 'em. Then the needle, my boy, and a long sleep. Lee, hurry out to the kitchen and get the fire going. I want hot water, and plenty of it."

Brisk, efficient, cool and immense. Dr. Mulray attended to Bony as gently as he might have attended a duke. He had the half-caste undressed and inside his spare pyjamas before Lee could appear with the hot water, and when Bony lay luxuriously between sheets he asked the old man:

"You insist that I stay here?"

"Of course! Think I am suggesting that you run up and down the street? How did you get here from Nogga Creek?"

"Walked—when I wasn't lying down."

"Ah! A long way for a man in your condition. About what time did it happen?"

"A little after one o'clock."

"Humph! Quite a long time ago. And what were you doing on Nogga Creek at that hour?"

"I'll tell you … I will be happy to explain when Lee returns."

"All right! All right! Don't worry. Hi, Lee! Stoke up that confounded fire."

"Flames are shooting out the top of the chimney, doctor. The water is nearly on the boil."

"That's right, Lee. Never mind about the chimney. I always clean it every three months by setting fire to it. And then Mrs. Mumps has a fit and I have to dose her … with brandy."

Dr. Mulray demonstrated that he was an excellent nurse as well as a good doctor. Lee submissively obeyed his orders, and presently Bony lay with his neck tingling from the application of hot cloths.

"Any pains in the chest or the back, Joe?"

"No, doctor."

"Ah! Humph! Yes! Lungs not damaged, apparently. You can thank your coat-collar for a lot. Now Lee will want from you particulars about this terrible attack, so you need say nothing more than necessary at this time."

Bony managed to smile. His neck and throat were feeling much easier, and his nerves were already steadying.

To the worried Lee, he said, "Explain to Doctor Mulray who I am. Doctor Mulray will respect the confidence, I know."

As the constable told who Bony was and the business which had brought him to the district the doctor barked:

"Inspector! Incognito! Bless my soul! Humph! Ah! Yes! Simone knew nothing? Ha ha! That mountainous fool! That gutter-bred Charlie Chaplin detective! That champion chess-player!"

"In explanation of my absence from the homestead last night, doctor," Bony took up the tale, "I said that you and I would probably be playing chess the night through to finish a close and interesting game. Let that stand." To Lee, he said, "Can you manufacture an excuse to visit Wirragatta this morning?"

"Yes. Or rather, there need be no excuse. There is a small matter of a choked bore-drain I wish to see Mr. Borradale about."

"Very well. Mention to him that I have played chess all night and that I have accepted the doctor's kind invitation to stay the day. He will probably want to know what a detective means by playing chess all night and then sleeping all day, but no matter. It is important that you find some pretext to interview Donald Dreyton and Hang-dog Jack and note if they behave abnormally—if they show any signs of having been struggling, even of gunshot wounds. If you can overlook all the other men, do so. Then ride across to the Storries' and have a look at Fred and his son Tom.

"I was attacked on the north bank of the creek under the trees approximately opposite that tall leopardwood-tree growing out on the plain. I made a distinct cross on the clay-pan on which I regained consciousness. I want you to search for my pistol and torch. I was too ill to do so myself. Make a thorough examination of the locality for clues and tracks. Tracks there will be none, I feel sure. You may find a shred of grey flannel cloth. Is that clear? Oh, and you will say nothing to anyone of my adventure."

"Perfectly, sir—er—Bony."

"No more," interrupted the doctor, flourishing a hypodermic syringe. "That'll do for the present, Lee. Take a stiffener before you leave and tell your good wife to keep her mouth shut. I'll be having that Mrs. Mumps here in an hour, and I'll have to explain about the fire being lit so early. And now, Inspector Bonaparte, you are going to indulge in a nice long nap. Where will you have it? In the arm is as good as anywhere. That's the idea. I like a man with guts, because I have none myself. I wouldn't have loitered about Nogga Creek at that hour for the price of Wirragatta itself. Bless my soul! And Simone's arrested the wrong man! Ha ha! Now close your eyes and sleep."

When Bony awoke, the sun was striking full on the lowered blind. The wind no longer heaved and strained at the roof iron and drummed on the walls. The house stillness permitted the sounds of Carie's life to penetrate into the room—the not unpleasant sounds of goat and cow bells and a blacksmith's hammer on ringing iron.

He was feeling much better in himself, and his throat felt much less painful. Save for the stiffness of neck muscles, he had almost recovered from his ordeal, and he earnestly blessed Dr. Mulray—and his coat-collar. He was smoking his second cigarette when the old man came into the room. "Ah! Humph! Smoking, eh!" he exclaimed in noticeably subdued voice. "Mrs. Mumps thinks that we had a night of it together and she is now preparing dinner for us, with plenty of Worcestershire sauce in the soup. Great stuff, that sauce. Her husband always drinks a full bottle after one of his benders in order to settle his stomach—what's left of his stomach, I mean."

"I am almost completely recovered, doctor, thanks to you," Bony said as he swung his legs to the floor and so came to sit on the edge of the bed.

"Good! Excellent! Lee is in the study. If you can manage it, I suggest that you dress and come along. We must not arouse the suspicions of my housekeeper. I'll examine the neck first, though."

"Show me the bath-room, or may I use the washstand here?"

"Whichever you please. The shower is on the back veranda. I'll run out and see if Mrs. Mumps will favour us with a pot of tea." The ponderous old man rolled away to the door, but before opening it turned and smiled and said, "We can add brandy to the tea if we choose."

Fifteen minutes later the detective was sipping tea and smoking a cigarette in the study. In his workaday station-hand's clothes, he did not appear as disreputable as he might have done had Dr. Mulray's clothes looked better than they were. Lee was in uniform, and the wearing of uniform had a distinctly official effect on both his appearance and his mind. "I gave your excuse to Mr. Borradale," he began his report. "He didn't believe it, but it hardly mattered. He was more relieved with the wind having gone round to the south'ard early this morning, when it lost its power to raise the dust. Dreyton looked all right. Smart as always. As for Hang-dog Jack—well, his eyes were red from lack of sleep and his temper was bad. The others were normal. Fred Storrie is in bed with a mild attack of influenza, which he says he got down at Broken Hill. Tom looked and behaved all right. He's doing the cooking and looking after his father while the women are down in Adelaide.

"I found your gun and torch at the edge of the claypan you scored with a cross. The torch is all right, but the gun is empty and clogged with grit."

"So Fred Storrie is in bed with influenza, is he? Did you see him?"

"Yes. He's got it sure enough. I hope I don't catch it …"

"Could Storrie successfully trick a layman into believing he had influenza, doctor?"

"He might. He wouldn't trick *me*, though," asserted Mulray. "But surely— —"

Bony stood up and sauntered to the window, before which he lingered. The doctor glanced at the policeman, and Lee placed a finger to his mouth, indicating the advisability of silence. Opposite the doctor's house was the hall and drawn up outside the side entrance was a car and a man pouring water into the radiator. The scene recalled to Bony's mind the car driver who filled his radiator only after the static electricity had been allowed to drain from his car. When he turned back to the doctor and Lee, his eyes were smiling.

"I am going to take you both into my confidence, not because I love you so much, but because I need your assistance. It is not really the detective's business to take anybody into his confidence, but then, you see, I am not a real policeman," Bony told them.

"When I first came here, Constable Lee prepared for me a list of the names of everyone living in and around Carie over the last two full years. I have struck out all but eleven names. Among the remaining eleven is the Strangler. I haven't proof of it, but I yet believe it. Your name, doctor, is one of the names struck off. I am about to strike off your name, Lee. That will leave ten names."

Rapidly Bony related all that he had seen and experienced during the night of terror, and the discerning Dr. Mulray came to understand the real measure of Bony's courage. Lee listened intently, and twice essayed to take his long and narrow note-book from his pocket.

"I never saw my assailant," Bony concluded. "That he is exceptionally strong in the hands and arms, I was given ample proof. Understand, a man who is strong in his hands and arms need not be strong in his legs and body, and he need not be a big man. What caused him to fling me aside before he had killed me we shall probably never know, unless it is that I winged him with my pistol, or that its reports frightened him. You say, Lee, that all the cartridges were expended?"

"Yes; the gun was empty. It seems evident that we'll have to put that cook through the hoops. Hang-dog Jack's the man right enough. Why, he's strong enough to hold me. Is he on your list of suspects?"

"He is," Bony admitted. "And yet we will not question him or permit him to think we suspect him. I had you among the eleven suspects, Lee, because you *could* have killed those two and attacked Mabel. I have taken you off the list because you wear a nine-size boot. Who the other eight on the list are I will not inform you just yet."

Lee grinned ruefully.

"You're a strange fellow, Bony," he said.

"Ah! How many times have I heard that? I wonder now if Dreyton is responsible for the introduction of it into this district. Well, there are quite a number of strange fellows here. Tell me, doctor, can you guess what Dreyton was before he left England? It is sometimes easy to tell a man's profession from his gait, his eyes, even the cast of his face."

"Dreyton!" echoed the doctor, and he drew in his breath and distended his pendulous cheeks. "Yes, I can guess with reasonable certainty of being correct. I'd wager a bet that he was once in the Royal Navy. I'd wager ten bets that he was an officer. There is not a great deal of difference between the face-cast of the military and the naval officer, but there is certainly a small distinction."

"He would be, then, of that class commonly called the 'upper class' in England?"

"Yes. Dreyton would belong to the 'County' class. Probably, nay, almost certainly, he comes from a long line of naval officers."

"Thank you. Now would it be too much to ask you to visit Fred Storrie in order to be sure that he does suffer an attack of influenza?"

"Not at all, inspector. I could go along right away."

"Good! Try to remember, doctor, that to all my friends I am Bony, and I would like to count you among the number. While you are away Lee and I will get to work on the details of a little plan I have conceived. With your permission we will use your writing materials. And then, at dinner—if you will invite me to dinner—we will discuss the moon and madness and static electricity."

Chapter Seventeen

Dr. Tigue's Case-Books

In this community, doctor, there is a man suffering from a brain lesion,"
Bony was saying as his host and he smoked and drank coffee after dinner.
"This man is not a lunatic to the degree that he could be easily located and as
easily certified. Normally he is as rational as you or I or Constable Lee—but
you could be the victim of his mental trouble, as I could be, and the other one
of us would never suspect it. I believe that his trouble is hereditary, that it
did not seriously affect him until a few years ago, that it is now becoming
rapidly worse and will inevitably reach the stage when normality will have
ceased altogether."

"There's sense in what you say," conceded the doctor. "I have myself
thought along those very same lines."

Bony rolled himself another of his interminable cigarettes, stretched his
neck muscles, lit the weed and gazed solemnly at the medico.

"When a young man, doctor, I committed a grave mistake. Through a
broken love-affair I threw up my post-university career and went bush. It
was a mistake I have always regretted. Certain friends of mine wanted me to
study for a medical degree and take up work among the blacks. Had I done
that I would have known today more about the human mind than the
average layman."

"But you would not have been a detective."

"Perhaps not." Bony sighed before smiling. "The greatest evil of life is the
shortness of its duration. We are not given time enough to learn anything
before we must prepare for death. The older I become the more clearly do I
see that the creation of a man's brain is almost wasted effort, because the
mortal span does not allow him to develop it. The more he learns the more
clearly he understands that what he has learnt is but a drop in the ocean of
what he could learn did he live for, say, a thousand years. I am repeatedly
faced with a problem which would be no problem at all were I the master of
all learning."

"And your present problem?" asked the entranced Dr. Mulray.

"This—does static electricity affect the human brain, and, if so, to what extent?"

"Help!" cried the pendulous man. "You would have to be an Edison and an Einstein, not an ordinary doctor, to answer that. On that subject I, like you, am a layman."

"Well, then, let two laymen tease it a little by discussion," Bony urged, and then proceeded to relate the phenomenon of static electricity stored in the car he had met in the dust-storm. "That day there was no thunder, no manifestation of electricity in the atmosphere. The driver said that it was produced in his car by the incessant bombardment of sand particles, the dry tyres providing almost complete insulation. It appears to me to be quite a reasonable theory and, if correct, would account for several mysterious air accidents when the aeroplane is disintegrated. There must be a point when the charged object cannot carry more electricity. As you say, it is a problem for an Edison. Where it more closely concerns us is the probable effect on certain types of human beings of this singular electrical manifestation."

"What the devil are you driving at?" asked Dr. Mulray.

"You will see in a minute. I have been told by many old people that the weather, or, rather, particular phases of it, affect their rheumatism. Can you tell me why?"

"Not with any authority," confessed the doctor. "That the weather does affect rheumatic sufferers is, of course, correct."

"Well, then, do these dry wind-storms have their effects on certain patients?"

"Ah! I can answer that. Mrs. Nelson's nervous system is affected by them. I have prescribed a sedative for her to take when they begin. Then I have known two men and three women who become prostrate when a thunder-storm breaks. Admittedly, in the case of one the effect was caused by the shock of seeing her husband killed by lightning. The others suffered, in my opinion, by the atmosphere being overcharged with electricity, which affected their nervous systems. As a student, I used to think it was the result of sheer funk, but I do not hold that view today. They have a natural antipathy to electricity just as other people have a physical antipathy to lying on horse-hair, to eating strawberries, by contact with a cat."

"We are progressing, doctor," Bony said with great satisfaction. "Now, bear with me a little longer, please. Our Strangler operates only during a sand-storm. At first I believed he was sane enough to choose the conditions provided by these storms in order to conceal as much as possible evidence which might reveal his identity. I am beginning to think now that this might not be so. He might not be actuated by his own safety, but impelled to seek to satisfy his lust to kill by the electrical phenomenon accompanying these fierce wind-storms.

"Further. I have been seeking a man who knew, when normal, just what he did when abnormal. Now I recognize the probability that, when he is normal, he might not know what he does when insane. If this is so, then my task is made ever so much more difficult, because I could not trap him through conversation. He would not betray himself, being unaware of his guilt. Proof positive of his guilt can only be obtained by catching him in the very act of killing."

"Then he might be—anyone?"

"He might be anyone, as you say, doctor. Still, lacking the requisite knowledge of a combined Edison, Einstein and Curie, we cannot consider this aspect of the case to be anything more than a theory, and, perhaps, a wild theory at that. To arrest Hang-dog Jack might be to commit as great a mistake as that committed by Simone when he arrested Elson. Even if I found the Wirragatta cook climbing along the Nogga Creek trees I would not be justified in ordering his arrest. There is no law against him climbing trees, even at two o'clock in the morning. I am not going to order the arrest of any suspect before I am certain of his guilt. I have never yet done such a thing and I am not going to do it in this case. It is the toughest nut I have ever been asked to crack, but I'll crack it if I have to stay here for ten years —and am sacked by my chief for not giving it up."

Dr. Mulray pushed back his chair and clawed his way to his feet.

"Come along to the study," he suggested. "I think, perhaps, I can give you a hammer which might enable you to crack the nut."

Dusk was falling swiftly upon Carie as they entered the doctor's most comfortable room and drew the heavy leather chairs to the open window. With many grunts and sighs the pendulous doctor settled himself deliberately, as deliberately put the tips of his podgy fingers together before he spoke.

"Professional secrecy is generally an excellent thing, but sometimes it is not excellent. In the interests of justice, which will have to act quickly if another life is not lost, I will acquaint you with one or two matters which may have an important bearing on your investigation. All these people here have been, are, or will be, my patients. There are two men and one woman who stopped growing mentally when they reached the age of five. One of the men should be certified. Despite what you have said this evening, I long since have reached the conclusion that the genesis of these crimes is to be found in the very roots of the place. Here is a peculiar thing. From what I learnt recently, I believe that many years ago Mrs. Nelson almost met her death by strangulation."

"*Ah!*" breathed Bony, his eyes suddenly blazing. "How did you learn that?"

"I was with Mabel Storrie when she regained consciousness, and the first thing she said, with great difficulty, was, 'Will my neck be disfigured like Mrs. Nelson's?' I reassured her and commanded her not to talk, but a few days later I asked her about the old witch's neck. She then was loath to talk about it, saying she was sorry she had mentioned it, as she was under promise to Mrs. Nelson. I was interested, however, and I was firm, less because I was curious than because I could see the girl was suffering from some inhibition. It came out that at the time I got Mabel to nurse Mrs. Nelson when she had an attack of neuritis she saw on the old witch's neck several peculiar scars.

"I have never seen those scars. Mrs. Nelson always wore a nightdress with a high collar at those times I visited her when she was in bed. According to Mabel, Mrs. Nelson would never remove the nightdress to wash herself or to change it whilst the girl was in the room. One day when Mabel returned from a visit to her aunt in the town she found Mrs. Nelson asleep and the collar of the nightdress undone. The scars were visible to her, and on awakening and discovering that her nurse knew about them Mrs. Nelson was very angry."

"This is all very strange, doctor," Bony interjected.

"'Tis so," Mulray agreed. "In a young woman this shyness which dictated concealment of ugly scars could be put down to vanity. What is so interesting is Mrs. Nelson's determination to conceal such scars from her doctor and her nurse. Here is another peculiar matter. After the old witch got better, or well enough to be attended by Tilly, she presented Mabel with a most expensive ring. I know the old woman fairly well. She's made a fortune out of that pub, and in business she is as hard as steel. In other ways she's very generous, but even so, to give a nurse an expensive ring in addition to five pounds a week seems to call for an explanation."

"You are sure that the scars were caused by attempted strangulation?"

"Almost sure from the description of them I obtained from Mabel."

"Thank you, doctor. You have given me material with which to build many theories."

"I have more material to give you. I have been here fourteen years, as you know, and I have never attended Mrs. Nelson for wounds of that nature. Practising here before me was a Frenchman by descent named Tigue, and he left all his case-books here in this house. I'll come back to them in a minute, for I must begin at the beginning.

"Old Tigue fell mortally ill early in nineteen twenty-two, and at Mrs. Nelson's expense I came up from Adelaide to see him. I found Grandfer Littlejohn's wife nursing him. After Tigue died I returned to Adelaide, and a few weeks after that I received from Mrs. Nelson an offer of a hundred and fifty a year and this furnished house rent free to practise here. Further to this was the somewhat singular addition of a case of spirits per month.

"For several reasons I decided to accept the offer." The old man smiled when he added, "It was the spirit, perhaps. Of course, the hundred and fifty a year and the house was compensation for the lack of many practice fees. As Mrs. Nelson explained, it was an inducement to a medical man to reside and practise here when his normal work would not be remunerative enough to feed him. She thought it was up to her to hand back a fraction of what she took from the public in her hotel. I think that as she is getting old she fears the devil. I send in my bills to her as with the rest. She is an extraordinary character. I've known her foreclose on several properties because the mortgage interest wasn't kept up. And yet no one in real trouble appeals to her in vain."

Bony was staring unseeingly into the darkling night. He had met Mrs. Nelson but once, and he now was wondering if her acts of philanthropy were actuated by some ulterior motive, such as the gift of a valuable ring to Mabel Storrie to seal her lips.

"Mrs. Nelson has been very generous to the Storries, hasn't she?" he asked.

"Decidedly. Not only did she waive Fred's half-yearly mortgage interest, but she gave them a cheque for a hundred, and told Mrs. Storrie that if she wanted more for Mabel she was to wire for it. I saw the note she wrote to Mrs. Storrie. Lastly, she almost ordered me—*ordered* me, mind you—to accompany the girl to Broken Hill and see that a nurse was engaged to take her on to Adelaide."

"Ah! Very interesting, doctor, very. There is something else, though, isn't there?" Bony suggested.

"Yes. When I heard about the scars on the old witch's neck, and knew I had not treated her for the wounds from which they resulted, I thought of Doctor Tigue's case-books. They were all in a wood chest in this room when I first came here. I went through the lot.

"Each book is devoted to the cases in one year and the range of years is from 1909 to 1922—one book for every year Tigue practised in Carie. He was a methodical fellow, and at the end of every book the cases in it are indexed. In nearly all of them there is a reference to Mrs. Nelson's ailments, but a leaf from each of the books devoted to the years 1910 and 1914 are missing. They have been torn out. In all the range of books these are the only two leaves missing, and according to the indexes both leaves referred to Mrs. Nelson ..."

"Go on, doctor!" Bony cried softly.

"The missing leaf in the 1910 book was numbered pages eleven and twelve, and according to the index page twelve was devoted to Mrs. Nelson, and page eleven to Mrs. Borradale. In the other book, the year 1914, the page numbers of the missing leaf are one hundred and thirty-seven and one hundred and thirty-eight. Here again the index shows that page one hundred and thirty-seven concerned Mrs. Nelson, and page one hundred and thirty-eight dealt with a certain Henry Wagstaff, since deceased. Now for what did old Tigue attend the old witch on or about 5th January, 1910, and again about 15th June, 1914?"

"Hum! I suppose that the case following the missing leaves does not concern Mrs. Nelson? Doctor Tigue could not have made a mistake, or dropped a blot of ink and merely torn out the offending page and directly continued on the next?"

"I don't think so. If he had done, why did he index the material on them?" countered the old man. "They were torn out for a purpose, and the person who removed them didn't think of the indexes or thought that the indexes were of no importance."

Through the tobacco-smoke Bony stared hard at his host, and observing the stare the doctor realized how dark it was becoming and heaved himself upward to light the lamp. Bony lowered the window and fastened it and drew down the blind.

"Let us have a drop of my allowance of spirits," Dr. Mulray suggested. "Bring the chairs over to the table, my dear fellow. This detective business is just as interesting as chess. Would you care to look at those damaged case-books now?"

"Later, perhaps, thank you. Do you know Mrs. Nelson's history?"

"Yes—from the year Tigue came here to practise, in 1906. At that time Mrs. Nelson was living with her husband in one of the poorer houses in Carie. Her husband was Cobb and Co.'s groom. In February, 1910, she, and not her husband, bought the hotel."

"One of the pages in the case-book for that year is missing, is it not so?"

"It is."

"As the wife of a horse change-groom, where did Mrs. Nelson get the money with which to purchase the hotel. Do you know?"

"She has said, and I have heard it from several people, that she inherited the money from an aunt."

"Well, what other important dates are there?"

"In 1914 Nelson died, and from that year Mrs. Nelson prospered. I understand that he was an alcoholic."

"Ah! And the year 1914 is also remarkable for the missing leaf in the case-book devoted to it."

"Yes, but he died towards the end of the year, and the missing leaf deals with notes made in June. The notes concerning the death are still in the book."

"There is no reference in all the case-books to the wounds which caused the scars on Mrs. Nelson's neck?"

"Nothing."

"The wounding might have been done before Doctor Tigue came to Carie?"

"But it wasn't," Dr. Mulray almost shouted. "Across in old Grandfer's son's house is a photograph of Mrs. Nelson and her husband and a small crowd taken outside the hotel at the time she purchased it. In the picture Mrs. Nelson is wearing a low-cut blouse."

"Dear me!" Bony sighed, to add sharply, "What more do you know, doctor?"

"Nothing. And yet I have often scented a mystery enveloping the acquisition of the hotel by Mrs. Nelson. Old Dogger Smith once told me that Mrs. Nelson never had an aunt to die and leave her any money. There are two men who could tell us quite a lot about those early days—if they chose. One is Dogger Smith and the other is Grandfer Littlejohn. For heaven's sake don't ask Littlejohn anything. He would be sure to tell Mrs. Nelson."

"There may be no connection between the scars on Mrs. Nelson's neck and the Strangler," Bony said slowly. "I must mentally chew all you have told me. Did Mrs. Nelson have any children?"

"Yes—one. A male child. It died a day or so after it was born."

"What was the date of the birth?"

"The fourth of January, 1910."

"Oh! And the leaf torn from Tigue's case-book for that year bore reference to Mrs. Nelson! I must see those casebooks ... now ... with your kind permission."

Dr. Mulray was absent from the room only two minutes.

"I am a great believer in intuition," Bony told him on his return. "This matter of Mrs. Nelson's neck scars may be the essential clue in this extraordinary case I am looking into. I have been baulked and baffled for a lead, and this may well be it. Now for those dates as I write them down, thus:

1st March 1906—Tigue begins practising in Carie. Mrs. Nelson and husband living in poor house. Nelson is Cobb and Co.'s change-groom.

4th January 1910—Mrs. Nelson gives birth to a male child. Child dies a day or so after birth.

February 1910—Mrs. Nelson purchases Carie Hotel, as it was then named, with money from a legacy. Leaf in case-book for this year, probably dealing with the birth of Mrs. Nelson's baby, is missing.

20th June 1914—Near this date another leaf is missing in the year's case-book. One page of this leaf also devoted to Mrs. Nelson.

27th November 1914—Nelson dies of alcoholic poisoning."

"What do you make of it all?" inquired the interested Dr. Mulray.

"Nothing of much import just now, doctor," Bony replied in that clipped voice which betrayed mental excitement. "The missing leaves in these case-books provide us with a mystery, the solution of which may solve the identity of the Strangler. It is a thought, however, which might well be father to the wish. We can, with assurance, guess what concerns Mrs. Nelson on the page torn from the book devoted to the year 1910, the birth of her child and its death. By the way, from your examination of the books, do you think Tigue would note its death on the missing page?"

"Yes. That is why I assumed its death. It is not noted elsewhere. Further, I had heard that Mrs. Nelson's only child died in infancy."

"Oh, indeed! Then as yet we have not proof of its death. I wonder, now, for what Dr. Tigue attended Mrs. Nelson about 20th June, 1914? Did he attend her for wounds on the neck caused by attempted strangulation?"

Bony stood up, and Dr. Mulray always remembered him as he looked at this moment—slim and yet indicative of power, his eyes lit with the flame of mental vigour. "Doctor, I thank you," he said gravely.

Chapter Eighteen

The Warning

The new book-keeper for Wirragatta arrived on the morning of 1st December. The next day he took over the office from Donald Dreyton, and the day following Dreyton departed, with his camels, on another inspection of his one hundred and eighty-three mile section of boundary-fence.

As usual, this morning of 3rd December, Bony, as Joe Fisher, accompanied the men to the office at half-past seven, where they received orders for the day. As usual, promptly on time, Martin Borradale emerged through the wicket gate in the homestead garden fence and walked briskly towards the knot of waiting men.

He had a nice way with his employees, which went far in retaining their loyalty. He would always halt several yards from the gathered men and, after giving a general good morning, would call each to him in turn and give his orders in quiet, confidential tones.

This morning he called first Harry West, and what he had to say occupied a full five minutes. Having received his orders, Harry came away with a stony face and paused beside Bony to whisper that he was to take the ton-truck with wire and fencing-tools out to a place called Westall Corner and there assist Dogger Smith, who had accepted a few week's work fence repairing.

If there was a man Bony was anxious to meet it was this Dogger Smith, and when, on having called him, Martin Borradale asked with a smile what work he would like to be given this day, Bony requested to be sent with Harry West.

"All right, Bony. Are you looking for a spell of real work?"

"Physical work always bores me, Mr. Borradale, but it invariably improves my digestive organs."

"How is your investigation going?"

"Slowly but surely."

"I am glad to hear that," Borradale said warmly. "My sister, having guessed who you are, has been talking to me quite a lot about you. You know old Stanton and the Trenches at Windee! Jolly fine people, aren't they?"

"They are among the finest I have met," Bony agreed with equal warmth. "I hope you do not take it amiss that I have not confided in you about my investigation, but I always work along certain lines. However, it is due to you to know that I wish to examine this man called Dogger Smith. Can I have your permission to use the truck should I desire to return here before the fence repairing is completed?"

"Certainly—but I would like you to leave the camp with sufficient water to last for three or four days. Would you inform me on one point which has bothered me for some time? I cannot think what motive the Strangler has in killing people. Do you think he is a lunatic?"

Bony looked deep into the candid grey eyes and then examined in a split second the boyish, kindly face. Slowly he shook his head.

"I don't really know what to think, Mr. Borradale. Were he a lunatic he would not select the time and the place when opportunity presented him with a victim. Were he a lunatic he could not hide his lunacy from his associates for long. I may be wrong, of course, but that is what I think. The Strangler is a man who is controlled in exaggerated form by the lust to kill. This same lust, in much lesser degree, finds expression in the normal man who shoots pigeons released from traps, and who kills animals and birds when not bound to do so for food. I should say that the Strangler is a man who has never mentally matured."

"You think, then, that Simone arrested the wrong man?"

"Yes, I am sure he has."

"How will Elson get on?"

"He will be charged and probably remanded. I feel confident, however, that the Crown Prosecutor will not be satisfied with the evidence set before him by Simone, and that Elson will be released."

"I hope so, Bony. The lad was all right, you know. He was a bit wild with the girls and all that, but he's not vicious."

"I think with you. I would not be surprised if the Strangler turns out to be a stranger to everyone here. It is quite an interesting case."

"I wish you luck with it. I may take a run out to the camp in a day or so. Dogger Smith will take a peg or two out of young Harry's ladder. The young blighter is afraid of nothing. I expressly told him not to ride Black Diamond, and, as you are aware, he rode the brute to Carie to see his girl. He has let me see he would like to be promoted to the boss stockman's place and live in the married people's cottage, with Tilly for his wife. Because I would like to promote him and see him married to Tilly, I have decided to teach him a lesson. The young rip is a born horseman and a good sheep-man, and he looks on manual work as terribly degrading."

They laughed together.

"It will probably do him a great deal of good," said the delighted Bony.

"I think it will. He has many excellent qualities. Please do not mention to him what I hope to do for him. Ah, here is my sister on the veranda. She wishes to speak to you, I think. I'll go back and finish the orders."

Martin nodded, leaving Bony at the wicket gate to pass through to the garden and so to the veranda, where Stella waited, cool and charming.

"How are you getting on with the investigation?" she asked.

"Slowly but surely, Miss Borradale," Bony replied. "There are many little matters I have to straighten out."

Her warm hazel eyes became swiftly serious.

"I am not going to be dangerous this morning," Bony gravely told her, whereupon she laughed deliciously and her eyes told him he should dare to try. "I am going with Harry West to work at repairing a fence, and I shall be away for several days. Would you grant me a favour?"

"If it is not impossible, certainly."

"It is this. While having no intention to alarm you, or to be melodramatic, I would urge you not to leave the house at night without escort, not even to step into the garden. And in future, after a day of wind and dust, keep your bedroom window and door locked, no matter how uncomfortable that may be. And, too, instruct the cook and the maids to do likewise."

"Surely there is no danger to us in the house, is there?" she asked, her face now drawn and revealing the horror which had been in her heart for many a long month.

"The reason why my namesake, the Great Napoleon, won so many battles, Miss Borradale, was because he took every possible precaution against defeat. It is during the night following a day of high wind and dense dust that every man, woman and child in and south of Carie is in grave danger. All that I ask is that all sensible precautions be taken specially throughout such a night."

Stella expelled her breath in a slow sigh. "Very well," she assented.

"Thank you. Within a week or two I shall have removed the danger for all time."

"Then you suspect someone?"

"Alas! I suspect ten people," he replied. "One of the ten is my man. Have no uneasiness. I shall get him in the end. I have never yet failed to finalize a case."

"Never failed?"

"No, never. As Colonel Spendor says, and says truly: I am a damned poor policeman but a damned good detective. Permit me to leave you. I must roll my swag and assist Harry West to load the truck."

When she bowed her head slightly in assent, he bowed to her and wished her *au revoir*. Watching him walk to the gate, she felt like crying after him mockingly. Then she remembered the expression in his blue eyes and turned to enter the house for breakfast. Had he been dressed in evening clothes and with a jewelled turban on his head he would have been the living likeness of her idea of an Indian prince—polite, assured, dignified.

By the time the truck was loaded with rolls of wire, shovels and crowbars, rations and a tent and swags and a round iron tank, it was nearing noonday. Hence it was after one o'clock when Bony and Harry West and Harry's five sheepdogs left Wirragatta for the scene of their coming labours.

Two miles below the homestead the outback track crossed the now empty river over a roughly built but stout bridge, and thereafter the road ran southward for several miles before bearing again to the west. During the first half-hour Harry maintained a grim silence. There was no cabin to the truck and one of the dogs stood with its jaws resting on Harry's shoulder, another crouched against Bony, while the remaining three rode the load. All enjoyed the speed.

"Make us a smoke," requested Harry dismally. He handled the truck as though it were his greatest enemy.

"Certainly, my dear Harry," consented Bony, rolling him a cigarette. "Why are you so depressed this calm and warm afternoon?"

"Depressed!" snorted the youthful outlaw-rider. "Stiffen the crows! What bloke wouldn't be depressed at coming down to a fence lizard? Which ends of them shovels do you use to dig with, any'ow? Fencin'! Come down to fencin' and you want to know why a bloke's depressed."

With one hand working the steering-wheel, Harry struck a match and lit the rolled cigarette. The track wound sharply across a wild range of sand-drifts, and the detective regarded the slim, brown hand clutching the wheel with some misgiving as the speedometer was registering forty miles an hour. The cigarette alight, Harry reinforced his right hand with his left and savagely pressed down on the accelerator.

"I reckon I done me dash for that married cottage," he moaned. "Last year a bloke done some crook work, and the boss set him scrubbing the house verandas. You see, the boss don't ever sack a man. If he wants to get rid of him, he sets him to work such as scrubbing floors, knowing that no bloke will stand that for long before he asks for his cheque. I got a good reason to ask for mine, too, 'cos this fencing to a horseman is just as crook as scrubbing floors is to a fencer."

"You must swallow your pride, Harry," Bony said softly. "You listen to one who is possessed of much worldly wisdom. We should always mould our conduct on the examples set by the great men in history. Er—Nelson, Napoleon, Marlborough and others learnt in their youth how to obey. Having learnt how to obey, they were fitted to demand obedience. There arrived a point in the lives of all great men when they could and did put telescopes to their blind eyes and otherwise intimate to their superiors that they could—er—retire to the equator. The secret of success, Harry, is to know just when you can tell a superior to retire to the equator without resultant disadvantage to oneself."

"I didn't exactly tell the boss to go to hell, Joe. Some fool went and let the ridin' hacks outer the yard when I wanted one to ride to Carie. Black Diamond was in a yard by himself and they hadn't the guts to let him out. Any'ow, I can ride that cow on me nose."

"I don't doubt that, Harry. The circumstances, I admit, were annoying, and the business urgent. The boss said not to ride Black Diamond. You said 'I *will* ride Black Diamond.' Inexperience permitted you to disobey the boss when you expect advancement. Impulse blinded you to the obvious way of disobeying without subsequent unpleasant result. Now, Black Diamond is black all over. If you had thought at all, you would have stolen some white paint and given him a forehead blaze and white hocks. Then no one in Carie would have recognized him."

"Gosh, Joe! You're a corker," Harry said with great earnestness.

Bony laughed.

"I have the idea that the boss is merely testing you by putting you to real work, Harry. You see, if he thought of making you boss stockman, he would want to be sure of your character, that you would have strength of character to lead the men under you. In any case, why worry; why be depressed? As I pointed out, it is a beautiful day and you find yourself in good company."

The young man's expression of gloom persisted for another half-minute, when it swiftly changed to normal cheerfulness. He slapped Bony on the shoulder with his left hand and put on additional speed.

"You know, Harry, I think you are eager to get going on the business end of a crowbar and a shovel," Bony murmured, or rather his voice sounded but a murmur above the roar of the engine. Harry turned to face his companion, and the truck shied violently.

"Me eager——! Cripes! What you mean?"

"To me it appears obvious. You seem to be so eager that you are endangering both our necks in order to reach the work as quickly as you can."

The engine ceased its roar and the speed dropped to five miles an hour.

The grinning youth said, "I never thought of that."

Chapter Nineteen

Dogger Smith

Dogger Smith had for many years lived in a world all his own—a world in which human beings had a quite secondary part. The supreme being in this particular world was Dogger Smith himself, and the lesser beings were the wild dogs against whom he pitted his cunning and the wiles of his trade. Beings of much less importance were the other human inhabitants, but, notwithstanding, Dogger Smith knew every one of them intimately. He appeared to draw their secrets and the details of their lives out of the air, for he was seldom in touch with any human beings, black or white.

He was of immense stature, the most remarkable thing about him being the snowy whiteness of his full beard and hair. He might have been seventy years of age, and then again he might have been over a hundred. He was one of the "immortals" created in the 1860's, hardened by a diet of meat, damper and tea, and an annual "drunk" at a bush pub. The remnants of these "immortals" are still to be found camped in the pensioners' communities along the Darling, ancients blessed with agility and mental alertness to be envied by modern men of half their age.

Early this day he had arrived with a flourish at a narrow belt of mulga crossing a section of the fence which had to be repaired. The flourish was given by the roar of an ancient Ford engine lashed with fencing-wire to a truck chassis, clouds of following dust, and a really terrible stench. The grinding of iron and the dust having subsided, Dogger Smith made a fire and boiled a billy for tea.

He was oblivious, or impervious, to the stench, and drank black tea and smoked black tobacco in a short-stemmed wood pipe with evident appreciation. Being refreshed, he set to work cutting forked poles and straight poles and tree-branches, the whole of which he fashioned into an efficient wind-break. Having accomplished so much, he drank more tea and once more filled his pipe with the jet-black plug tobacco.

Harry West unwisely stopped the station truck to leeward of the decrepit Ford, and, as one animal, his five dogs jumped to ground with noses twitching with delight and raced up-wind to the dogger's truck, where they pawed the ground and whimpered.

"Good day-ee!" roared Dogger Smith. "Come and 'ave a drink er tea."

"Gosh!" gasped Harry. "You gotta dead horse on that hearse of yours? Cripes, she stinks something awful!"

"Haw! Haw!" came the bellowed roar. "That's only my secret dog attractor."

"Secret? There's nothing secret about *that!* She's worse'n a loud-speaker at full blast. What's it made of?"

"Coo! Like to know, wouldn't you? Why, I bin offered a 'undred quid for that secret attractor. She's caught more dogs than you got hairs on your head, young feller. Who's your lady friend?"

"This here's Joe Fisher," replied Harry, to add with pride, "Friend of mine."

"That is a wonderful dog-lure you have," Bony said, looking again at the five dogs who were standing on their hind legs and pleasurably sniffing at Dogger Smith's gear on the truck.

From above a height of six feet a pair of keen hazel eyes looked down into Bony's smiling face. There was nothing rheumy about those eyes, and there was no mark of spectacles on the bridge of the big Roman nose.

"Glad-ter-meet-cher," was the non-committal greeting. "You're a stranger to this district."

"Yes. I've come over from the Gutter for a change," Bony admitted. "Er— that secret attractor has a very powerful influence over Harry's dogs. I suppose you get used to it in time?"

"Well, she takes a bit of getting used to, I allow, but she ain't so crook as the lure what Boozer Harris worked with back in ninety-two. I generally parks the truck well to lee-ward, and I'll shift her now you've come. You gonna get water today, Harry?"

Harry decided that he would, and Bony, who decided he could not endure the stench a moment longer, elected to go with him. They unloaded the truck without discussing the weather, and then took the tank four miles away to fill it at a dam. During their absence Dogger Smith removed the offence and cooked the dinner—boiled salt mutton and potatoes.

The first night in camp Bony and Harry West were entertained by vivid descriptions of a dozen most gruesome murders, and Dogger Smith averred that never before or since his time had there been a cement-worker surpassing Deeming. Throughout the following day the dog-trapper proved that his interest in labour was equal to his interest in murders, and when the second evening of this association arrived Bony was indeed thankful that the sun did not permanently remain above the horizon.

The weather was clear and hot and calm, and constantly the detective looked for signs of the next wind-storm. As none appeared, he delayed his questioning of Dogger Smith in order not to arouse the old man's suspicions and thus shut off a valuable fount of knowledge. It was the unfortunate Harry who unconsciously gave the lead when, a few evenings later, he complained of Martin Borradale's decree of banishment to fence work.

"I ain't gonna hear nothing against young Martin Borradale," sternly said old Dogger Smith, his great white head thrown back and his hazel eyes hard with sudden wrath.

"He's the best boss you ever worked for, me lad, and he's just the man to keep you young fellers in your places, like his father before him."

"Oh, all right," snarled Harry, really too weary to argue about it.

"Has the boss owned Wirragatta long?" Bony slipped in conciliatorily.

Anger subsided like a spent wave.

"Since his father died. He was born on Wirragatta. I mind the time he was born. It was on the third of January, 1910. The day he was christened I'll never forget. Old man Borradale and Mrs. Borradale—she were a fine woman, to be sure—was that proud of having a son and heir that they give a grand party in the shearing-shed. Every man on the run was called in to the homestead the day before. Most of the townspeople were invited, too. The day of the christening there were barrels of beer and a special dinner, in the shearing-shed, and the barrels were tapped quick and early. Old Grandfer Littlejohn then was old man Borradale's horseboy, old Grandfer even in them days being considered past real work. He always was one of them tired sorta blokes. Any'ow, 'im and the woman wot was cooking at 'Government House' got that drunk that they hung onter each other on the dance floor and cried. And then Mrs. Littlejohn was told, and she came on the scene and started to screech at the cook, telling her in about ten thousand words that she was no lady. Then the cook, she hauled off and clouted Ma Littlejohn, and Ma Littlejohn, she clouted the cook. Then all hands fell down together and went orf to sleep for two days and two nights."

"It must have been a great day," encouraged Bony.

"Too right she was. Old man Borradale was never as generous before or after as he was when young Martin was christened. He was a hard old bloke, but he was just. He married the best woman ever the back country saw. She near died giving life to young Martin."

"The boss appears to be well liked," Bony craftily pursued. "He's worried, though, about the Strangler, he being a Justice of the Peace and all that."

"But," objected the old man, "they got Barry Elson for it, didn't they?"

"He never done it," Harry interjected warmly. "And there's a lot of people think like me, too."

"And a lot think he done it," dryly persisted the old man. "Still, I don't think it's him. I reckon it's that there bunyip old Snowdrop has been yelling about for years. Wot-in-'ll's the reason for doing of it if it ain't a bunyip. There's more in them blacks' ideas than you'd think. What we wants is a real detective to prove the Strangler is a real bloke or a bunyip."

"Sergeant Simone——" began Bony, but the old man cut him short.

"Him!" he exclaimed with withering contempt. "I means a real detective, not a drunk-pincher. We wants a proper bush detective."

"I agree there," Bony said dryly. "Whoever the Strangler may be, I think he is a little mad—someone who goes mad now and then. Do you know a man just mad enough to arrange his killings without being caught?"

Dogger Smith chuckled. He was blessed, like many lonely men, with a sense of the ridiculous.

"Only old Stumpy Tattem," he said, and now his eyes were alight. "Now and then poor old Stumpy rams his hat on a fence-post and says just what he thinks of it. Me and him was putting up a division fence in Yonkers' paddock when Mabel Storrie was nigh killed. It blew like the devil, you remember, and that evening I baked a damper, the best damper I ever baked. Old Stumpy went crook because it wasn't perfectly round. Then he went for me and nearly bit me 'and in two. I had to clout him hard with me other, and when he comes round he gets up and clears off into the scrub, and I don't see him again until next midday."

"And the night he was away from your camp Mabel Storrie was attacked. Where were you camped that night?"

"Eh!" exclaimed the ancient, staring hard at Bony. "Crummy, I never thought of that! Why, me and Stumpy Tattem was camped only three miles south-west of Nogga Creek! Now, I wonder— — No, of course not. Old Stumpy wouldn't go and do a thing like that. Not poor old Stumpy, with his wooden leg and all. He goes off his rocker now and then, but he's as 'armless as a dove."

"Where is Stumpy Tattem now?" asked the half-caste.

"Stumpy! Why, he's working away across on Westalls'. He's a decent kind of bloke, is Stumpy, even if he gets a bit rampageous now and then."

Bony recalled having removed the name of William Tattem from his list, and now he considered putting it back again. Stumpy would certainly have to be followed up. He must work Dogger Smith right out now this opportunity had come to find the old man in the proper frame of mind.

"How long have you lived in the Carie district?" he asked.

"Close to fifty years."

"What was Carie like back in those early years?"

"She was good-oh! When I hit Carie the first time there was three pubs in her!"

"Indeed! More people, too, I suppose?"

"Too right there was. Real people, too. Hard doers, all of 'em," Dogger Smith pridefully replied. "In them days the bush was thriving. Wool was worth only round about sixpence a pound, and sheep could be bought for a shilling a time, but the money them days went a thousand miles farther than it does these. They can have their high wages an' all that, but give me them times and low wages, when the wages we did get went farther. The squatters had plenty of money, and they spent it, too. When the companies took over and put on managers and talked about their flaming shareholders, that was the finish of the bush as it was in them days. The runs carried more sheep to the acre, and places what now employs a dozen 'ands uster employ fifty or sixty. Now blokes has to go to the cities to find work. The know-alls blame the sand-drifts, or the over-stocking, or the rabbits, but old man Borradale knew more'n all the perfessors when he said that the root of all evil in the bush was the stupid leasehold system of the land."

"How's that?" asked Bony, his interest switched off from his investigation.

"It's simple enough. People who lease land are no different to people who rent a farm or a house. They don't know what is gonna happen to them in the future, and they naturally gets all they can outer the land before they gets chucked off be the government. They overstocks and don't do more improvements than they must. Why, they would be fools to rest paddocks and clean up the rabbits and do real improvements for some other bloke to step in and collar the benefits, wouldn't they?"

"I heartily concur," Bony said vigorously, although it was a national problem which had not and did not interest him. Had Dogger Smith said that the Prime Minister ought to be hanged he would have agreed without reservation. Having got the old man "warmed up", he did not hesitate to put this question:

"How far back did Mrs. Nelson go into the hotel at Carie?"

"Away back in 1910. She come into some money from an aunt, so she said, but her mother was a Rawlings and she didn't have no sisters, and her father only had one and she died in 1902."

"She is a character, isn't she?" Bony pressed, giving the old man no time to reflect.

"She is that," Dogger Smith agreed. "Some reckons she's pretty hard, but it ain't my opinion. When she first took over the pub she had a fine way of getting rid of cheque-men after their money was cut out. She would go round the tables herself and she'd ask each feeder what he'd have. 'Will you have goat or galah?' she'd say. 'Course every one would say, 'Goat please, Mrs. Nelson.' When a bankrupt chequeman said that, she'd say, 'Indeed, you won't. You'll have galah.' And galah they would get—the toughest birds ever stewed half-way through.

"She only made one mistake in her life, and that was marrying John Nelson. A fine-looking, 'andsome bloke he was, I give that in, but he was a born boozer and gambler like his father before him. Ma Nelson tamed him some after she married him, and if it hadn't been for her, he wouldn't have lasted as Cobb and Co.'s groom as long as he did. And then, when she bought the pub, his end was quick and sure.

"I gets into Carie one morning and I finds Ma and the yardman and Trooper Halliday all trying to hold John down on his bed so's Doctor Tigue could get to work on him with a squirt thing. John is that powerful that he's heaving 'em all around like they were straws. He's well in the horrors, and he's roaring that he'll do 'em all in. There wasn't nothing I could do but grab him, stand him up and place him right, and then clout him a good un under the chin to quieten him and to give old Tigue a chance to prod him with the squirt.

"Oh, yes, John Nelson was a doer all right. What he drank no one kept tally, and in the end Ma got tired of trying to keep 'im off it. Any'ow, I don't think she did much trying after she bought the pub. Some says she oughtn't to have bought it, knowing what John was, but buying it made no difference either way. Jail or the South Pole was the only place for him. He got to be like old Stumpy Tattem, wanting to bite everybody. Now, he could have done all these murders if I hadn't meself laid him out in his coffin what was a foot too small for him, but made up in width."

"Never had any children, did they?"

"One—a baby boy. It was born in the worst sand-storm I ever knoo."

"Indeed! What happened to it?"

"Died. Might have been just as well—with John Nelson for a father. Aye, a fine, 'andsome bloke was John Nelson. He was dark and soft spoken, and all the gals tore their 'air over him."

The old man stirred the fire sticks together and in the growing blaze they saw that Harry West had dropped off to sleep beside them.

Chapter Twenty

Grandfer Littlejohn

The heat had been excessive all day, but such was the low humidity that none felt ill-effects when along the seaboard 118 degrees in the shade would have provided death with a harvest. And now the crimson sun was throbbing above the western scrub-line, the bluebush plain was painted with purple and blue, and Mrs. Nelson sat in her chair placed at the southern end of her balcony.

In the street below stood the dust-covered mail-car, its driver and passengers being waited on at dinner by Tilly, the beloved of Harry West. Near the car, talking to Constable Lee, stood the Wirragatta book-keeper, and a little farther along the street, on the far side, old Grandfer Littlejohn sat on his empty petrol-case seat outside his son's house and conversed with a stranger to Carie, the man known there as Joe Fisher.

The sun disappeared and the distant sandhills changed colour from orange to red. Now and then Mrs. Nelson glanced down through the uprights of the balcony rail at the men standing by the mail-car, when she smiled only with her lips. Now and then she looked back to Bony and the town ancient, and then not even her lips smiled. At those times she glanced upward at the colourful sky her eyes narrowed and her beautiful hands trembled.

Presently the mail-car driver appeared, a tall youth dressed in city fashion, smoking a cigarette, wearing a vast cloth cap with the peak drooping over his right ear.

"Going to the 'Ill?" he asked the book-keeper.

"Yes. When, do you think, will we be starting?"

"When I've got me mails. I'm going for 'em now."

The driver went into his seat stern first, as had become the correct mode. The engine roared and cigarette-smoke mingled with exhaust fumes as the heavy car was turned round and driven to the post office. It was then that Fred Storrie stepped out to the veranda from Mrs. Nelson's sitting-room.

"James said you wanted me to run up, ma'am," he drawled.

From his elastic-sided riding-boots Mrs. Nelson's beady eyes lifted their gaze to note the worn riding-slacks, the large, red, long-fingered hands, the faded khaki shirt, and finally the man's sun-darkened face and its long black moustache and pale-blue eyes.

"Yes, Fred," she said crisply. "This morning James told me that yesterday a man and his wife camped at Catfish Hole. Do you know anything about them?"

"Not much. The woman slipped into the tent when I went there this morning. I don't know the man. Said they had come up from Menindee. He's a prospector."

As Fred Storrie did not know these people, Mrs. Nelson was sure she herself had never seen them.

"Well, did you tell the man it is not a good place to camp at?"

"I did. I told them what had happened to Mabel near by, and the man laughed. Said he was afraid of no one."

Mrs. Nelson remained still. Her passivity was one of the several remarkable things about her.

"What's his name? Did you find that out?"

"Yes. His name's Bennet. He's thick-set, muscular, about forty-five. Tough-looking customer."

The mail-car drew up again before the hotel, and the driver shouted:

"Come on, now! All aboard!"

Long accustomed as they were to watching the mail-cars depart, Mrs. Nelson and Fred Storrie broke off their conversation to watch this one away. All was bustle down below them. The book-keeper and several others climbed into the car whilst the knot of bystanders and James called farewells. The usual mob of children ran about it. Constable Lee took no notice of them. They no more feared him than they feared old Littlejohn. The driver derisively tooted the horn, and then the car slid away, with a boy standing on the running-board to go as far as the Common fence and open the gate. And so on to Nogga Creek and Broken Hill.

"That book-keeper didn't last long at Wirragatta," stated Mrs. Nelson with sharp disapproval. "Couldn't stand being so far away from the pictures, I suppose.—Now, Fred, about that couple at the Catfish Hole. We can't be sure that that fool of a Simone arrested the right man, and we don't want another murder. To allow that couple to camp at Catfish Hole is flying in the face of Providence. They are on your place and you must move them first thing in the morning."

"I can't shift 'em, ma'am, if they don't want to go," asserted Storrie.

"You can't shift 'em!" echoed Mrs. Nelson. "Fiddlesticks! Haven't I been generous to your Mabel and you? Haven't I pensioned old Mrs. Marsh?" The claws began to be shown. "I'm not a benevolent society, Fred. I have lost a lot of money over these murders, what with Sergeant Simone coming here and upsetting Lee and keeping my bar shut at nights. I am not going to sit quiet here and have more people murdered, do you hear? You can't shift 'em! Say you want the water. Say you've got sheep watering at Catfish Hole! Say *anything*, but move them on first thing in the morning."

"They won't go, and I can't shift 'em," Storrie persisted. "I told the man that Catfish Hole wasn't healthy. He said the climate suited him. I then told him he was on my land, and he asked if Catfish Hole was inside the freehold of the selection. When I said it wasn't he flashed a piece of paper at me—a miner's right. He says he intends pegging a claim to include the sand-bar at the bottom end of the water, 'cos he reckons it'll wash gold. He says I ain't gonna shift him; the police can't shift him; and with that miner's right me and you can't shift him, either."

Standing there leaning against the veranda rail, Fred Storrie looked down into the beady eyes of the leader of Carie.

"Gold!" she snorted. "Gold, my grandmother!"

"Might be gold there, all the same," Storrie dared to argue. "My father once found colour two miles up Nogga Creek."

Mrs. Nelson permitted her gaze to wander over the plain from which the sunset colours were being drained away.

"I tell you, Fred, I don't like it," she said. "If the man is murdered, I won't support the woman, or do anything for either of them, but that Simone will come again and I'll have another period of bad trade. It's not good enough. Still, if that man holds a miner's right and he pegs a claim, no one can move them by law. I'll have to concoct some plan. I must think it over. Go down to the bar for a drink, and then stroll up along the street and tell that half-caste talking to that old dotard of a Littlejohn that I'd like him to come up."

Storrie nodded, evidently pleased that the interview was over, and departed with silent, cat-like tread. Mrs. Nelson turned to face squarely to the south, then to observe the colour-shot dust raised by the mail-car, still floating above the track all the way to the emerald tree-line that was Nogga Creek. The hot colours were now fading from the sky across the blue-orange dome, beneath which hung ghostly white streamers of cloud mist. Tight-lipped, the old woman regarded this ominous sign.

Down in the street, Bony was comfortably seated beside Grandfer Littlejohn, who had been listening with the interest of the confirmed gossip to the details of Harry West's banishment to a fence.

"Old Dogger Smith and young Harry will enjoy theirselves," he said, his voice cracked and never for long remaining at the same key. "It'll do that young rip a lot of good having to work properly, and Dogger will see to that. Times ain't what they uster be, when men could ride 'orses without being threatened with being charged with riding to the public danger. Still, he had no business to ride Black Diamond, night or day."

"Have you been living hereabouts for long, Mr. Littlejohn?" Bony asked soothingly.

"When I fust come to Carie it wasn't yestiddy," came the emphatic answer.

By now the evening was well advanced, and after the heat of the day the air was cool and languorous. The old man, who was dressed in the usual stockman's regalia of elastic-sided boots, skin-tight moleskins and a "weskit" over a cotton shirt, spat with accuracy at the first of the yellow-and-black night ants, and then decided to proceed.

"When I fust come to Carie, there was whips of cotton-bush and wild spinach and wild carrots and things growing all over the country. Now, the country is turning into a desert. You seen them sandhills away over the Common to the east? Well, they wasn't there forty years back. What the rabbits have done to Australia ain't nothink to what the sand is gonna do."

"I understand that Carie was much bigger in those far-off days," led the crafty Bony, who was like a wise riverman, sometimes allowing the current to take charge of the boat, sometimes steering it.

"It wasn't what you'd think," retorted Grandfer with a hint of asperity pardonable in one of his undoubted age. "'Course, the post office wasn't up then. It uster be at the store when the present man's father ran it. Nor was the hall and the court house up in them days, but there was three pubs, more houses, more people and a hell of a lot more money. The hotel across the way was one-storied, and," the old man chuckled, "one-eyed, too. It was kep' by a

158

feller called Beaky Evans. When a man asked him, 'How's the galah's perch today, Beaky?' he uster get wild and chuck out all his customers and shut up the pub for a coupler hours or so."

Bony gave an encouraging laugh.

"When was the hotel rebuilt?" he asked carelessly.

"Back in nineteen-o-eight. Watkins, who had the place, pulled it to bits and did the rebuilding, but he didn't do no good. He sold out to Ma Nelson for four thousand pounds. He wasn't meant to make money—like Ma Nelson."

"She appears to be a born business woman, Mr. Littlejohn," Bony said, knowing that the conversation would be repeated to the leader of Carie, but no longer disturbed by the probability.

"Ah, she's all that, young feller," agreed Grandfer. "She's always had her head screwed on right, but even she didn't do no good till after poor John Nelson shuffled off."

"Drank hard, didn't he?"

Grandfer's clean-shaven chin sank to rest on the backs of his palsied hands, which, in turn, rested on the root handle of his stout mulga stick.

"John Nelson didn't drink like you or me," he said slowly, and Bony knew that he was no longer in the present. "He never had no swaller as I could see. I fust knew him when he was working on Wirragatta, when he was a smart lad and a terrible fine horseman and a mighty good-looking chap. But the drink got him early, and it got him bad. He pulled up a bit when he was a-courting of Ma Nelson. She was cooking at the pub. Then he got the job of change-groom to Cobb and Co. in this here town and married her.

"Well, well! Ma was as pretty as pretty then, and poor John was as handsome as the devil himself. Any other man would have worked the flesh off his hands for a woman like that—but no, he went on the booze a week after they were married. He got locked up time and again, and old man Borradale uster threaten and roar at him from the bench something terrible. And when John was coolin' off in jail Ma uster ride out for the change horses for the coach, and me and the others uster hitch 'em in for her."

"Plucky!"

"She was that, Joe Fisher. And so she is to this day. We knew something of what she uster put up with, but not all of it. We could hear poor John on his way home—they lived at the far end of the town—and he would be roaring drunk. Sometimes someone would go out and stop him and persuade him to come in and camp the night. It musta been a happy day for Ma when he shuffled off."

"That was in 1914, wasn't it?"

"Yes, it was in 1914, in December—the year the war broke out."

"What did he die of?"

"Delirium tremens, of course. He could die of nothink else."

"Was he ill long?"

"Well, yes, he was," replied the old man. "He had a terrible strong constitooshon, did poor John Nelson, and he took a lot of killing. You see, Ma Nelson come into some money—her aunt left her a tidy sum—and she bought the hotel in 1910. From then on John Nelson got going properly. Nothink could stop him. Between bouts of boozing he got bouts of praying, holding meetings in the bar parlour. There was no more keeping him off the praying than there was off the drink.

"Well, it got worse and worser, and the beginning of the end come when poor John walked round and round the pub all one afternoon and night, wearing a track so plain that it lasted eight months. That side fence joining the hotel to the postmaster's house wasn't up then, so John had a fair go.

"A coupler days after that he fell down in a kind of fit. The policeman—not Lee, but a man called Halliday—the yardman and Ma Nelson carried him up to bed and sent for old Doc Tigue. Then there was Ma and the yardman and the policeman all trying to hold poor John down so's Tigue could quieten him with morphia or something. Dogger Smith, he come on the scene and quietened John with a punch. Then old Tigue got to work, and John slept a bit. John always was a bit looney, but that time he was a raging madman. And then he busted a blood vessel one evening, and that was his finish."

"Horrible!" murmured Bony. "Were you with him when he died?"

"No. Old man Borradale was short of a horse-boy and I was on that job for more'n five years. You see, I was getting past real work even in those days, and the job was easy. The missus, rest her soul, and me had this very house behind us, so when me and the boss wasn't out on the run I could get home at nights."

Memory silenced Grandfer Littlejohn for several moments, and Bony wisely waited. Then:

"We're gonna have another wind-storm be the look of that sky tonight," predicted the old man. "It bin a rare year for wind-storms, this has. Not as bad as seventy-one though."

Bony recalled the conversation he had had with Dr. Mulray, when he had complained about the shortness of life, and now he glimpsed the comfort old age drew from the store of memory. Grandfer's body was old, but his mind was young. How strange it is that while the mind remains healthy it seldom grows old and feeble like the body. Bony saw himself fifty years hence. God willing, what a store of memories he would possess then!

Softly he said, "I wonder! I wonder if John Nelson would have pulled up if his wife had had children."

"Ah!" exclaimed Grandfer as though this was a question he had often debated. "You know, she did have one baby. It was early in 1910. I remember quite well when it was born, because it was in the middle of the worst sand-storm I ever seen. Fortunately for Ma Nelson, poor John went on the booze something terrible two days before the little un come along and the policeman locked him up for Ma's good. Old man Borradale—he was the sitting Justice, as his son is today—he gets the policeman to charge John with assault and battery and resisting arrest, and obscene language, so's he can give fourteen days without the option. As it happened, John was just plain drunk—so drunk that he couldn't resist and assault no one, and he couldn't swear, because he couldn't speak. Every one knew it and every one was glad he got the fourteen days.

"That give Ma Nelson a bit of peace and quiet. My wife, rest her soul, tended her, and when the baby was born the father was stone sober and quite safely out of the way. When he was told about the baby, he swore off the drink and implored the policeman to let him out so's he could see his son and heir. But the policeman, he says, 'No, Nelson. You stays where you are till your fourteen days is up. When we lets you out your wife will be strong enough to take care of herself and the baby.'

"Then the baby died, and when John got out, instead of going home to Ma, he walked direct to the pub and started drinking again. That finished Ma with him. She was never the same to him again, and I don't blame her. Watkins had no business to serve him, and ever since she took over the pub, Ma watches the married men, and if she thinks they're boozing too much she puts 'em on the Blackfeller's Act, and James keeps 'em out. If that baby had lived, poor John might have gone straight, but I doubt it. He was too far gone."

"Hum! Very sad, Mr. Littlejohn," murmured Bony. "Your wife, I suppose, assisted to prepare the little body for burial?"

"She did, young feller, she did," Grandfer replied shortly—so shortly that Bony did not expect him to continue. However, after a space of five seconds, he went on: "Old man Borradale was very good to Ma Nelson. He provided the coffin and things, and the baby was buried up at the cemetery, old man Borradale reading the service, and crying over it, too. Yes, my wife, rest her soul, was Ma Nelson's greatest friend, and when Ma came into that bit of money she wasn't forgotten."

"That was kind of Mrs. Nelson."

"Too right!" Grandfer instantly agreed. "She gave my missus, rest her soul, a clear thousand pounds, although no one never knew anything about it afterwards. I—I——"

The ancient ceased speaking, and Bony could see him peering down at him.

"I shouldn't have told you that," Grandfer said anxiously. "I promised Ma I never would. I never even told my son and his wife about it, nor anyone else. It sorta slipped out, you see. Don't you say a word about it to anyone, there's a good lad."

"We will both forget this talk, Mr. Littlejohn," Bony suggested quickly. "If you say nothing of our conversation this evening, I'll say nothing about that money. What do *you* say to a pint of good beer?"

The ancient leapt to his feet.

"That beer what arrived the day afore yestiddy oughta be well settled be now," he said brightly, no longer living in the past. "Still, I can't shout back, Joe. Me daughter-in-law don't let my son slip me more'n two bob a week terbacco money."

"Then I will shout twice," suggested the very pleased detective.

But Bony walked pensively to the hotel, with Grandfer Littlejohn hopping along beside him like a sprightly sparrow.

Chapter Twenty-one

Two Appeals

If the evening when Bony talked with Grandfer Littlejohn hinted at yet another wind-storm, the next morning most plainly predicted it. There was an entire absence of wind and not a leaf stirred among all the great river red-gums. A tenuous high-level haze produced in the sunlight a distinctly yellow tint, while the flies were far more sticky than usual, and the seeming lack of oxygen had a depressing effect on both men and animals.

When Bony entered the office a few minutes before noon, he found Martin at work at his writing-table.

"Hullo, Bony!" the squatter said wearily. "Sit down, will you. My book-keeper left yesterday, as probably you know, and I'm up to my eyes in office work."

"Isn't Dreyton due in?"

"Today or tomorrow," was the reply, spoken irritably. "I do wish he would stop here for good. Dependable man, Dreyton. When he's here, everything goes with a swing. Have you seen that couple who are camped at Catfish Hole?"

"No, but I have heard they are there."

"Then you probably know that the man is about forty, and his wife slim and light-weight and only half his age. Lee tells me he has warned the fellow of what has happened along Nogga Creek, and what might happen to the woman if they persist in staying there. Then the man produced a miner's right this morning and pointed out the corner pegs of a claim he intends working just below the water."

"And that waterhole being on Crown land, no one can argue with the miner and his miner's right," Bony said calmly while rolling the inevitable cigarette.

"I am not so sure," Borradale countered with a show of temper. "I'm not so sure that they can't be moved away. I am the sitting Justice. Here are Lee and yourself, representatives of the law. We ought to be able to devise some action to remove them from what I think is still a grave danger."

"Yes, it could be done, of course," conceded Bony. "I could complain to Constable Lee of being assaulted by the man. Lee could arrest him, and you could remand him for the Divisional Magistrate to deal with. We three would have to stick together in the frame-up. If it came out——"

"What the devil are you driving at?"

"I am outlining one way we could adopt to move that couple from Nogga Creek," Bony calmly answered. "There are, of course, other methods. You and I could kill a sheep this side of the boundary-fence and then swear we saw the miner killing it."

"This has gone far enough," Martin almost shouted, his eyes blazing with indignation. "If you think I am a liar and a perjurer you are——"

"I fervently hope not, Mr. Borradale," interrupted the now smiling Bony. "I was merely suggesting ways and means—not that you would even consider them. I would, of course, never lend myself to anything so gross. The fact is that the man has legal right to be where he is, and we have no legal right to move him from where he is. He has been made conversant with the ugly history of Nogga Creek, and, if tragedy comes to his wife or himself, you and Lee and I can be held blameless."

"But all that does not remove the very grave danger, to the woman especially. I am more or less responsible for this district, and every day since Simone arrested Barry Elson I am becoming more convinced that he has arrested the wrong man." Martin vigorously banged a clenched fist down upon the table. "Is it not your duty to prevent a crime if possible?"

"It is, I believe, the duty of an ordinary policeman," Bony gravely admitted. Then, although his face remained serious, his eyes began to twinkle. "I like crimes to be committed. A cleverly executed crime is ever a delight to a man having my brains to solve it."

"Ye gods!" Martin cried despairingly.

"What on earth would I do for a living; how would I maintain my wife and children and keep the eldest at the university if people did not commit crimes? Oh, no ... I certainly would never attempt to prevent a crime, especially a first-class murder."

Borradale sighed with exasperation.

"Then it is a pity that Sergeant Simone arrested Elson and took him away to Broken Hill. He would have moved on those people."

"Sergeant Simone is a man capable of doing anything, Mr. Borradale. On the other hand, he is very tiresome when his somewhat original personality begins to wear on one. Honestly, though, that miner cannot be moved against his will. I will see him this afternoon and try to persuade him to go somewhere else. I can at least paint a word picture which will keep the woman inside the tent after sundown."

Martin swiftly became his normal self.

"If you would do that, it would be something," he said. "We can't do more than our best to move them away. By the look of the sky today we are in for another wind-storm. It will be a snorter, too, so late in the year as this. You understand the incidence of those crimes taking place during a wind-storm?"

"Yes. The fellow is clever enough to choose his time when his tracks are certain to be wiped out very shortly after he commits a murder. He has his wits to that extent."

Martin fell to staring hard at the detective.

"Would it be too much to ask if you have any inkling of his identity?" he asked.

"By no means, Mr. Borradale. I have in mind at least three men, one of whom could be the Strangler. It has been a very difficult case and yet one profoundly interesting. Solving a crime mystery depends largely on the element of luck. I have read of no prolonged investigation which did not contain the element of luck to make it successful. It has become the fashion to sneer at coincidences, as though coincidence was never found mixing the destinies of men and women. This case has been exceptionally barren of coincidence, but my investigation has been attended with luck. However, the detective's greatest asset is patience, and patience is my greatest gift. When investigating a crime I permit nothing to disturb me, not even this private letter from my revered chief, Colonel Spendor. Listen."

Bony had produced a plain envelope, and from it he took a sheet of notepaper. He read:

> You cannot expect to succeed every time. Should you think Mr. Borradale's case will occupy you for very long, return at once. You are urgently required at Roma. Perhaps at a later date you could take up Mr. Borradale's case again. Convey my warmest regards to him and to his sister. This is no time for you to go on a walkabout. Report at once.

"Here we have, Mr. Borradale, a very mild effusion pounded out on a typewriter by Colonel Spendor at his private home. It illustrates the dear old man's inherent impatience. If I took the slightest notice of it, I would get nowhere. Still, I promised him in my letter, which left on the mail last night, that I would finalize this case within seven days. I think I can assure you that I shall keep to my time-table. I believe that this coming wind-storm will give me the Strangler."

"You do? I am glad to hear it. The beast has cast a shadow over us ever since Alice Tindall fell a victim to him. You must have a lot of sway over Colonel Spendor. My dad used to tell me he was the greatest martinet in Australia."

Bony chuckled, and now his blue eyes were beaming.

"Long ago," he said, "I discovered the secret of managing Colonel Spendor. By the way, I have come up against another mystery. Do you know anything about Mrs. Nelson?"

"Quite a lot. What's the mystery?"

"Do you know how she came to possess at least five thousand pounds early in 1910?"

"From an aunt, I think."

"But Mrs. Nelson had only one aunt, and she died years before 1910, I am told. Your father took a great interest in the district, did he not?"

"He did."

"And he helped several people over very bad stiles, I understand?"

"Yes. Why do you ask?"

"I learnt that both he and your mother had deep sympathy for Mrs. Nelson in her affliction—John Nelson. I have been wondering if your father assisted her financially to take over the hotel."

"I am sure he did not, Bony. My father was a very methodical man and he kept accurate records of all his transactions. After his death those records provided me with much interest. You know, he was thought to be a hard man, but the records prove his secret generosity."

"Thank you. Knowing the first Mr. Westall, who was living in that year, 1910, do you think he might have advanced her the money?"

"It is quite possible," agreed the squatter. "Those were the times and those the men when generosity in the bush was a by-word. It was my father who set up the first Storrie on that selection, which was taken away from

Wirragatta."

"Thank you. It is rather puzzling and, therefore, interesting." Bony rose to go. "Throughout my career I have always had to fight down the temptation to expend time and thought on a mystery having no connection with my investigation. I am like a young dog who is always dashing off one scent to follow another. Ah! There is Hang-dog Jack smiting his triangle for lunch. What a case he would present to an anthropologist! *Au revoir*, Mr. Borradale. I will certainly visit that couple camped at Catfish Hole."

"Thanks. I hope you are successful. It would be a heavy burden off my mind if they were moved away."

Bony having departed, Martin worked on till the homestead gong called him to lunch.

He was again at work at five o'clock, when Dreyton entered the office, and at sight of the tall and lean fence-rider he cried, "Hullo, Donald! I'm mighty glad to see you. Sit down."

Dreyton's sun-puckered eyes glanced at the empty book-keeper's table and then at the book on which Borradale was employed.

"That chinless ass left for Broken Hill last night," Martin said.

"What was his hurry?" asked Dreyton.

"Fright."

"Fright!" echoed the fence-rider, his body jerked abruptly tense and his eyes as abruptly wide open. "What gave him the fright, Mr. Borradale?"

"A kookaburra's laughter and a branch breaking from its parent trunk to crash to the ground."

"But surely——"

"The evening before last my sister and Payne were playing tennis until quite late," Martin explained. "Stella says that from one of the river trees there reached them a long chuckle of devilish laughter which made her shiver and caused Payne nearly to drop. Then a heavy branch snapped and crashed to the ground, and a few seconds later the same laughter reached them from somewhere down the river."

"Strange!" Dreyton murmured, his face muscles strained so that his mouth was nothing but a line.

"There is nothing strange about it," objected Borradale. "At any time during these quiet summer days a gum branch is liable to snap off. They are the most dangerous trees in the country. Then, too, the kookaburras always laugh and chuckle a little after sunset. I got Joe Fisher to have a look at the ground along the river and search thoroughly about the fallen branch. He assures me that what Stella and Payne heard was a bird and that the branch snapped off because the sap, which the heat had driven down to the roots, had been prevented from as quickly returning to the branch by a growth."

"Miss Borradale—— does she now believe what Fisher says?"

"I am afraid not," Martin replied. Then he was on his feet, his eyes blazing with passion. "Why the devil don't you stay here with me? Can't you see that I am almost worried to death by this Strangler business and the responsibility of running Wirragatta? On top of it all there is a miner and his wife camped at Catfish Hole, who won't go away and who can't be made to go because they have a miner's right. I wouldn't care a tinker's curse if my sister didn't own a half-interest in this place. I keep awake nearly all night debating if I will do this or that, and gripped by fear that whatever I do I will make a mistake. With you here in the office my mind is relieved by half the responsibility. You'll have to stay this time, Donald. You can ask what salary you like."

He stood, young and good-looking and passionately earnest, glaring down at the seated fence-rider, who knew quite well just the measure of anxiety such a property as Wirragatta would lay on the mind of its owner.

"What I want is a long holiday. I should go to Europe for a trip," Martin went on, the gust of anger having subsided. "I have never had a holiday since I came home after my father's death. If I owned the place, I wouldn't worry about making a bloomer now and then. In fact, I'd sell it and go to Sydney to live. But Stella won't sell with me. Says we would be betraying our father by doing such a thing. Say you'll come back to the office, Donald."

The pleading in the young man's grey eyes touched Dreyton as no argument had ever done or would ever do. Martin hurried on:

"Here is this problem of two thousand hoggets I have to decide before tomorrow. I'm offered twenty-four and three-pence a head. The market is inclined to rise and I am not short of feed. But a good rain down in the Riverina will cause the market to fall. What shall I do—sell 'em or hold 'em?"

Dreyton rose to his feet and thrust a hand deep into a trouser-pocket. He spun the penny he took from it, neatly caught it and laid it on the back of his hand.

Looking up from the coin, he said, "Sell them, Mr. Borradale. Forgive me, but you are too prone to magnify problems which are often of no importance. I will start here in the morning, and if you give me more responsibility I may presently be able to manage the place while you go for that holiday."

"Good man! That's splendid. But you start tonight by dining with us. No, I shall accept no refusal. Bring across your gear now. I'll slip over and tell Stella. Why, we might get in a game of tennis before dinner."

They left the office arm in arm.

Chapter Twenty-two

Trap Setting

Inspector Napoleon Bonaparte certainly agreed with Martin Borradale's verdict that the evidence he found concerning the broken branch and the devilish laughter, which had so frightened the tennis players, proved the causes to be perfectly natural. Now, while the squatter and Donald Dreyton were talking in the office, he sought for and found Stella Borradale reclining under an orange-tree in the garden. The quick smile with which she greeted him but proved the strain still controlling her.

"Hullo, Bony! Have you come to talk to me?"

"Yes. May I sit here on the ground at your feet?"

"Why not bring a chair from the veranda? It would be much more comfortable."

"I like comfort, Miss Borradale, but it is good for a man not to indulge in it too much. I wanted to assure you again that your uneasiness the other evening really had no foundation."

"Oh!" she breathed, the corners of her expressive eyes become tight.

"I climbed the tree this morning and thoroughly examined the branch again, as well as making a careful examination of the ground. What I saw confirms my opinion of yesterday, and that was based on a superficial knowledge of the action of tree sap at certain seasons and in certain temperatures. Excessive heat drives the sap out of the branches, down the trunk and into the roots. Permit me to give an illustration. You know, of course, what is colloquially called a needlewood-tree. If a surface root is laid bare and broken off, and then fire is set to the foliage, the sap will be driven down the trunk to the roots, so that should a billy-can or other receptacle be placed under the broken root it will collect quite drinkable water. Over about three parts of Australia there is no need for anyone to perish if means are to hand to make fire.

"Well, then. What happened to the gum-tree branch was that the heat of the day had driven the sap down towards the roots, and when evening came the sap began its journey up into the branches. At the junction of the branch which snapped off from the parent trunk there was growing what I believe is called a tree cancer. The sap from the branch had taken a long time to pass round this cancer to the trunk, but it was not allowed to get back again quickly enough, and the first of the cool evening breeze was too much for the limb to resist. The laughter you assumed had human origin was, of course, made by a kookaburra. As you know, Miss Borradale, at times even the crows make a noise not unlike a man being choked."

Stella sighed with relief. Bony smiled up at her.

"I am surprised by you," he said in his disarming manner. "Imagination is our greatest gift and blessing, but when it is uncontrolled it can be a curse. And for an experienced bushwoman to be bushed by a new-chum book-keeper — —"

"Please, Bony!"

"Oh, I know," he said swiftly. "The longer we live in the bush the easier can we become frightened by it. I become horribly frightened by it sometimes."

"Well, I am glad to hear what you have said about the branch and the laughter," she told him half-laughingly. "Probably I would not have been so foolish if that stupid man had behaved normally. Why, he was a perfect coward. But, oh, I wish you would catch this beast who is so frightening every one. Do you know why I am sitting here?"

"Because it is cool and quiet and wonderfully pleasant."

"No. It is because I am becoming so fearful that I despise myself. I am forcing myself to sit here under this tree. I am defying fear and deliberately allowing my imagination to do its worst. Martin told me that he believes the beast dropped out of a tree to attack his victims, and when I discovered the other evening that I dreaded being under a tree for an instant I determined to sit under this one."

Bony, seated on the ground and smoking one of his badly-made cigarettes, regarded the small and attractive face turned down to him.

"The procedure is excellent," he said. "To control fear one must exercise the will—which is always good. Still, it is not always desirable to carry that too far. I can most earnestly assure you that there are no grounds for fear during the day-time, and there need be none during the night if you do as I suggested: keep your bedroom door and windows fastened. Even that is merely precautionary, as the wearing of a hat is a precautionary measure against sunstroke."

She was now leaning forward, her lips parted, her gaze fixed on his eyes.

"Do you think you will ever clear up this terrible mystery?" she asked.

It was one of Bony's grandiloquent moments.

"I should be utterly astonished if I did not," he said gravely. "After all, Miss Borradale, it is what I have come from Brisbane to do. I have never yet failed to clear up a mystery, and it would be absurd even to contemplate failing to clear up this one. Within a week I shall vanquish the ugly cloud hanging over Carie and Wirragatta."

"You will?"

"Yes. I will make it a promise. You see, Colonel Spendor is becoming annoyed by my absence. He is a very impatient man. My wife, too, becomes unduly impatient when I remain away from home for a little while." Bony's face lit up from the smile originating in his eyes. "Like myself, my wife is a half-caste, but, unlike me, she has not the gift of patience. So you see, Miss Borradale, I have two impatient people on my tracks who simply will not allow me to take the time I would like on an investigation. Marie, my wife, tells me that she finds life almost unbearable when I am away from her. That, of course, is very nice of her. May I express the wish that some day soon you will be as happy as my wife says she is when I am home?"

The girl's eyes abruptly sparkled, and she cried softly, "I told you once before, Mr. Napoleon Bonaparte, that you are a dangerous man. I ought to be furiously angry with you, and I cannot understand why I am not."

"It is a problem somewhat common among my—my friends. I may regard you as a friend?"

"Yes ... my dangerous friend, Bony," she answered and laughed at and with him. Try as she did, she could not control the trembling of her lips or cease to wonder at her complete acceptance of him. "You know, Marion Trench used to make me smile over her letters about you. I understand her now. I think you are the most dangerous, the most discerning, the most sympathetic man I've ever known. No one, not even a woman, could hide a secret from you. Tell me, why did you so laud Harry West to my brother when we stopped at the fencers' camp the other day?"

"I am, Miss Borradale, not the only discerning person present," he told her, utterly pleased with her and with himself. "I will lay bare *my* secret. I think quite a lot of Harry West, and on two occasions I have met his sweetheart. Harry is young yet, but he is possessed of moral courage beside physical courage, and he is considerate to others as well as being terrifically keen on his work. Tilly, when she smiles, is lovely. Alas! romance is my one weakness. If we can assist a dream to come true, why not?"

He saw her eyes become quickly diffused, and he looked away.

"Yes, why not?" she echoed. "I will see to it that this one *does* come true, even if others do not."

Bony rose to his feet to stand before her, hat in hand.

"I must be going—if you will permit it," he said grandly.

"I promised your brother I would pay a visit to the prospector and his wife now camped beside Catfish Hole."

"It is extremely foolish for them to stay there."

"Yes, it is. A miner's right, however, is a powerful document. Now, please, do not allow fear to trouble you. I shall soon banish the cloud, and I hope most earnestly that the result of the long investigation will not spoil a most valued friendship. *Au revoir!*"

Looking after his retreating figure, Stella Borradale permitted herself to blush. Only by exerting tremendous effort had she delayed it so long.

Once out of the garden, Bony sauntered up-river, humming a lilting tune. He was feeling elated as he always did when having spent time in the company of a good woman, and one whom he could completely blind to the facts of his ancestry. That was balm to his stupendous vanity. To make a white man or woman forget his social status and the stain of his skin was always to him a wonderful triumph. It was the eternal eagerness to be regarded with equality which had produced in him the exception of the rule that all who have the aborigines' blood in their veins must in the end go back to the life and conditions of the bush nomads.

The hot sun was westering, but the birds as yet remained quiescent in the branches of the slumbering river trees. By walking along the dry bed of the river, Bony managed to pass the men's quarters without being observed, and, after he skirted Junction Waterhole, he walked up Nogga Creek over its dry, shingle bed. Now, however, he maintained a wary watch of the tree-branches beneath which he was obliged to pass. These rows of bordering trees were to him like old friends, despite the being who used them at night. Every one he knew intimately: every one knew the secret he was so persistently teasing from them.

Coming to the boundary-fence and the Broken Hill road, he paused long enough to be sure that no chance traveller was approaching. Satisfied on that score, he jumped the fence and slipped across the road, and from this point he flitted from tree to tree until he was behind that one nearest the prospector's camp.

Beyond the tent stood an old half-ton truck and beside it a much-repaired shaker. The man was washing sand at the edge of Catfish Hole, and the woman was tending meat grilling on the fire coals. She was slim and of medium height. On her feet were snakeskin shoes. On her shapely legs were silk stockings. Her skirt was of white duck and her blouse of white muslin. A mop of fair, short hair was the only untidy thing about her.

Bony stepped from the tree and gravely bowed. "Good afternoon, madam," he said.

Uttering a sharp exclamation, the woman sprang up and about to face him.

"Oh!" she cried. "Oh! Hullo, Mr. Bonaparte!"

Bony smiled and bowed again, saying:

"You make quite an attractive woman."

"Do I? I hope so. I am trying to be as attractive as possible."

"Good! I see your husband approaching. You must introduce me."

The man walking swiftly to them was grey of hair and moustache. His shoulders were broad—very broad—and his hips were narrow—very narrow.

"Bill, this is Mr. Bonaparte," said the woman.

The granite-hard expression on the prospector's face relaxed.

"Pleased to meet you, inspector," he said in deep bass tones. "I was hoping you would come along."

"I would have come earlier, but there was no real necessity. What is your name and rank?"

"Smithson, sir. William Smithson, sergeant."

"Champion boxer and champion wrestler in the New South Wales Police Force," added the woman.

"Not now," corrected the sergeant. "Still, I can take care of most of 'em. Satisfied with Elson's get-up, sir?"

"Quite. Barry makes quite an attractive woman," Bony replied, and studied Barry Elson with open admiration. "Did the Commissioner explain

174

to you why I requested your services and those of your—er—wife?"

"Only that I had to report to Broken Hill, meet Elson, hire a truck and a prospector's outfit, and come here with Elson dressed as a woman and armed with a miner's right. Of course, Elson has told me all about this strangling gent, and I can make out what is wanted of us."

"Good again. I will explain further. Perhaps meanwhile you might invite me to dinner. We can talk over the meal."

With approval Bony noted that these two acted their parts with credit. The sergeant washed from a basin, and his "wife" continued the preparation of the meal until "she" called them to dinner.

"How was Miss Storrie when you last heard, Barry?" inquired the detective as he was given a plate of grilled chops, a slice of damper and a pannikin of tea.

"She is well forward to complete recovery, Mr. Bonaparte," replied Elson. "I think she has forgiven me. She will, I know, if we can trap this strangling brute. I'd like to thank you properly for what you did for me as well as for giving me this chance to clear myself."

"There are many people here who do not believe you attacked Miss Storrie, Barry. I suppose Simone was most disappointed?"

"He was, by the look of him. The inspector down at Broken Hill had me in his office and almost apologized. Then when I got your letter asking me if I would offer myself as a bait—why, I jumped at the idea."

"Ah! I was hoping that Simone would be annoyed."

"Strange how that feller got on as well as he has done," growled Smithson. "He's been mighty lucky all through."

"He is an unpleasant person after one has become accustomed to his ego. However—— Are you still willing to carry on with this scheme of ours, Barry?"

The young man's rouged and powdered face flushed and his eyes grew bright with enthusiasm.

"Too right!" he said earnestly. "Only by bringing this sneaking scoundrel to book can I avenge Mabel and clear myself."

"I must impress on you that you will run a grave danger," Bony pointed out. "I don't myself like the idea now. If anything very serious should happen to you, I would always regret planning this trap. How does that iron collar fit you?"

"Comfortably. It will take very strong fingers to bend that iron against my throat. The police blacksmith made a good job of the collar. It protects all my neck right up hard against my chin, and it is light and easy to wear."

"Doctor Mulray brought the acid paste?"

"Yes. It's good stuff, too."

"I should say," agreed the sergeant. "I got a pin-head of it on a finger and it burned like fire."

"It doesn't tend to melt and run on account of the heat?"

"No," Elson answered. "I was out last night, and the night before last, just to let the Strangler know I wander out of camp. If ever he gets his fingers round that iron collar his hands will be that blistered that they won't heal for a month."

"It's a neat little scheme, Mr. Bonaparte," the sergeant said admiringly. "As per orders, Elson walks up and down along the creek from here to the road several times during the late evening. If the Strangler attacks him, he'll be branded plain enough. Should he get away—which he won't from me— all we'll have to do is to go through the population for him."

Bony was pondering with his fine brows knit.

Presently he said, "I want you to remember this, sergeant. The fellow's capture, should he attack Elson, is of far less importance than Elson's personal safety. Once the fellow gets his hands smeared with the acid on the collar, it does not matter if he gets away, because we can very easily pick him up when his hands are well blistered. We have to remember that he is exceedingly strong in the arms. He must be allowed to attempt to throttle Elson, but must not be given time enough to injure Elson, which he might attempt to do when he finds he is unable to strangle him. Therefore, Elson's safety must come first.

"I do not anticipate an attack until the night following the next day of wind and dust, and by the signs in the sky this evening another wind-storm is due to break on us. Both you and I must never be far away from the bait, but we have to exert every possible precaution against giving the Strangler the suspicion that Elson *is* a bait and thus frighten him from the trap. Now listen carefully. This is what each of us will do from tomorrow night, as I do not require Elson to parade the creek-bank tonight."

Lucidly and with remarkable detail, Bony planned their individual parts. In his woman's clothes, wearing his iron collar on which would be smeared the doctor's acid preparation, Barry was to walk from the camp to the road and repeat this walk until two o'clock every morning. If attacked, he had to resist the impulse to struggle until he was sure that the criminal's hands were clamped round his iron collar. Then he was to shout for help. The sergeant would lie hidden from early in the evening at a spot approximately one-third the distance to the road, and Bony would be keeping watch on the road itself. Barry was not to begin his promenading before nine o'clock, at which time the watchers would be in their respective positions.

"Have you any idea who the bird will turn out to be?" rashly asked the sergeant.

"Yes. I am not a gambling man, sergeant, otherwise I would lay short odds against a particular man, one of ten I have had remaining on a list for a long time."

"Who is he, Mr. Bonaparte?" urged Elson, and Bony smiled.

"I would not dare to tell you," he said. "Should I prove to be wrong, I would never forgive myself, and you would never again regard me as being a great detective. I must remain silent until we get him, and then I can always say I knew who it was. Now I must be off."

The sky this evening was one of splendour. The sinister high-level haze was now transmuted into streamers and banks of crimson velvet, the reflection from which stained the tops of the plain's bluebushes with brown while leaving their under-portions a brilliant blue-green. Despite the lateness of the hour, the flies were particularly active, and no evening breeze came to stir the pointed leaves of the box-trees—leaves which drooped as though too long without water in a hot room. Deeper yet in shade became the ominous but glorious sky, until, like a curtain, night was drawn down to the western horizon.

Bony at length reached that box-tree against which he had sat for several hours, and from behind which an unknown man had watched the passage of Hang-dog Jack, when the detective saw not far distant the shape of a car standing on the track. It was the Borradales' single-seater, and because the hood was down Bony saw that no one was seated in it.

With tautened nerves, his mind at once sensing an important development, Bony edged to the creek-bank and proceeded with the utmost caution. He came eventually opposite the car, and he had reached this point with absolutely no sound betraying him. His right hand gripped the comforting butt of his pistol.

The sky was still faintly lit by the departed day, and a sound directed his attention up and into the tree immediately beyond him. On one of the lower branches he saw a man, and then, when this man's head moved out from a branch above him and became silhouetted against the sky, Bony recognized him as Martin Borradale.

At once realizing that if Borradale was the Strangler he would certainly not leave his car standing on the track, yet unable to grasp what the squatter was doing, the detective waited, his body pressed against the tree-trunk and invisible to anyone but a yard distant. Borradale was not climbing farther into the tree, and he was not coming down out of it. He appeared to be doing something to the branch above that one on which he was standing. There he remained working for some few minutes, whilst Bony's muscles were tensed like steel springs. Four or five long minutes passed, and then the squatter descended to the ground, walked quickly to the car and drove away to the homestead.

Without delaying, Bony climbed to the branch on which Borradale had stood. The tree, even in the near darkness, was as familiar to the detective as his own house near Brisbane. It was a unit composing one of the many sections along the creek in which the blacks' bunyip leapt and swung from branch to branch.

Standing as Borradale had stood, the next higher branch was on a level with Bony's face. It was a branch used by the "bunyip's" feet, and with great care Bony raised a hand to it and felt along its worn surface. His fingers came in contact with slack string, and following this string to the trunk of the tree the brown fingers came in contact with the warm metal of a double-barrelled shotgun.

Having found the gun, Bony proceeded to examine it by lowering his head and bringing it against the sky. He saw now that it was lashed to the trunk of the tree and that its two barrels pointed slantingly upward along the branch.

Bony understood.

Anyone coming to step on the branch from swinging to it from another at a higher level would tauten the string, which in turn would discharge the weapon and kill him instantly. As Smithson might have said, it was a very neat little trap.

Martin Borradale's action was a revelation. Bony was really delighted and could hardly forbear to chuckle. Borradale had discovered—or, more likely, had been told by Dreyton—that the Strangler climbed from tree to tree, and here he was determined to end the suspense by bagging the Strangler himself. After all, he had had but a poor opinion of Detective-Inspector Bonaparte, and, like Colonel Spendor, was become impatient of delay.

Standing there up in the tree, Bony pondered. If he left this trap set, it might well kill the Strangler. Then it would come out that the great Bony had been beaten by a young pastoralist, and the said pastoralist would certainly get into hot water for using such means. That would not do. No, of course not. In any case, if the gun went off and killed anybody, it would not provide proof that the person killed had strangled two people and had come close to strangling two others.

Bony permitted himself to chuckle softly as, with great care not to discharge the weapon, he broke open the breech and extracted the two cartridges. He would take his turn in providing a first-class mystery and proving that the Strangler was as cunning as a whole flock of crows.

While walking on to the homestead, he visualized the squatter's face when he went to examine his trap. Afterwards, when the case was finalized, he would explain everything to Martin and his sister. Altogether, Bony was feeling very pleased with himself.

Chapter Twenty-three

The Vigil

The weather portents did not disappoint several men who had been waiting for the calm, hot spell to break. Shortly after the dawn following the evening when Bony watched Martin Borradale set his gun-trap, the wind rapidly freshened from the north. It sent scudding over the ground the debris of bluebush and river tree; it sent the galahs and the cockatoos and the crows whirling in the air like pieces of paper, and when Bony set off for Carie to fetch the mail it was raising the sand high over the bluebush. And the bluebush now was painted a brilliant purple on the underside of every curiously shaped leaf, and the sun's shadows were tinted ash-grey.

When in Carie Bony spent half an hour with Constable Lee. The northerly wind swept down the main street and caused Mrs. Nelson to desert her balcony. It assisted the detective on his way back to the homestead, but its angle gave the flies shelter against his face and chest.

Two among his several letters provided much interest. One was written by his wife, in which she carefully noted a hundred and one details concerning their children and herself. The second letter was typed and was signed by the New South Wales Commissioner of Police. It was, however, the enclosure which was of greater importance, for it dealt wholly with the career of Donald Dreyton prior to his arrival in Australia.

When Captain Malcolm Dreyton, R.N., was accidentally killed on the China Station in 1912, his son, Donald, was at school at Stubbington, Hampshire. An uncle, Vice-Admiral Sir Reginald Dreyton, became the boy's guardian and supervisor of his career. In due course the boy went to the Naval College at Osborne and subsequently graduated into the Royal Navy. Promotion was normal, and the young man reached the rank of Lieutenant-Commander and became the commander of a destroyer.

Then one afternoon when Dreyton was taking his ship into Portsmouth Harbour in the teeth of a fierce out-rushing tide-rip it had collided with one of the small ferry boats, with fatal results to three of its passengers.

At the Court of Inquiry the evidence regarding an order issued by

Dreyton at the crucial moment, before the collision, was conflicting, but yet hostile to the young commander. Dreyton was dismissed from his ship and placed in the retired list.

The writer of the report, Bony noticed, was plainly sympathetic. According to him, subsequent evidence had come to light which cast grave doubt on the justice of the court's verdict, but was not sufficiently strong to base a demand for a fresh inquiry.

Broken and disgraced and disinherited by his uncle, Donald Dreyton had disappeared from England and had never drawn his retired pay.

The writer of the report asked for Dreyton's address for several reasons. Opinion in naval circles had veered strongly in his favour. The quartermaster on duty when the collision had occurred had admitted collusion with Dreyton's junior officer in giving hostile evidence. The admiral uncle had reinstated his nephew in both his affections and his will, and was only then beginning a wide inquiry to locate him.

"This certainly urges me to remove Dreyton's name from my list." Bony murmured. "It is highly improbable that a man having Dreyton's heritage and training would lust to kill. If he had sunk beneath the injustice of fate, he would have taken to drink or committed suicide. Instead of which he continues to live a clean life, determined not to sink farther than the Court of Inquiry ordained even if unable to rise again to his former status. Anyway, this report confirms a little theory concerning Mr. Dreyton. He has behaved exactly as the nephew of Vice-Admiral Sir Reginald Dreyton would behave. Yes, breeding does count—but only when allied with training."

At noon there was hell created on this fair earth. The people of Carie shut their shops and barred the doors and windows of their houses. White-faced and anxious on her lover's account, knowing him to be working with Dogger Smith in a camp having no protection, Tilly crept silently about the hotel, while James sat in his closed bar trying to read.

The wind was not of cyclonic strength, not of the destructive force of the cyclones which cut into north-western Australia from the Indian Ocean. It was not the wind so much as the sand which was become a blinding, choking menace. To be sure it was the wind that stirred the sand off the ground, raised it hundreds of yards in the air, but it was the sun's heat which was the major force lifting the sand-grains ever higher and ever in greater density, so that for ten minutes after noon there was complete darkness.

"I'm gettin' fair sick of these wind-storms," Hang-dog Jack shouted to make himself heard above the pandemonium of roof iron and shrieking wind. "It's all right for you blokes. You don't have to work—not that you work properly any time."

"I had to go to Carie for the mail this morning," Bony ventured.

"That ain't work," snorted the cook. "You orter be only too glad to call in on James. How did the beer taste?"

"The bar was shut."

"I'd have made 'im open up mighty quick," Young-and-Jackson stated with extraordinary emphasis.

"I'd have stopped there with the flamin' mail all day," said Bill the Cobbler, his bald head streaked with sand-dust. "Hell, what a day! Old Dogger Smith and Harry West will be 'aving a lovely time of it—just lovely."

"Do young Harry good," growled Hang-dog. "The young nip is too cocky by a long way. Looks down on them as has to work for a living. I thanks the boss for lowerin' his dignity a bit."

"Cripes! This is about the worse storm we've had for years," complained Young-and-Jackson. "Me and Bill has been trying to concentrate on a game of draughts. How Joe, here, and the doctor can play chess all night beats me."

"It's merely a matter of will-power," asserted Bony. "The doctor and I have been engaged on one game for the last two nights, and we intend finishing it tonight if it occupies us till morning. Sand or no sand, I am going to Carie tonight."

Barred in their own quarters, it was impossible for the men to do anything but sit on their bunks and try to read. Even to talk for long was impossible. The substantial building rocked and creaked and rattled. From without, the roaring wind was now and then blanketed by the flying sand to a moaning whine. It was the worst sand-storm in Bony's experience.

Not until six o'clock, when the sun was westering and the temperature was slowly falling a few degrees, did the sand waves begin to subside. The wind, however, blew no less strongly. The sun's heat waning, the wind's power over the sand waned, too, and now there were passing rifts between the waves when the sky was revealed the colour of a shark's belly.

At seven-thirty Bony announced his intention of setting off for Carie and the game of chess with Dr. Mulray. No one saw him slip the pistol into a coat-pocket, and no remark was passed about him wearing a coat this hot and most unpleasant evening.

When he reached the open bluebush plain he knew that the sun was setting. There was, of course, no sign of it, and the red light which would indicate fine weather to come was absent. Great waves of sand-filled air rolled over the plain to scream through the small and close-leafed bushes and to hiss over the tortured ground. Here, away from the station buildings, the wind's triumphant roar was changed to a low, sinister, throbbing hum. Of a certainty it would be an evil night and the morrow would be worse.

Arrived at the left of the two black gates in the Common fence when the early-come night was fast falling, Bony walked westward along the boundary for a quarter of a mile and there sat down. He was a little early for an appointment, and he filled in time by rolling and smoking cigarettes which always were thick in the middle and pointed at the ends. The town he could not see. When one of the sand waves was passing he could not see two yards.

Ah! A tall figure loomed into his radius of vision, coming eastward along the fence. It was Constable Lee dressed disgracefully in old civilian clothes and wearing an old cloth cap.

"You are on time, Lee," Bony shouted. "Come and sit here with me. It is a trifle early yet. Did you take care that no one in the town saw you leave it?"

"If anyone did, I was seen to leave it by the north end," replied the burly policeman, cheerfully smiling. "What a day it has been—and what a night it is going to be!"

"An interesting night, let us hope, Lee. Did you bring some blacking for your hands and face?"

"Yes."

"Then you can turn yourself into a black minstrel. Remember to keep your eyes semi-closed. The whites of a man's eyes can be seen in the darkest of nights when the eyes are turned at a certain angle. Listen carefully while you are making up for your part in this coming play. I am going to leave you at a place about forty yards out from Nogga Creek, and about midway between the camp and the road. Between you and the camp will be Sergeant Smithson, while I will be stationed on the Broken Hill road where it begins to cross the creek. We three then will have Elson almost constantly under observation as he will walk to and fro from road to camp. Is that clear?"

"Quite clear," replied Lee, who, having blackened his face, was now attending to his hands.

"Very well. Now, this is most important. Our first consideration is not the capture of the Strangler, but the safety of Barry Elson. Our objective is to permit the Strangler to brand himself and yet prevent him from injuring the young man who so bravely is offering himself as the bait of our trap. If we can capture the Strangler, all the better, but once he is branded we can take our time tracking him down. Therefore, be wary about using your pistol. If you hear Elson shouting for help, rush to his assistance. In such case, Smithson and I will be doing that, too. The point is that when Elson shouts for help we must render it as quickly as possible."

"All right! All that is simple enough. Does the collar fit Elson?"

"Perfectly. The iron is covered with white satin which not only disguises the iron, but holds the acid preparation. The Strangler will find it impossible to throttle Elson, but he is strong enough to do him some other grave injury if not stopped in time."

"If this birds falls into the trap, it will be a brainy scheme," Lee said with unusual enthusiasm.

"Smithson called it neat," Bony said, laughing.

"If we catch the Strangler tonight, who do you think he will turn out to be?"

"Up till last night I was almost positive who the Strangler is," replied Bony without hesitation. "Now I am back again in a fog which is worse than this dust. When I took your name off the list there were left the names of ten men. There are now five. They are:

Hang-dog Jack
Bill the Cobbler
Fred Storrie
Tom Storrie
James Spinks."

"It will be the cook, I'll bet," asserted Lee.

"I believe not. Hang-dog Jack is too obvious, and while the obvious is sometimes right I shy off it. No, my first pick is Fred Storrie, and my second his son, Tom."

"Who did you think was the Strangler up till last night?"

"That is an unfair question, Lee."

"Sorry, sir—er—Bony, but I'm all worked up about it."

"Then let us get going. As you said, it is a nice little trap, but I do not like it notwithstanding. It is a reflection on my ability to solve a mystery with my brains. Perhaps, Lee, it is human to seek excuses for failure, and I am but human. Never in my career have I been met with difficulties so great and clues so few and of such small importance. Never have I had less assistance from nature, with so little indication of common motive. It is because I believe it to be impossible to obtain proof of murder, even if we knew the identity of the Strangler, that I have conceived this trap."

"Well, it will be quite a sporting event," Lee said.

"I doubt it. I shall not feel in a sporting mood. Now, no more talking, and, of course, no more smoking."

When half-way to the creek, Bony led the policeman off the road, and Lee, who followed closely, was obliged to keep his gaze on the detective's figure so as not to lose touch. It appeared to Lee that they walked for some considerable distance before Bony halted, turned to him, and whispered:

"Can you see the Nogga Creek trees?"

Lee stared into the velvety night.

"No, but I can hear the wind in them," he admitted.

"I can see them," Bony said. "They are only a little more than a hundred feet away. You are to remain here—seated, of course. In two hours the moon will rise. In half an hour Elson will begin his promenading. If an attack is not made on him before the moon gets up, the moon will assist us; and it will assist the Strangler, too. Don't move from this place until you hear Elson shout for help."

Lee was about to give an assurance when Bony vanished.

The detective walked direct to the road and then along the netted boundary-fence to the creek. Arrived at the top of the incline leading down to the creek-bed, Bony went on hands and knees and crawled along at the foot of the protective fence, under the branching trees beneath which Mabel Storrie was attacked, and so almost to the bottom of the incline.

Now he sat with his back to a strainer-post which was a foot higher than the ordinary posts, and by looking to his left he had the top of the incline providing him with a dim and valuable skyline. He was now immediately beneath the trees, but for this he cared little.

Having reached this position, he felt distinct relief from an acute attack of nerves, and it must stand to his credit that, after his experience of the Strangler along this same creek, he proceeded determinedly. The strainer-post gave him a feeling of great comfort. Its height would prevent any man attempting to strangle him from behind. In the distance a dim glow marked the position of the "prospector's" camp, and the sense of complete isolation was less difficult to combat because of it.

Tortured by inherited superstitions, lashed by the contempt of reason, Bony maintained an incessant watch, visually searching for a monstrous figure slinking through this shrouded world of wind and noise. It was like waiting to spy upon one of those legendary half-dead people who are supposed to crawl from their coffins at sunset to roam the earth as living entities until sunrise. It was like a defiance of the bush bunyip, that horrific thing, half-dog, half-human, which, during the daylight hours, lurks invisibly in the heart of a bush, behind a tree, at the foot of the mirage, and at night takes material form to stalk venturesome blacks and half-castes who roam away from their rightful camps. This Strangler come from the world of light and colour into this living darkness with the wind and the stinging sand, and to the accompaniment of the wind's fantasia. Bony was opposed to something which had uncanny sight, which could progress swiftly from tree-branch to tree-branch, which could move without sound.

The wind was hot, and yet Bony felt icy cold. Reason and inherited superstitions warred within him with nerve-racking ferocity. After all is said about reason, it flourishes best in the sunlight and drawing-rooms. A dark night with a prowling, foul murderer at hand is apt to wither this flower.

Thus was the reasoning Inspector Napoleon Bonaparte assailed by fear and doubt. Neither reason nor instinct assisted him to maintain the will-power.

A noise not of the wind banished even fear from his mind, subconsciously tensed his muscles for instant flight. Someone was on the road, humming a tune, and Bony tightened his ears and taxed his straining eyes. He saw, passing by on the road, distant but four yards, the figure of a woman dressed in white, and he knew "her" to be Barry Elson.

The fellow had grit, to be sure. A wave of shame and self-reproach swept through the soul of the half-caste. For a young and not too robust man to walk alone under the creek trees and in this darkness, hoping and yet dreading to hear at any moment a quick, pantherish step behind him, and then to feel iron-strong hands gripped about one's throat, demanded courage of the highest degree. To do it night after night and never to know when the attack would come! To have no tree-trunk, no strainer-post comforting one's back! To be able to control oneself like that for love's sake and the honour of one's name!

Bony was strongly tempted to call out, to get up and assure the young man that he was guarded by a watcher at this end of his awful beat. Barry Elson was playing the major part in a dreadful drama, while he, the investigator, crouched like a rabbit at its burrow's mouth. But when the white figure passed again back to the camp, Bony kept silent and still.

After that, the minutes passed slowly, dragging out their allotted span. Above the dull glow of the tree-masked camp-fire was now growing an unearthly refulgence. Against this gradually came into being the ghostly outlines of the branches of the near trees, and Bony knew that the moon was about to rise.

The wind continued its blaring of fantastic music, now satanic, mocking, shrewish, then strident, roaring, triumphant. Of the little familiar bush sounds there were none. They long ago had fled, affrighted by this monstrous concert played on leaf, bough and fence wire.

When the dirty-red disk of the moon was high above the invisible horizon, the white figure again appeared. Only the mind of a madman would find no incongruity in a woman walking in such a place and at such an hour, but it was a madman Bony sought. Elson went on down to the creek-bed, and then turned and came back to "float" away towards the camp.

After the passing of another hour the moon's enormous disk, lustreless brown in colour, strove bravely to rise above the dead-black sand waves endlessly leaping upward to snatch it down into their inky depths. These waves appeared like lava and as solid, before they passed beneath the moon, when they became redly diaphanous and made the moon's light more terrible than the featureless darkness had been.

Another sound not of the wind appeared to originate above Bony's head.

Fear, like icy water, poured through his veins. Slowly he turned his head to look up and behind. He quite expected to see an awful face looking down upon him, but there on the top of the post perched a night bird, its white owl-like face and big fathomless eyes presented to the moon.

For some few minutes it remained there before taking to wing with an abruptness Bony was sure was not due to his presence. Another minute passed, and then the fence wires unmistakably tightened. Something was telegraphing its presence along them—something was climbing through or over them.

Bony's eyes were never still. All physical and mental powers had become concentrated on the effort to probe the gloom. Across his skyline ran a shapeless form, so grotesque, so indistinct, that to name it was impossible. One moment did Bony see it: the next moment it had vanished. Whatever it was it had either climbed through or over the fence. Its action had appeared too quick for it to be a man, but it had not the graceful movement of a wild dog or a kangaroo. Tensed, wondering, every nerve screaming protest, Bony waited.

The wind came in a mighty gust, a roaring, hissing, triumphant clamour, and in it or under it there reached Bony a long-drawn-out gurgling scream of human terror. It came from somewhere up along the creek-bank, and, figuratively, it kicked Bony to his feet, automatic pistol in hand. Muffled by the wind as it was, there was no mistaking the direction from which the cry had come. Then, likewise muffled by the wind, a revolver of large calibre cracked like a child's toy pop-gun.

Bony began a wild semi-blind race. He was roared at by the trees, jeered at by the wind, blinded by the dust, hobbled by the unevenness of the ground. He raced up the incline to the creek's bank, and then towards the camp obsessed by the necessity of reaching Barry Elson.

Ahead of him the revolver spoke thrice in rapid succession. He shouted to stop the firing, for in this ghostly darkness, friend might well receive the bullet intended for the enemy. A man cried out exultantly. To Bony's left, another shouted. He could now see the pin-prick of fire marking the camp-site. Still ahead, but closer, he heard Elson's hysterical crying, and a moment later he saw him, a white-clad figure, lying on the ground.

"Barry! Barry! Are you hurt?"

"No, not much! Down in the creek! Smithson's got him! Go on! Never

188

mind me!"

Recklessly Bony leapt down to the invisible bed of the creek. He was directed by the sounds of a severe scuffle. He heard the sergeant shout:

"Take that!"

"Ease up, blast you!" shouted a second man, his voice muffled by another terrific gust of wind.

Bony could see them now—two men struggling. Now one fell, and the other stooped menacingly over him. As the detective was about to charge, not knowing who the stooping man was, he heard the sharp click of handcuffs.

"You have him?" pantingly asked Bony.

"Too right!" replied the triumphant sergeant. "I only happened to see him getting away from Elson. He fired once at me, and I fired three times at him, but don't think I hit him. He's tough all right. I had to bash him with my gun-butt. Let's have a look at his face."

Lee came rushing to them like one of the wind gusts. They bent over the still form on the creek's gravel bed. and Smithson managed to strike a match and keep the tiny flame alight for a half-second.

It was Hang-dog Jack!

Chapter Twenty-four

The Brand

"I've tackled a few strong men in my time," growled Sergeant Smithson, "but never a man so strong as this one. He's an expert grappler, and he very nearly got a strangle hold on me. What beats me is that a gun will never jam when used in practice, but nearly always does when in action. How is young Elson?"

"Not severely damaged, I believe," replied Bony. "You take this man up to the camp, and I will go across to Elson. By the way, sergeant, where was Hang-dog Jack when you first saw him?"

Smithson paused, with his hands under the cook's arms.

"When Elson shouted, I headed for him at once. I saw him fall, and I saw this man jump off the creek-bank. From the creek he fired twice, and I shouted to him to stop or I would shoot. When I reached the creek-bed he was running away down the creek, and I again ordered him to stop before I fired at him. That stopped him, and he came at me like a bull."

"Well, the trap succeeded," Bony said slowly. "I am a little disappointed, because, after all, Lee guessed right. It has been a baffling case all through. Yesterday I was sure who our man would be. Today I was sure it would certainly not be Hang-dog Jack. My congratulations, Lee."

Bony left the policeman to carry the inert form of the Wirragatta cook to the camp, whilst he scrambled up the creek-bank to reach Barry Elson. The young man was seated on the ground.

"Are you badly hurt, Barry?" he said.

"Not much, Mr. Bonaparte. He got his hands round my collar all right, and I ... I couldn't help screaming. I couldn't, I tell you. Then he lifted me right off the ground and threw me down hard. My arm hurts, that's all. Did you get him?"

"We have him well entangled in handcuffs, Barry," Bony said soothingly. "Now we must be careful of the acid preparation on the collar. Come, let me help you back to the camp."

Elson laughed hysterically. "Who is he, Mr. Bonaparte?"

"Hang-dog Jack."

"I thought so. All my muscles are trembling and I can't stop them. Hang-dog Jack is it? I tell you I couldn't help yelling when he gripped me round the neck."

"It's all right, my dear Barry," Bony said. "It's all right now. Come, take my arm and we will get back to the camp and boil the billy. The job has been done magnificently and you did just the right thing by shouting when you did. Here is Constable Lee. Take his other arm, Lee. Barry is not much hurt, but he's a bit shaken."

Thus supporting the nerve-racked Elson, they reached the camp, where they made him sit on a case within the light of the replenished fire.

"I've got a bottle of rum in my swag and this is a good time to open it," Smithson announced. "You get it, Lee, while I remove Elson's collar. It's a good fit, but a trifle weighty, isn't it, Barry, old man?"

With care, the sergeant unlocked the iron band, when its two hinged sections opened wide to permit removal. The collar was deposited in the fire, and, with his knife, the sergeant cut away the protecting high collar of the blouse. Elson was shaking as though with fever.

"Here, Barry! Have a stiffener," Lee said kindly, proffering a tin pannikin.

"Thanks. I feel bad, but better than I did. Gad, that was terrible. I'm a bit of a coward, after all."

"Coward be hanged!" Smithson growled. "It took the grit of a regiment of soldiers to do what you done. You come and lie down on your bunk. We'll make a drink of tea, and we will take an aspirin or two with it."

Bony sat on the vacated seat and rolled a cigarette whilst the sergeant took Elson to the tent and Lee made the tea.

"'Bout time Hang-dog Jack came round," suggested the constable.

"Yes, Lee. We must look him over. It has been a good job well done, but I still feel the disappointment. I thought up till now that I was a good judge of men. Hang-dog Jack was too obvious to be true."

"The obvious is right more times than not, according to my reading of the newspapers."

"I agree, Lee, I agree. Sometimes I am blind to essential facts because of their obviousness. When all is summed up there was no other man in the district who fitted the meagre facts so well as Hang-dog Jack—after one other man. Let us examine him."

There was a bluish mark on the cook's right temple, which of itself did not account for the man's prolonged unconsciousness, but when he was turned over there was revealed an evil-looking wound at the back of his head.

"Can you account for this?" Bony asked the sergeant, who joined them.

"Well, sir, after I hit him with my gun-butt as he faced me, he fell on his back. Likely enough the back of his head struck one of those large, loose stones, lying half-buried in the creek-bed. That wound don't look nice. He'll want a doctor."

Bony stood up. He was dirty and weary.

"It cannot be far off daybreak," he said. "When you have had a drink of tea, Lee, you must return to the town, get a truck, and bring Doctor Mulray out. We cannot do anything for this man, and to move him before the doctor has seen him might well be dangerous."

Invigorated by the spirit-laced tea, Lee set off for Carie when the swirling sand swept across the dawn sky. Presently Elson joined Bony and the sergeant at the fire to announce that he was feeling almost recovered from his ordeal. He had discarded his women's clothes and washed from his face the rouge and the powder.

"It is not a nice morning, Barry, but it will surely prove to be a brighter day for you," Bony greeted him. "I am positively sure that you were not so nervous last night as I was when sitting back against the boundary-fence and watching you pass and repass."

"I wish I had known just where you were, Mr. Bonaparte," Barry said with an effort to smile. "I suppose I could catch the mail-car for Broken Hill and Adelaide tonight?"

"Of course, but Sergeant Smithson will be returning this evening or tomorrow morning. Why not travel with him?"

"Yes, I'll be going back, Barry," agreed the sergeant. "Unless I've to wait a little before taking down the prisoner."

"Ah, yes, sergeant. Doctor Mulray may want to keep him here for a day or so. Yes, Barry, you can go whenever you wish. And the very best of luck."

When Bony set off for the homestead Dr. Mulray had not arrived. The sky was white—a pasty, unwholesome white. The air in the comparative shelter of the trees was white-tinged—a ghastly colour. Long, low streamers of sand were sliding across the plain, and Carie could not be seen. Second by second the wind was gaining strength, and immediately the sun rose it raised ever higher the rolling sand-waves. When Bony arrived at the homestead the sky was no more.

Despite his slight disappointment that the Strangler had turned out to be the Wirragatta cook, Bony felt profound relief that the case was finalized. In this affair he had not experienced the pleasure of sorting out clues to establish the essential clues. He had built a structure from half-clues and theories which had proved to be like a house built on quicksand. He had wasted effort and time, and the carefully baited trap had shown him that he had backed the wrong horse.

Yet, although he had received a blow to his vanity, relief far outweighed chagrin. The case was finished. He had unmasked the criminal and provided proof of guilt. Now he could bid adieu to the several people he had met and to the two whom he had come to admire. He would turn a little out of his way to visit the people of Windee and stay a night with Father Ryan, who lived in the small town close by. Yes, after he had talked with Donald Dreyton and permitted him to read the report on his career before coming to Australia, he could say his farewells to Miss Stella Borradale and her brother.

Then, of course, there was the little matter of the gun-trap so carefully set by the squatter, who had so keenly desired to score over him, Detective-Inspector Bonaparte. Bony was chuckling over that as he neared the men's quarters, and Dreyton, who was standing outside the closed door, wondered why he was smiling.

"Another night of chess, eh?" the book-keeper shouted above the howling wind. "Mr. Borradale has been asking for you. He wishes you to go to him immediately you return."

Bony's brows rose a fraction.

"Mr. Borradale is about early this morning."

"He came to my room an hour ago," Dreyton said. "I am to show you right to his bedroom window if you come before the house staff are up."

As Bony accompanied the tall Englishman to the wicket gate, he was still smiling. So the trap-setter had been out early to his trap and had found the cartridges removed from the gun!

Dreyton led the way to the south veranda and indicated one of the pairs of french windows.

"I'll leave you," he said. "Better knock."

At the station-hand's knock one of the windows was opened by Martin Borradale, who was smoking a cigarette and was dressed in dressing-gown and slippers.

"Come in, Bony. Close and fasten the window after you. We're in for another filthy day, by the look of it. Have you been playing chess with the doctor?"

"No," replied the detective. "I have been playing chess with the Strangler."

"Ah! Who won?"

"I did."

Bony turned to the room. Martin stood behind a table set end-on to the foot of the bed. On the table was an oil lamp, its light accessory to the murky daylight coming through the windows.

"Cigarette?" asked Borradale.

"Thank you, but I prefer to make my own."

"Very well. Sit down in that chair and tell me all about your night's work. First, though, tell me the name of the fellow you caught."

"Hang-dog Jack," replied Bony, who, having removed tobacco, papers and matches, sank into the indicated chair. Martin seated himself at the table's far side. Briefly, Bony related the night's adventures.

"You do not seem to be very pleased with the results," Martin said, regarding the detective curiously.

Having lit the cigarette, Bony looked up.

"No, I am not too well pleased," he confessed. "I never really considered Hang-dog Jack as the guilty man. He did not—in fact, even now he does not—square with the steps of my investigation."

"That iron collar and the acid paste smeared on it was an excellent idea. Yours, I suppose?"

"Yes. You see, having myself been almost strangled to death one night on Nogga Creek, I came to have a great respect for the fellow's strength. He has hands of iron."

"Indeed!" Martin murmured, his expression tragic. "Like these, I assume."

Borradale's hands had been concealed below the table's edge. Abruptly they came upward. In the right was a revolver, which now steadily pointed

194

at Bony's heart. The left hand was held palm outward for Bony's inspection. It was red-raw and blistered.

"You see, Bony," Borradale said slowly, "your trap was cunningly prepared, but you have captured the wrong man."

Chapter Twenty-five

Bony's Unfortunate Friend

"Nothing, Inspector Bonaparte,", Martin said, making a great effort to speak calmly, "nothing would grieve me more than to shoot you. I have certain statements to make, certain requests to ask of you, and then a certain thing to do. Should you reach for your gun, or attempt to leave your chair, I shall kill you. I must!"

The almost placid expression with which Martin Borradale had first met the detective this morning was now distorted into the reflection of a terror-filled mind. Bony shivered, but his voice was steady when he said:

"The effect of the surprise given me by this denouement is much less than the blow given my pride. Not to have examined the cook's hands is one of the very few—but the greatest—mistakes I have ever made. However, all this is compensated for by the fact that after all I was sound in my reasoning right up to the moment I saw you setting a gun-trap in one of the Nogga Creek trees. Probably you will be good enough to explain just why you did that. If it was done to mislead me completely, then it was wholly successful. To retrieve my own self-respect, you could escape only after having killed me. Even so, you would have then to deal with Constable Lee and Sergeant Smithson, who so ably represented the prospector."

"You mistake me," Martin said, speaking rapidly. "I am not contemplating escape from you, but rather from myself—from this body and this brain. Let me speak. Lee and the sergeant will soon find that Hang-dog Jack's hands are not burned. So there is little time left. When I have finished, you will get up from your chair and leave me here without feeling the slightest desire to arrest me, for you are not a Sergeant Simone."

"That remains to be seen. Please proceed."

Borradale sighed, and the agony of his mind was portrayed on his face. The pain of his hands must have been severe, but he gave no sign that he was conscious of it.

"Until an hour or so ago I did not know who was the Strangler," he said, battling for control. "I am glad—immensely glad—that your trap has succeeded. But I must begin at the beginning.

"When I was at school I gave much trouble by sleep-walking. Sometimes I was rescued from sitting on the sill of the dormitory window with my legs dangling over a sixty-foot drop. Sometimes I was found on the roof of the building. Once I was watched climbing to the roof by way of a rain-spout. On another occasion I was followed to the park beyond the road where, in a line of ornamental trees, I climbed about like a monkey.

"On awakening I never could recall the details of these escapades. My school fellows used to regard me as something like a Tarzan of the Apes, and I took no little pride in my unconscious antics. My somnambulism almost came to be taken for granted. I never committed harm to anyone or to myself. Dieting had not the slightest curative effect. And then, when my father died and I had to come home to manage Wirragatta, I was assured by the head that I had grown out of my somnambulism, as I had not walked in sleep for several months.

"Arrived home here, I was claimed physically and mentally by Wirragatta and my father's old overseer, who almost took my father's place in my affections. I thought but little of my former somnambulism. It had never been real to me, because I recollected nothing of what I did. My adventures were related to me as though they were the experiences of someone else."

Bony's cigarette had gone out. Interest in what was being said, and speculation on what was about to be said, completely mastered him, but he noted with an underlying interest that the pistol in Borradale's hand never wavered off the direct line to his heart. He could see in Martin's face, as well as hear in his voice, the emotional tempest which was being chained by will-power. If the chain broke, then he might be presented with the chance to take charge of the situation.

"From my earliest memories," the younger man went on, "a violent wind-storm produced in me extraordinary effects. First would come mental depression. That would be followed by a period of acute nervous tension. When in this back country, both before and after I was at school, at the height of a dust-storm, I can produce vivid sparks by gently rubbing my hair. I retire to bed at the normal hour, feeling tired and yet nervously jumpy. When I awake the next morning every muscle in my body aches and my mind suffers great depression. These last symptoms are not singular to me. A woman who occasionally visits us suffers hysteria when a wind-storm breaks, and I have heard of a man who nearly goes mad with headache while the centre of the disturbance is passing.

"Now I must hurry. Like everyone else, I was greatly shocked by the dreadful murder of Alice Tindall. It was done, as you know, at the height of a bad wind and sand-storm. Simone came here, fussed and bullied a lot, and achieved nothing. The blacks cleared out after a while, and their action was attributed to their fears and superstitions.

"One windy night, when returning from Broken Hill, my car broke down opposite Storries' house. From there I walked home. It was after midnight. When on the creek track I heard someone coming towards me, and, wondering who it could be at that hour, I stopped under one of the trees and waited.

"It was Hang-dog Jack, and the following day I called for him and asked for an explanation. The earnestness with which he spoke prevented me from laughing. He told me that he had been deeply in love with Alice Tindall, and that after her murder he talked with the blacks, who told him that for some time they had known a bunyip to inhabit the trees. He had discovered that, bunyip or not, something haunted the bush at that spot, and he was offering himself as a victim, being confident of his own tremendous strength to deal with it.

"Because of Simone's behaviour, I decided to tell him nothing of what Hang-dog believed. When Marsh was murdered I again talked to the cook, and pointed out to him that it was improbable that the blacks' bunyip would wander so far from the trees. After some hesitation Hang-dog Jack confessed that he had found the body of Marsh on the Broken Hill road where it inclined to the bed of Nogga Creek, and that to frustrate Simone, or another detective, and so save the bunyip for himself to deal with, he carried the body to the Common gates."

"Why did you not inform me of all this?" Bony naturally asked.

"Because from the first I was sure you would find out about the bunyip and its activities in the trees, and because I did not wish to get the cook into trouble over moving the body of Marsh. I was convinced that Hang-dog Jack was not the Strangler.

"I thought you would question my conduct as a man of substance and a Justice of the Peace. You will find it difficult, inspector, to believe me, but it is the truth spoken by a man about to die. Please do not let me think you intend to act hostilely. I am a good shot, I assure you. But to proceed. …

"Not until some time after Frank Marsh was murdered did I have the faintest suspicion that I might be the murderer. I awoke one morning to discover in my left hand an ugly wood splinter. I could not recall how or when or where I had come to get it. The day before I had returned from a trip outback, occupying eight days. I had not been near a box-tree all that time, and I was convinced by a piece of bark attached to the splinter that it had come from a box-tree—and Nogga Creek. I sent it to an expert down in Adelaide and he pronounced it to be a splinter of box-wood. No matter how I concentrated my mind in going back over the preceding week, I could not account for the splinter being in my hand. I was positively sure it had not been there the evening before.

"It was the splinter of wood which first made me think about those old somnambulistic stunts of mine, and the question which became a kind of mania with me was: Had I committed two murders when in a state of sleep-walking? These two crimes were committed during the night of a dust-storm, and always had I walked in my sleep at school when a wind-storm was raging.

"If you will look to your left, you will see on a chair my day clothes neatly folded. It has been a life-long habit with me, first formed by my mother when I was a child, always to fold my clothes neatly and place them over a chair-back before going to bed. For many years I have never omitted to do that little task.

"It stands to reason that if I walked in my sleep at night, and went prowling among the trees along Nogga Creek, that the clothes I wore would reveal rough usage. My folded clothes never revealed anything of the kind. In fact, I have tied cotton round them before getting into bed and always found the cotton unbroken in the morning. It was the same with my pyjamas and dressing-gown. They were never torn or soiled, as the garments must have been had I worn them out of doors and when climbing trees.

"In short, inspector, I could never find any shred of evidence against myself. Am I plain?"

"Perfectly," Bony replied. "Please go on."

"Very well. I haven't much more to say. Obsessed by the idea that I might be a murderer, I took a trip to Sydney and interviewed my old head master and house master. Careful questioning brought to light a significant fact. I had never been known to walk in my sleep unless a gale of wind was blowing from the land, from the west. Sea gales never affected me. While in Sydney, too, I visited an authority on somnambulism, giving him a false name and address. From him I learned that sufferers from somnambulism had been known to commit crimes, chiefly theft, and that in Austria, before the war, there was a case when a husband cut his wife's throat when in a state of somnambulism.

"You will, I hope, begin to appreciate my dreadful problem. What should I do? Without any evidence against myself, I decided that to confess my fears would be foolish. A confession not based on some evidence would only cause my sister great distress and achieve nothing save possibly to have myself confined to a mental hospital for observation. If I could have been sure I was the murderer, then I could take my own life and no one need ever know the reason for the act.

"When Frank Marsh was so horribly attacked, I knew that something would have to be done. I appreciated the extraordinary cunning of this devil who went out and killed, but yet never attempted an attack on Hang-dog Jack, who could most certainly handle and kill him. He knew that. And so did I. Searching for evidence against myself became a frantic effort. I had to know the truth before I could even hint at my fears, even to my sister.

"Then I thought of you. We had heard quite a lot about you from Marion Trench and her husband, of Windee, and as my father knew your Chief, Colonel Spendor, I wrote to him, feeling fairly sure he would send you if it were possible."

"That you did not confide in me when I first arrived is to be much regretted," Bony said steadily, although the recital was tensing his nerves and sweeping him with a great compassion.

"It would have achieved little, and I might then not have found myself master of the situation. The crimes had been committed before you arrived, remember. After all, my suspicions might have proved groundless—the outcome of a too vivid imagination. If only I could have got evidence incriminating myself! If only I could have found the clothes I wore on those expeditions along Nogga Creek! A dozen times have I ransacked this room and my study. God ... can't you understand what I have gone through, and what I am now going through?"

Bony was mute. He had never seen agony painted on a man's face as it was painted on this virile young man's face lit by the flickering oil lamp and the sinister light of the day beyond the room. The wind mocked and screamed and bellowed in turn. The chairs on which they sat and the floor beneath their feet vibrated ceaselessly. Martin's voice was higher, and he spoke more rapidly when he continued:

"When Donald Dreyton found a scrap of grey flannel cloth in one of the Nogga trees, I searched again for clothes, this time for a damaged pair of grey flannel trousers. I never found them. I possess two pairs of light-grey trousers and these are in good condition and perfectly pressed."

Borradale paused to pass the back of his left hand across his wet forehead, but not for an instant did he remove his gaze from Bony, or move by a fraction of an inch the muzzle of the revolver aimed at Bony's heart. First despair, then rebellion, and now a great weariness was in his voice.

"No, I have never found a shred of evidence pointing at myself. I can't understand it. I have thought and thought about it until I thought I would go stark raving mad. I am not normally a vicious brute. I have never consciously thought of injuring anyone. Why, even to sack a man gives me pain.

"And then the other day—or was it yesterday?—you told me you would finalize your case within a week. I knew you would succeed, for I had summed you up and knew you to be not a boastful man. I thought if I really was the murderer, if I really was the man who swung himself from tree to tree along Nogga Creek, as Hang-dog Jack had shown me the murderer did, then I would set a trap for myself. You see, I intended never to stand on a drop with a rope about my neck or live my life in a lunatic asylum. So I arranged the shot-gun on the tree-branch I knew the murderer would leap to, and I aimed the gun so that when it went off it would kill him."

"I saw you setting your trap, Mr. Borradale," Bony cut in, "and after you left I took out the cartridges. I thought you were trying to get ahead of me by catching the Strangler. Had it not been for that trap, I would not have made the bad mistake about Hang-dog Jack this morning."

"I take it that prior to that trap-setting you guessed that I was the murderer. I would like to know how you guessed, but there isn't time for me to hear that. Last night I went to bed as usual. I awoke with the report of a gun in my ears and a violent stinging pain along my right ribs. I found myself clinging to a tree-branch, and in a kind of horrible nightmare I hung

201

from it, not knowing where I was, and yet knowing I was somewhere on Nogga Creek, and what I had been doing there. Can you imagine a more terrible awakening than that?

"Then at a little distance from me someone fired shots. I thought that they were directed at me, and I fell from the tree to a soft patch of sand on the creek-bed. I was feeling sick from the pain at my side. Close to me there were men shouting and fighting.

"I knew then, as I crouched on the bed of the creek, that I was the Strangler. I felt—for I made no effort to make a closer examination—that I was wearing old clothes and old tennis shoes. In my mind was the one idea—to get away and get back into this room, where I always kept the means to escape myself should I find the evidence of my guilt.

"So I crept away and then ran hard all the way back to this room, where I lit the lamp and found myself wearing a grey-flannel undervest of the kind I have never bought, a pair of dark-grey flannel trousers I never remember to have seen, and a pair of tennis shoes I remembered having purchased in Broken Hill. You will find the clothes and the shoes under the bed.

"Where I have kept them I don't know; I cannot tell you. I found my hands to be not only red-raw, but stained with green tree-bark. I have never seen that stain before, and on my return formerly I must have carefully washed them and then emptied the water out into the garden before hiding my old clothes and shoes—where, I do not know—getting into my pyjamas and then into bed.

"That, inspector, is all I can tell you. There is nothing I can add. The whys and the wherefores I cannot explain. Now for my requests. I know you will grant them. Afterwards, after I have escaped from myself, please relate all I have told you to my sister. Please try to convince her, as I have tried to convince you, that consciously I am entirely innocent of these terrible crimes."

"Yes, but——"

"There can be no buts. I have seen my road for so long that I cannot mistake it. I am a kind of monster—a Jekyll-Hyde man—but I did not make myself what I am. If I surrender to you, I may escape the rope, but I will surely be confined to an asylum for the remainder of my life." The steady voice broke at last. "I could not bear that; it would be too terrible. I don't deserve the agony of a trial. I am innocent, I tell you, innocent! But ... but look at my hands.

"I want you to tell Dreyton about everything, too. I want him to know that I am not a conscious monster. My sister loves him, and I have thought sometimes that he loves her, but would not speak on account of his poverty. I have willed him my half-share of Wirragatta so that no longer will he be poor. I wanted him in the office because I desired that he and Stella should be brought more often together, and because I was losing grip on the station's affairs. Lastly, I want you to ask my sister to be sure that young Harry West is made boss stockman and given one of the cottages to take his bride to. No, not last. There is something else. I am going to ask you to grant me this request as a favour."

Borradale stood up. His eyes were terrible and his gun hand was as steady as a rock. With effort, he mastered the trembling of his lips.

"I want you to plead for me with Dreyton," he said. "I want you to try to show Dreyton that, although I am a monster in human shape, my father and mother were normal, decent people, and Stella is clean and normal too. I want you to impress that on him, because he might think that my abnormality is a family trait. It may be that I am a kind of throw-back, like a colt sometimes is a throw-back over generations. I don't know. Will you try to make Dreyton see it in a sensible light? I'd like to know at the end that Stella would be happy presently."

"I will do that," Bony said simply.

"Thank you, inspector. Now please go," Martin said sharply. "You will get up from the chair and march to the window. You will pass out to the veranda and then shut the window. I would like to do what I must do away from the house, but I had to call you here to explain matters and ask you to grant those few requests."

Slowly Bony stood up. He stood then with his hands stiffly at his sides, less from fear of the revolver than from a perhaps unwarranted respect for the man before him. When he began to speak his voice almost failed.

"Mr. Borradale, yours is the most terrible story to which I have ever had the misfortune to listen," he said. "I am in the position to believe every word of it. I leave you of my own free will. To arrest you, assuming I managed to do so, and to thrust you into the torturing vortex of a murder trial, with its inevitable result, would be beyond me. I shall not make any attempt to bar your way of escape. At this moment I thank God I am not a real policeman, mindful of his oath, a Javert, a Sergeant Simone. I feel honoured by knowing you—a man who can think of others at this moment, and a man who sees clearly the road he should take and who has the courage to tread it."

Martin's mouth quivered.

"Thank you, inspector," he said, almost whispering. Bony's eyes were shining.

"My friends call me Bony," he said.

"Thank you again, Bony!"

"Good-bye!" sighed the detective who was not a real policeman.

At the window he turned to look back to see the squatter still standing beyond the table, the flickering lamp light giving a marble-like passivity to his agonized face. The revolver was no longer pointed at him as he said with his hand on the window catch:

"I am going straight across to the office, Mr. Borradale. The garden is large and the wind is loud. A shot here may frighten Miss Borradale. You may trust me, for I am a man of honour."

Bony bowed, opened the window, left it invitingly open, and walked direct to the picket fence, jumped over it and so crossed to the office building. In the office he found Constable Lee talking with Dreyton. Dreyton stared hard at him, and Lee said:

"I am glad you have come in. Can I now speak to you officially before Donald Dreyton?"

"Yes," Bony said very, very softly. He appeared to be listening, and Dreyton thought it peculiar. About them the storm roared and whined. Beyond the windows was nothing but a blank wall of red sand.

"Very well, sir. We have found out that Hang-dog Jack's hands are not burned with that paste stuff. Elson swears that the Strangler got his hands pressed to the iron collar. Sergeant Smithson reckons that we made a mistake."

"The sergeant should reckon that *he* made a mistake, not us," Bony pointed out. Still he listened, and still Dreyton regarded him curiously. Lee was addressing this half-caste as *sir*, whom he had known as Joe Fisher.

Bony expelled his pent breath. Then he said, still very, very softly, "If, my dear Lee, it is not the cook, it must——"

Above the yelling of the wind there came to them the sound of the shot.

"—— must be the cook's master," Bony whispered.

"What the hell are you talking about?" Dreyton shouted.

Lee and Bony were staring at the featureless wall of sand-dust sliding eastward beyond the opened office door. Bony turned to the frigid constable.

"From now on, Lee, you will exercise extreme reticence," he said with unexpected firmness. "Do you understand?"

Constable Lee stood at attention. His eyes were full of knowledge.

He replied, "Yes, sir."

Chapter Twenty-six

The End—And A Beginning

Carie's one street with its flanking buildings, the flock of goats passing the police station, old Smith standing at the door of his shop, and Grandfer Littlejohn holding audience with two men and three women: the distant line of trees bordering Nogga Creek, the far sand-dunes, and the nearer Common gates—everything and everyone was seen this evening by Mrs. Nelson as though in her spectacles were red lenses.

Above the township and the bluebush plain hung vast red cloths black within their deep folds. The wind had dropped almost to a calm, and it was coming, cool and sweet, from the south. The sun was setting and its oblique rays were being filtered through slowly falling sand-mist to strike full upon the celestial draperies now being majestically drawn away to the east.

When Mrs. Nelson, who was standing at the south end of her topmost veranda, held out her hands for inspection she saw them to be as though recently dipped in blood. There was no escaping this colour out of doors. It even transmuted the diamonds and sapphires in her rings into rubies.

Only now had she been able to leave her rooms in which she had been imprisoned for two days by the sun-lifted and wind-driven sand. She stood straight and sturdy, thankfully breathing the cool air, wonderingly watching the amazing sky above her coloured world. The soul of this woman was stirred, and she suffered vexation when a light step behind her broke a train of thought.

The man she knew as Joe Fisher stood before her when she turned. His blue eyes were soft, almost appealing.

"Madam, I am the bearer of sad news," he said gently. "It is of your son about whom I have come to speak."

Instantly the dark eyes widened and the fragile lips were compressed. For three seconds she stared up at him before saying sharply, "My son!"

"Your son, Mrs. Nelson!"

For the first time Bony saw this woman shrink.

"My son! What do you know? Who are you?"

"I am an investigating police officer. Will you not sit down and invite me to bring a chair from the sitting-room?"

Mrs. Nelson nodded, her face white, her eyes anguished. When Bony became seated a little to her front she said softly, "My son! Tell me, please."

"When I was told that old man Borradale wept when he read the service over the body registered as your child I knew that he wept over the body of his own son, Mrs. Nelson. You must prepare yourself for a great shock. Your son, known as Martin Borradale, is dead."

"*Dead!*"

Bony averted his gaze from her stricken face.

"Dead," he repeated. "He died this morning a brave and an honourable man—by his own hand."

Swiftly Bony related everything he had that morning been told by the young man in the Wirragatta bedroom, and of the trap prepared to ensnare the Strangler.

"I did not enlighten your son regarding his parentage," Bony continued. "The only people who know that are Miss Borradale, Dreyton, Doctor Mulray, and our two selves."

"Tell me all you know," the woman commanded.

"Your son was born on the third of January, 1910. Doctor Tigue attended you and Mrs. Littlejohn nursed you. The following day Mrs. Borradale's baby was born, and it died. Mrs. Borradale and her husband had been eagerly looking forward to the coming of their first born, and so ill was the lady that Dr. Tigue feared to tell her it was dead. Mr. Borradale and old Grandfer Littlejohn——"

"Yes, yes!" Mrs. Nelson interrupted. "Mr. Borradale thought of me and my baby and of John, whom he had caused to be locked up for safety's sake. Mrs. Borradale was crying for her child … and it was dead. Mr. Borradale and old Littlejohn brought the dead baby to my little home. He pointed out to me that my child would be badly handicapped by his drunken father, and he offered me five thousand pounds to make the exchange.

"You and the others who know, and the world who will know, must not be too hard on me. It wasn't all on account of the money. My husband was fast being ruined by something other than drink. His father was mad before him, and my John was mad, too. We were very poor, but up to the time my son was born I didn't mind that so very much. Underneath everything, despite his goings on, my John was a wonderful man. But ... there was the creeping madness and the drink. Mr. Borradale offered my baby a life filled with opportunities if I consented to the exchange. He paid me five thousand pounds and Mrs. Littlejohn another thousand pounds. And I am glad I allowed the exchange. I am glad, glad, glad that I sold my baby for five thousand pounds. I have watched him grow up a fine man, a wealthy squatter, a Justice of the Peace.

"When Dr. Tigue died without kith or kin, he willed me all his few possessions. I already owned the house and furniture. From his books I tore out the page relating to the babies, and I tore out the page concerning the neck injuries I got when poor John nearly strangled me in one of his frenzies. His father was put away because he almost strangled a woman."

"That injury left scars, did it not?" Bony said. "When Mabel Storrie accidentally saw them you closed her mouth with the gift of an expensive ring."

Mrs. Nelson nodded.

"You seem to know everything," she said. "Yes, my poor John was always queer. Before Martin was born he nearly strangled me one night when he returned home. He was perfectly sober, I know. He very nearly killed me after we had taken over the hotel, and it was then that I got these scars. Ah, me! What chance did Martin ever have, what with his father and his father's father back of him? What chance did he have for all his wonderful upbringing? Somnambulism! It was something much deeper than that—an inherited evil which came with the wind.

"Yes, I knew who killed Alice Tindall and Frank Marsh, and who almost killed Mabel Storrie. It could have been none other than John Nelson's son, my baby, whom I sold for five thousand pounds."

The small, blue-veined hands were being twisted over and over each other. The little china-white face was kept turned to Bony, and the small, dark eyes, anguished and tear-filled, began suddenly to search his.

"What could I have done?" she asked plaintively. "Could I denounce my own son? Could I give up to the police my own child? I didn't, anyway, and I'm glad, glad, glad that I didn't. As for poor John! No woman ever loved a man as I loved him. Even when he was the cause of selling my baby I didn't cease to love him. But I bought this hotel in order that he would die before he was taken away to an asylum, if he didn't murder me. I have made money, my friend, but I have done a little good with it. I have worked and suffered, but I have been repaid with years of peace and happiness watching my son grow to splendid manhood. I ... I. ..."

The small voice trailed into silence.

"He is to be buried tomorrow, and Miss Borradale thought you might like to see him," Bony said gently. "Perhaps we could arrange a secret visit to Wirragatta tonight."

"That is kind of Miss Borradale. She takes after her sainted mother. But ... but I will not see Martin. I want to remember him as he was—the Squatter of Wirragatta."

Bony noted her pride in the fact that her son had become a squatter. In her young years squatters had been like powerful princes of the bush.

Then Mrs. Nelson said, "So you are a policeman. What are you going to do with me?"

"Do with you? Why, nothing," he replied, astonished. "For Barry Elson's sake, as well as for the peace of mind of the people here, it must become public that Martin was responsible for these tragedies. Nothing, however, will be made public concerning Martin's parentage, for no good to anyone could be derived from such a disclosure. You will accept my very sincere sympathies, will you not?"

The white-haired head nodded and sank forward, to be supported by the beringed hands. Bony stood up.

"I must leave you now," he said. "Is there anything I could do?"

"No, thank you, excepting to ask Tilly to come to me."

And so Bony left her. In the dining-room he found Tilly.

"Tilly, your mistress wishes you to go to her. She has had bad news, but she will want you not to question her."

Tilly's plain face bore an expression of anxiety.

"All right, Joe. Did they—have they had any news of Harry out there at Westall's? That sand— —"

Bony said firmly, "Harry will be coming back in the near future to become boss stockman at Wirragatta, and to marry a certain young lady. Good-bye, Tilly, and life-long happiness."

On his return to Wirragatta Bony asked to see Stella Borradale, and was shown into the morning-room, which already had been cleaned. Stella greeted him bravely enough, but the signs of tears were still evident.

"Will you sit down?"

"Thank you, Miss Borradale," he said. "I have been talking to Mrs. Nelson and she confirms my history of Martin's birth. She does not wish to see him, wishing to remember him as he was. That part of this very sad and terrible case will never be made public. She was very brave about it. Now that we know everything we must admit her sterling qualities."

Stella compressed her lips to stop their trembling.

"I will go to her ... after ... tomorrow evening. I shall always remember him as my dear and splendid brother. Oh Bony! He was so fine and generous. It wasn't ... it wasn't really Martin who did——"

"No, Miss Borradale. The man who left his bed to climb among trees was not Martin Borradale, but Martin Nelson. The man we knew was Martin Borradale. The other was born during a raging sand-storm. He inherited his father's mental disease and was controlled by the peculiar conditions of these wind-storms, which affect his mother and many others as well. The man we knew took the brave and the honourable course by slaying that evil born in a sand-storm."

"My brother Martin! I can't help it, Bony."

Bony continued to talk to her for some little while, telling her of Martin's wish concerning the advancement of Harry West, and of Hang-dog Jack, whose injuries were not as serious as had at first been thought, and which would permit him to return to work in a few days.

"I have a long report to write," he said, presently, rising to stand at her side. "Donald Dreyton wishes to see you. May I ask him to come here?"

It was strange, he thought, that Stella Borradale should be seated just as Mrs. Nelson was seated when he left her.

Stella nodded, saying with forced calmness, "Yes, I will see him here."

The brilliance of the stars was remarkable. Without being conscious of it, Bony filled his lungs with the cool fragrant air several times during the crossing to the office building where, at his table in the office, Dreyton was found, his pipe forgotten, his eyes expressive of anxiety.

"I thought you would not object to me writing a long report here, Mr.

Dreyton," Bony exclaimed. "There is, too, a matter I wish to discuss with you."

Dreyton nodded.

"Very well, Mr. Bonaparte."

Bony drew a chair to the opposite side of the table at which Dreyton sat, and at once began the manufacture of cigarettes.

"You have not been very helpful, Mr. Dreyton," he began, "but then you did not know I was supposed to be a police officer. Had you confided in me as you did in Mr. Borradale—for we will always refer to Martin as Mr. Borradale—about that piece of cloth you found in the tree and one or two other discoveries you made, I would have been saved a portion of mental labour. However, I think none the less well of you.

"I have just left Miss Borradale in the morning-room. Naturally she is still profoundly shocked, but she is thinking of Saint George and the Dragon. Er—in the course of my investigation I found it necessary to know all about you. I want you to read this document. It concerns you."

The other's blue-grey eyes stared from the detective to the pinned pages of typescript slipped across the table. Without speaking, Dreyton accepted it and began to read. Bony, with a cigarette between his lips, lay back in his chair and found much of apparent interest in the lamp suspended above them. He heard Dreyton exclaim. He heard the papers rustling. Then he heard Dreyton sigh. When again he encountered the blue-grey eyes he saw in them a great hope.

Bony said, "Before Martin Borradale shot himself he informed me about a matter I have not mentioned to anyone. He said that he had long desired to have you in this office, and for several reasons. He wanted you here because he felt he was losing his grip on affairs generally, and because he liked you very much, and his sister liked you, too. He had a particular idea concerning his sister and you, and in his will he has bequeathed you his half-share of Wirragatta.

"Wait, please. Your preference for the fence-work over this office work, with its accompanying privileges, mystified me not a little. Even now I am not absolutely sure of that reason. However, I rather think that the reason was worthy of the nephew of Admiral Sir Reginald Dreyton, and the son of Captain Dreyton. Pardon my seeming impertinence—I may be excused, for I am serving the dead—but I believe now that the reason no longer exists.

When I left Miss Borradale I told her you wanted to see her at once. She is waiting to receive you in the morning-room. My dear man, if ever a woman needs comforting——"

With a clatter, Dreyton's chair was pushed back, and he was on his feet. He looked like a man gazing on a glorious vision.

"You are a strange fellow," he said, and almost ran to the door.

"And you," loudly asserted Detective-Inspector Napoleon Bonaparte, "are another!"

CPSIA information can be obtained
at www.ICGtesting.com
Printed in the USA
BVHW03s0355140618
518973BV00002B/69/P